Archetypes in Literatures and Cultures

Rahilya Geybullayeva
(ed.)

Archetypes in Literatures and Cultures

Cultural and Regional Studies

In Collaboration with
Sevinj Bakhysh and Izabella Horvath

PETER LANG
Frankfurt am Main · Berlin · Bern · Bruxelles · New York · Oxford · Wien

Bibliographic Information published by the Deutsche Nationalbibliothek
The Deutsche Nationalbibliothek lists this publication in the Deutsche Nationalbibliografie; detailed bibliographic data is available in the internet at http://dnb.d-nb.de.

Cover Design:
© Olaf Gloeckler, Atelier Platen, Friedberg

Layout:
Kumpernatz + Bromann
www.kumpernatz-bromann.de

ISBN 978-3-631-63467-7

www.peterlang.de

Table of Contents

Preface

The idea for the project "Archetypes in Literatures and Cultures" as well as the idea for the previous projects "Literary Contexts" (2006), "Stereotypes in Literatures and Cultures" (2008), hosted by Baku Slavic University, arose in hopes of strengthening discussions about *We and Others, Mine and Others'* in culture and art, which are supposedly significant components of national identity. This idea also was realised at the "Cuisine: Taste of Others" conference (2010), launched jointly by Prof. Didier Francfort and Dr. Denis Saillard, and hosted by Khazar University, Baku.

The formation of new countries after the collapse of the Soviet Union and the Eastern European block necessarily brought about an increased awareness of the problem of national identity and has given rise to more urgent attempts to define national literary and cultural facts. Among the matters to be discussed in this context are the circulation of similar cultural motifs, situations, symbols, plots, genres, words, and rituals. Such a situation gives rise to questions concerning both things that were constructed over centuries and relatively new archetypal plots and situations created by different authors, in different periods and in national literatures. For example, how does translation influence the migration of plots? Does the blurring of borders between sources and re-interpretations make it difficult to distinguish the original and the "kidnapped" texts? The forms of archetypes have changed and continue to change, creating a hyper-text. Taking these things into consideration, the question arises: "Where are the borders between an original text, influence, and plagiarism?"

Research questions in this context concern both what has been constructed over centuries and relatively new archetypal plots and situations created by different authors, of different periods and national literatures. The topics of research range from adaptations of the heroic story of Troy by English and Italian authors, the medieval story of Romeo and Juliet as interpreted by Italian and English playwrights, the plot of Leili and Mejnoun as re-narrated by Azerbaijani, Persian, Uzbek, as well as contemporary Georgian and Russian poets, or the story of Doctor Faust as interpreted by German and English authors. They also include adaptations of plots from diverse periods and national literatures, such as Biblical plots as they appear in literary fiction created by European and Islamic writers, or in modern literature, such as the representation of the Italian Pinocchio as Buratino, and the English Winnie the Pooh as Vinni Pookh in Russian culture.

Another question is how to consider "nationality" in the construction of a tale or in epic stories that require the hero to overcome compulsory tests with magic powers? How is one to distinguish the song and verses of Mowlana and their adaptation in music by American authors? And what about the similarity of melodies in the classical mugham of Bayaty-Shiraz and in "Toccata D Minor" by Johann Sebastian Bach?

Other possible themes and questions raised at the conference were: how does a translation influence the migration of plots? How is one to define the "nationality" of "Kalila and Dimna", the Arabic translation of the Indian "Panchatatra" tales? Does the blurring of borders between source and re-interpretation allow one to distinguish the original and the "kidnapped" texts?

The forms of archetypes have changed and continue to change from one migrant plot to "fan-fiction," from folklore to movies, from literature to music, from music to movie, thus creating a hyper-text.

Taking into consideration above mentioned, the question arises: "Where are the borders between an original text, influence, and plagiarism?"

Baku Slavic University (BSU) co-jointly with Azerbaijan Comparative Literature Association (AzCLA) held the conference "Archetypes on Literatures and Cultures" in October 22-23, 2010. The scope of submitted papers by scholars from Australia, Sweden, United Kingdom, Netherlands, Turkey, United Arab Emirates, China, Russia, Bulgaria, Azerbaijan, Georgia, Kazakhstan covered different aspects of the above-mentioned themes and questions and included archetypal symbols, motifs, plots, situations and their reflections on languages, comprising archetypes in art forms.

Kamal Abdullayev, Rector of Baku Slavic University
Rahilya Geybullayeva, editor, Head of AzCLA

Acknowledgements

I would like to express my gratitude to the people who worked to bring this book to its completion. First and foremost, I thank all of the authors who contributed to the book. I am particularly grateful to the rector of the host university Kamal Abdullayev, and feel indebted to Izabella Horvath and Peter Orte for professional support. Tremendous support came from Sevinj Bakysh, who carefully re-translated many of the papers. I gratefully acknowledge the moral and financial support received from Hilal Sadigov, who has always been there for me. I am also indebted to the publisher Ute Winkelkoetter for support and advice.

Part 1
National or Transnational, Source or Interpretation

From Archetypal Situation to Archetypised Words or Words as a Unit of Semantic Reinterpretations

Rahilya Geybullayeva
(Azerbaijan)

The word "archetype" as a carrier of the meanings "primary" and "module-type"

Etymologically the word "*archetype*" in Greek means initial, primary sample; the first part of the word *arche* means primary model; a *type*, a pattern supposing reiteration.[1] Classification cannot be made without repetition, so type implies the recycling of a pattern. Any recycling, even an imitative recycling cannot present an identical copy of the primordial type or any previous type, namely the archetype. Time, space, and the individuality of the author are inevitably imprinted on the new version, thus creating variation. Thus archetype presumes both an archaic type (an invariant) and the modification of the type.

Regarding the term *primary*, it means *the first* not only in time, but in rank as well. The second meaning is reflected in such words as archangel (a principal angel)[2] archbishop, archeries (the highest rank in the Eastern Orthodox and Catholic Churches), archon (the chief magistrate in Ancient Greek city-states).

"The term "archetype" occurs as early as Philo Judaeus, with reference to the *Imago Dei* (God-image) in man. It can also be found in Irenaeus,[3] who says: "The creator of the world did not fashion these things directly from himself, but copied them from archetypes outside himself." In the *Corpus Hermeticum*, God is called … archetypical light (Harrison, Charles 2003: 379). In some of Plato's dialogues, Socrates describes the material world only as an image or copy of the real world. The forms are types of real things. Therefore, a type is the core recurring and repeating in different forms.

---

1 *Online Etymology Dictionary*. http://www.etymonline. com/index.php. "Archetype – original pattern from which copies are made", 1540s, from L. archetypum, from Gk. arkhetypon "pattern, model, figure on a seal", neut. of adj. arkhetypos "first-moulded", from arkhe- "first" (see archon) + typos "model, type, blow, mark of a blow" (see type). The Jungian sense of "pervasive idea or image from the collective unconscious" is from 1919".

2 Usually the archangel Gabriel has been viewed as a mediator and messenger between God and the human race; he related the text of the Quran to the prophet and announced to Mary that she was to be the mother of Jesus.

3 Saint Irenaeus, bishop in Gaul, Roman Empire, 2nd century AD, circa 130- 202.

Types of archetypes

Archetypes can be sub-divided into several *types or groups*:

- archetypal *sujets (plots)* from ancient times (in religious books, such as in Bible, Koran and through them in classic and contemporary literature; Leila & Majnun)
- archetypal *situations* (three tests for marriage, keeping a promise, etc.)
- archetypal *melodies* (Mozart's *Alla Turca March* and Beethoven's *Marcia Alla Turca* based on *Yanussary March*; *Bayati-Shiraz*, Bach's *Toccata D Minor); dancing (Caucasian* type, *Central Asian* strukture, plastic motions of arms and hands in Indian dancing in modern Indian dancing and Arabic belly dance, their recycling-improvisations, imitating the plastic gestures, of ancient temple dance rituals.[4]
- archetypal *symbols* (mirror, apple, treasure, underground, invisibility, fire, water, magic wand, etc.)
- archetypal *images* (Biblical, mythological, realistic; Virgin Mary, Faustus/ Iblis/Devil/Mephistofeles, beloved /ashig/Majnun, King Arthur/ knight, holy fool/man of motley, geisha/vestalis)
- archetypal *genre* (imitation – *mimesis* (in Western culture)-*nezire* (in classic Islamic literature); *mirror for princes*-hagiography-didactic; *metqel* (devoted to Kerbela martyrs in VII century, from Arabic *qetl* – execution;[5] *Panchatatra* (Indian) or *Khamsa* (five framed in Islamic literature), *divan*;[6] *mugham* or *makam*,[7] sonatina, rhapsody in music; *manga* (Japanese drawing style for comics-cartoons))
- archetypal *words* (shabbat-subbota-sabbatical; sacral words, distributed in different languages through a dominant people-or a carrier of a dominat religion)
- archetype as textual *method* (travel, ascension to the heaven, three tests for the hero before marriage, slumber, retrospection; five-frame composition in Islamic carpet and narrative)

---

4 For example, Киноконцерт – Махмуд Эсамбаев. "Золотой бог".[Kinokonsert – Mahmoud Esambayev. "Zolotoy Bog" – Golden God]. 28 май 2010. http://rutube.ru/tracks/32 82375.html.

5 Metqel literature started in Arabic literature from the time of the battle of Kerbela between supporters of Imam Hasan and followers of Muaviya –bin-Abu-Soufyan in 680 AD. It was written as narrative, describing significant stages of the life of the hero and the social-political core of these historical events.

6 A Divan is a collection of works in Medieval Islamic literature.

7 Mugam or makam is a system of slow melody types, borrowed with Islam, based on the technique of improvisation. It appears somehow also in the music art of non-Islamic people, such as Greeks and Assyrians.

- archetypal *ritual* (Friday, Saturday or Sunday in monotheistic religions for revival and recreation, sacrifice both in paganism and monotheism, zikr-prayer-sacralized remembrance days)

Some *methods of formation* of archetypes are:

- canonization (the Bible's standards for approving texts, images)
- representation of historical fact or belief in fiction or art
- adaptation (depiction of depicted texts, units in different texts and art genres)
- translation (into different languages)
- plagiarism (in the light of the above, as the borders between copying and new interpretation are fluid)
- hypertext (borrowing the known archetype and making a new interpretation)
- fan-fiction (continuation of a known text, or character, by fans in their reinventive creation)

Archetypes can be conditionally divided into the following *several categories:*

- collective unconscious (K. Jung) – prototypes, something inherent to the psyche of a person, rather than acquired through experience, thus forming a particular behavior mode
- conscious application, adaptation of a known example or pattern
- even copying, such as the modern movement's of *appropriation* existing in the visual arts.

Traditionally, the field of research of archetypes includes notions of symbols, motifs, plots, and situations. Another type of research comprises archetypes in the different art forms. Thus we can talk about different forms of archetypes, which embrace images of religious motifs in *pictures* in church and palace walls and ceilings, in ritual and/or hunting rock *paintings*; *situations*, *elements of plot*, images, and symbols recurring in folklore, mythology, literature, music and cinema; *verbal units* reflecting the semantic transformation of beliefs in different periods, indiscernible at first sight.

One can consider as a form of archetype the reappearance of myths, lore, legends in literature, films, music, sculpture, and most importantly its layering with the atmosphere of a current time, so the new reappearance could be termed as an *adaptation, recycling culture, convergence, or fan-fiction.*[8]

The formation of an archaic image occurs from time to time through the practice of beliefs, traditions, and rituals. Beliefs integrate into religions, and

8 Adaptation – adjustment of the text for television, music, movie, painting; fan-fiction – continuation of the text by amateurs or professional writers, recycling culture – combination of these two points, interpretation of known content in the new text.

migrate from one religion to another, gradually forming the primal image, which is usually defined as an archetype, at times leading to alterations in words, reflecting basic sematics. This image or motif reflects not only the ritualistic or symbolic on the plot level, but it reveals also cultural layers that appear as semantic carriers, transmitted on the verbal level. Myths, rituals, and beliefs affected the formation of the academic and professional as much as colloquial language and dialects.

The archetypes mentioned above are expressed in language through proverbs, phraseology, words. The purpose of this essay is to reveal and identify the expression of archetypes, that is, the scheme of a primal image and motif, enclosed in words, or to be precise, in the roots. To distinguish the archetypal words from pure lexical loans and coincident words in related languages we used both examples, thus making an attempt to *disclose their arhectypal-prototype* culturological meanings, those enclosed in the word, which sometimes appear unusual at first glance.

Interestingly, in various religions the repetition of the same rite with some variations (for example, the types of 'zikr'-rhythmic repetitions of certain *actions* (such as rhythmic motion of heads) and words in Buddhism, Islam, shamanism, or rites in Zoroastrianism, Greek mythology, and Christianity, related to the belief of purging fire) result in repetition with the same regularity in *language*. In this sense, the *history of language* is not merely a *linguistic* science, since at the same time it reflects the *history of an ethnos and a nation, their cultural crossroads and encounters.*

Any plot, situation, or image can be archetypal or not. Consequently, a word can be (or not be) an expression of a primal image. The primal images are created and transformed in any particular period of time, including the modern.[9] Tracing the archetypal function of a word allows for discovering how it originated or is related to a primordial belief system. The interesting fact is that, the same type of a semantic footprint can be observed in ethnicities of distinct language groups and distant geographical areas, and their semantics can be identified as a carrier of an archetype. The objective of this research is mostly a study of the form of ***expression of archetypal ideas in certain words*** rather than their chronological appearance. The material for research consists of words encountered by the author on numerous occasions and in different places and checked in dictionaries, including online sources, wherever possible.

9 For example, iconoclasm appears with the Egyptian pharaohs, old Greek and Eastern gods, in monotheistic saints' icons and political leader's portraits.

Words, related to a religion, as the linkage point for different civilizations

Apostasy[10] – separation from the main religion, beliefs

Apostrophe – separation of two syllables in Azerbaijani and other languages, using Arud rhythm, for construction of length of syllables in the words; in Latin rhetoric: to *interrupt* speech to address to someone; *apostr*opha (Latin) in court to address to the adversary

Apostle – eventually the apostles changed their beliefs, *differed, separated* from their fellow countrymen by *conversion* to a new religion. The mission of the twelve Christian apostles was a branching off from Judaism, to convert people to another religion.

Apostolic – synonym of *papal,* because the pope is a chief successor of Apostles.

This group consisting of disparate lexemes, such as apostle (12 apostles of Jesus Christ, or an indicator of the length of a syllable in Azerbaijani and other Muslim alphabets, and a sign of English alphabet, reflects an *archetype of differentiation.*

Schism – division, rupture, breaking out

Shiism – one of the confessions, which separated, broke out from the main Sunni movement of Islam

Schizophrenia – mental illness, characterized by the *breakdown* of thought,

Sacrifice – священный, что и предполагает суть – ***sacrum*** – священный предмет, facio (fact) – делать

Sacral – related to ritual

Sacred – religious

Sacred mushroom – English name of a hallucinogenic mushroom, used in religious rituals of American aborigines. In this sense insane can be understood as a quality of being close to God.

Sacrament – a religious symbol or a rite, such as Baptism and the Eucharist.

Секрет (Russian) – *secret*

Rites and prayers are used for calling ton sacred power, to reveal intentions. This group of words consists of sacred, mystic, secret symbols. The word ***zikr (secret)*** related to the above mentioned group is worth considering.

10 Here and after most of the references are checked from ABBYLingo-12 Online dictionary.

Zikr (or ***Dhi-kar***)(Arabic, remembering, reminding) – an Islamic *religious ceremony*, a devotional practice representing a way of *reminding oneself of God* used in Islam and *especially by Sufis.*

Zikr – In Sufism, Islamic Mysticism, a term used both for the regular activity of remembrance and for the litanies and prayers involved in the acts of remembering. The act of rhythmic recital accompanied by head movements from left to right is close to that of shamans and Buddhist rituals. (To achieve a higher consciousness one is required to repeat) The partial loss of consciousness in this practice brings closer to the *sacred* group of words another archetypical word *insane.*

Ziggurat – a temple of Sumerian origin in the form of a pyramidal tower, consisting of a number of stories and presenting the appearance of a series of terraces (to achieve a highest pinnacle one required to repeat steps).

The archetypisation of *zikr* related to the 28-th Ayat of the 13 Surah of the Quran: Those who believe, and whose hearts find satisfaction in the remembrance of Allah: for without doubt in the remembrance of Allah do hearts find satisfaction. The fourth Surah shows the importance of *zikr* practiced by a group: When any group of men remembers Allah, angels surround them and mercy covers them, tranquillity descends upon them, and Allah mentions them to those who are with Him. (Muslim) Quran (Surah 4: Verse 190) (Qurani-Kərim 2006: 131).

Each Sufi order has its own distinctive zikr practice. The tradition of *zikr* implemented not only Sufis and dervishes devotions, but also funeral rituals. Relying on personal experience, even in Soviet times, funeral rituals in some areas of Azerbaijan, i.e. Zagatala, were performed with use of *zikr* practices of the Naqshbandi order. This tradition with some deviations continues nowadays in different parts of Azerbaijan and in the areas of Georgia and Armenia inhabited by Azerbaijanis.[11] We can compare the origins and the primal meaning of *zikr* with the word *ziggurat*. One of its meanings is related to the *weird* group of words.

Weird – involving or suggesting the supernatural; unearthly or uncanny, fantastic; concerned with or controlling fate or destiny.

Weird – a region in Southern Sweden

Wyrd (German) – a destiny

Wert in Indo-European languages – cyclic rotation

---

11 For example, in the novel "The Violent Kur-river" (1967) Ismail Shykhly describes zikr, inherent in the Nigarits order of Sufism, still popular in Kazakh region of Azerbaijan.

Vird (Azerbaijani, Turkish) – type of *Zikr*, one of the Sufi or dervish rituals, in other parts of the world it is called wird (Arabic)
Virtue – a good or admirable quality or property
Virtues – the fifth of the nine orders into which the angels are traditionally divided in medieval angelology

The words of this group come from different language groups united by symbolism of attaining a magic, secret, transcendental world. The Sufi ritual of *vird* is used for the achievement of a stability of heart. In this case, the most important thing is not a rotation of the body and head, but a certain repetition of the word "Allah" or names of Allah. *Wird* (Awrad – plural in Arabic) means source or place of return (compare with *zikr* or *dikr*). Another origin of this word according to dictionaries and encyclopaedias could be found in Indian and/or Saxon. The lexical line in Indo-European and Turkic languages indicates the same function as the of archetype of ritual.

Bog (Russian) – God
Bog – a swamp
Bhagavan (Sanskrit –literally "possessing fortune, blessed, prosperous") – in some Hindu traditions used to indicate a Personal God
Baku – capital of Azerbaijan, *Bak (Bhagavan)* is associated with God and sun
Bogud (Latin) – Brother and companion of Mauritanian ruler Bokh[12] (circa 31 BC)
Богатырь (Russian) – a man of distinguished courage or ability, a personage from heroic myths and legends (compare to Turkic *bahadur, batir*, Sanskrit *Bhagavad*-Gita –(Song of God), sacred scripture)
Boguz (Chagatay), ***bogaz*** (Azerb., Turk. – throat) compare with aphorism "can *bogazdan* kecher" – "life (soul) goes through throat", with the belief that the soul leaves a body through throat.

This group of words consists of such notions as the name of God – *Bog*, an extraordinary hero – *bogatir* etc. deriving from different language groups (from Sanskrit and Slavic to Turkic). It exposes a meaning that seems prior to monotheism.

The analogy to *Bog* – *God* also designates a certain cultural layers.

God – A Supreme Spirit
Good – morally excellent; virtuous, right, favourable etc.
Guten (German) – good, favourable, reliable
Gutlu – (Old Turkic) – happy, favourable

12 Compare: Bokh – Vakh lexical line.

Gutadgu – bilik ("The path to happiness") – the name of the book by Yusuf Balasaguni
*Gor**gut*** – name of Turkic mythical prophet
Kutlu olsun (in modern Turkish and some Azerbaijani dialects) – be full of goodness
These examples show the positive qualities related to God, and godliuness.

Sabbath (Hebrew) – is the seventh day of the Jewish week and a day of rest in Judaism (like Friday in Islam, and Sunday in Christianity). It recalls the Biblical Creation account in Genesis, describing God creating the Heavens and the Earth in six days and resting on the seventh. It may also be the reason why the witches' Sabbath happens on this day.
Sabbatical year – every 7th year in Bible,
Субботa [subbota] (Russian) – Saturday
Şənbə *[*compare: *sabbath]* (Azerb.) – Saturday
In all cases, the archetypal plot reflects the abovementioned Biblical story of the Genesis of the world (Exod. 31: 17).

Shiva – one of the main *gods* in Hinduism, "the *Destroyer*," the third member of the Trimurti (Holy Trinity in Hunduism), along with Brahma the Creator and Vishnu the Preserver.
Shivah (or siva) – the *mourning* period, following the funeral and lasting traditionally for seven days indoors, observed by Jews for a deceased (compare: *destroyer* function) parent, sibling, child, or spouse, sitting on low stool; *sit*
shivah – to observe this period; to mourn (compare with the pose of a mediating *Shiva*).
Şivən qoparmaq (Azerb.) – to wail, to weep, to make a loud noise (not only during funerals and mourning periods).
The expression completes the semantic-archetypal line with changing details.

Mi'raj or ***Meraj*** (in Islam) – the ascension of the prophet Muhammad to heaven (661 AD) on the fantastic steed Al-Borak given by the archangel Jibriil (Gabriel) to the throne of Allah, (Qur'an, sura 17 (Al-Isra), ayah1). During the flight God gave him ninety nine thousand revelations; (compare – the Ascension Day in Christianity, on the fortieth day of Easter, related with Ascension of Christ into a heaven). Another holy transportation occurs with Abraham, who was taken on Al-Borak to his wife Hagar and son Ismail (compare: the Ascension Day in Christianity, in fortieth day of Easter, related with Ascension of Christ into a heaven; Elijah's rapture to heaven in order to sake him; ascension of the Virgin Mary into heaven after her earthly life.

Mirage – an optical illusion ***Mirror*** (English) – a reflecting surface, usually made of glass; apart from this everyday meaning, something that gives a minutely faithful representation, image, idea of something else (compare with the archetypal genre of literature known as Mirror for princes (*principum specula* in Latin) in Byzantyne[13] and popular in Medieval Islamic literature[14] as well)

Мир (Russian) [mir] – the universe as a whole; assuming the being of what is first, and what is the reflection (*mirror*); the world – supposedly, as the mirror, which *reflects* an image of heaven; peace (the homophone)

Mir (Arabic) – mirror, derivated from the verb *R'a* (see) and noun *M'i* (device)

Miror, miro, mirum (Latin)- to marvel at, admire, to be amazed

Миро, мирра [mirra] (Russian) – a myrrh tree, and the aromatic oleoresin which is used in rituals of the Eastern Orthodox Church for anointments during chrismation.[15]

Myrrha – mother of Adonis, transformed into a myrrh tree

Archetypes in words with different roots in the same semantic area

Дышать – **душ**а [dyshat' – dusha] – to breath – a soul
дыхание – **дух** [dyhaniye-duh] – a breath (spirit)
воз**дух** [vozduh] – **air**
Havva – Eve (women's name)

Traditionally spirit, **soul** (дух) was not related to women. Although biblical Eve was created from Adam's rib, the other meaning of it in Hebrew was breath (air). Thus a man – a body created from clay, and a woman, created from rib

---

13 A genre of political writing known as mirror for princes, which directly instructs kings on certain aspects of rule and behavior; Hellenic tradition had an influence on both the European, and Slavic moral genre through translation in the Xth centure. The Islamic literary genre, the Oriental tradition, originated in India (Panchatantra) and had a different form (animal fables) which transformed into Islamic Kalila and Dimna.

14 In Islamic literature "Siyasat-Nameh" (The Book of Politics) by vizir Nizam-al-Mulyuk, is known to have been written in Persian for Sultan Malik-Shah, third ruler of the Seljuk's Empire (the end of XI centure), who was the shah's master since the sultan was 17 years old. (See: A.E. Крымский. Низами и его современники. Баку: Эльм, 1981, стр.128, 116, 117). Another sample of mirror for princes or mirror literature (literature zersal) was "The Wisdom of King's Glory" written in Turkish by Yusuf Khass Khajib from Kashqar, Central Asia, in 1069, during Karakhanid's governing.

15 The Russian expression "одним миром мазаны" (literally 'anointed with the same myrrh') and meaning "tarred with the same brush," originates from this ritual.

were not alive, until they were given a breath (air, soul, spirit). One can parallel it with Sumerian "ti" which had double meaning as "a rib" and "to give a life".

The same aspect can be found in a belief of Jesus Christ as a child of the Holy Spirit and a mortal woman, Mary. Thus this lexical chain, unlike the previous ones, reflects the **archetypal plot of creation of a human being and in general of all living things.**

Nəfəs *– breath;* ***nəfs*** *desire* (Azerb.). Atfirst sight they bear diffrent meanings, but the chain "breath – air – spirit – soul (look: in Russian ***дышать*** *–* ***душа, дыхание*** *–* ***дух***)" shows that the Azerbaijaani expression *nəfsini saxlamaq – to control desire* is connected to a spirit, the moral attribute. The archetype of controling desire often appears in Turkic, Persian and Slavic fairy tales as a protection of a extra-ordinary apple from an ugly monster, *dev*.

The word ***hal*** (Azerbaijani) [condition] can contribute to the chain of *breath-spirit-soul.*

In**hale** – to breathe

Hale – healthy, ***heal*** – cure

Hal (Azerb. from Arabic): ***hal****-əhval* – condition, əhval-***ruh***iyyə – here the bold part of a complex word means spirit.

Hal *arvadı* – a personage from Turkic mythology, in corellation with *Havva* (Eve), specifically signifies a female image. It is worth mentioning that the use of different variations of *hal* in Azerbaijani occurs as often as does *spirit* in Latin.

Hal*itus* (Latin) – *breath*. This unexpected windfall endorses in semantics of the archetype "*душа* (in Russian from "дышать – to *breath*") – *душа* (soul, spirit) – *hal* (condition)," which we have encountered in the search of an origin and variants of Latin *Halleluija* (praise to god), which has resulted in similar archetypal carrier words:nin icons *halo* – light, radiance (compare: in Greek *halo* means disk, circle.) and an aura round a face, with the meaning "to breath, to breath out, to smell sweet."

Let's come back to the example of ***Həvva.*** Although the chain *breathe – soul – spirit* does not play by certain rules, the semantic perspective reveals new issues.

Eve – first women according to the Bible

Evan*gelie* (Gospel from Greek) – a part of a Bible

Parole *d'****Evan****gile* (French) – a fact

The interesting fact is that *Evangelia* in Latin has another meaning as a ***dig****estum*.

Evan *–* ***euan*** (Latin) – *Bacchus* – is the name of a Greek god; the call for him (Francis Edward Jackson Valpy 1838:149.). As Jesus is the son of a mortal woman and a cosmic power – spirit, Bacchus is the son of Supreme god,

Zeus, and a mortal, Semela. After the death of Semele a prematurely born Bacchus was bound by Zeus to his leg, consequently he received the name bimater (with two mothers).

Thus, the chain of words connected with archetypal motif of binarity – the synthesis of worldly, bodily and cosmic, spiritual.

In its turn:

Digestum (Latin) – The Bible (Evangelie), also Codex
Digest – to understand, to absorb, to grasp
Dig – to excavate, to search

We can assume, that the lexical chain of Havva – Evan – Eve – Evangelie – dig unites the archetype of searching – a call to God.

Ewe – lamb
Ewe – one's **ewe** lamb – the only child, a treasure

Root ewe originated in Latin **ov**is (compare: in Russian **ов**ца [ovsa]).

This meaning is a thematic carrier of an *archetype of sacrifice.*

This can be explained by the Biblical statement that the social status of many prophets (Moses, David, Jesus) was connected to a lamb and shepherd. The archetypal link goes far beyond the Biblical plot of sacrificing a lamb instead of a child, to the well known plot of the Golden Fleece in Greek mythology, where a golden lamb was sacrificed to Zeus by his own request (http://fatetattoo.ru/index).

Let's return to the previous semantic field of the first woman, *Eve*. The question arises: Is Eve herself – and later on all women – the first sacrifice? According to the religious code for thousands of years it was believed that childbirthing pain was a woman's punishment for succumbing to the Devil and tricking Adam to eat the forbidden fruit. This concept can be interpreted as a transformation of the archetype of sacrifice.

The same function of the concept of sacrifice as torments can be continued as the martyrdom of Jesus. Thus, the crucifixion of Jesus (a son of a mortal woman and the Holy Spirit) brings to life the symbolization of the 3 main elements of Christianity: his blood as red wine; the bowl where his blood was gathered – the Holy Grail (*Мифы народов мира*. 1980: 184, 317.); and the Shroud; the different interpretations of the relics' symbolization created new movements in religion.

One of them as an archetypical plot becomes the storyline of Dan Brown's bestseller *The Da Vinci Code.* Jesus himself became a symbol. *The Holy Spirit* is used in the Trinitarian formula,"in the name of the Father, and of the Son, and of the Holy Spirit". Saint Mary (Eve as a representative of women's ancestry) as a mother of a son sacrificed for humanity, a mother who witnessed the torments of her son became one of the popular symbols of Christianity and archetypical plot.

Mary became one of the admired images of art, her numerous statues sometimes accompanied by baby Jesus are popular in churches and palaces.

Another very popular Christian symbol is Jesus the Redeemer (being sacrificed for sake of people. The symbol is expressed not only through a cross – crucifix and in the christening ceremony, but also on the monument in Rio-de-Janeiro, where it became the symbol of the city. The grandeur of the monument becomes the sign of the future greatness of the Resurrection of Jesus.

Here the archetypal motif is reproduced verbally as *Ewe – my ewe, one's ewe lamb.*

Thus the motif of sacral lamb and motif of sacrifice are connected through different times and plots. **Ewe – Agnes – Ram – Lamb – Sheep** – the line has been encountered in many versions in the world mythology.

The transformation of this archetype is also reflected in the white apron of Freemasons, once made from the *white lambskin.* Although the Masonic apron developed from the apron worn by real masons in the middle ages, it also had a symbolical meaning conveying the idea of being pure and *innocent*, and ready for *sacrifice* at any time for the maintenance of purity. The white colour being a sign of purity is also related to Hiram Abiff, the mason of Solomon's Temple. According to legend, masons, who wanted to prove their innocence, came to his funeral in white aprons and white gloves. Since then, it has become a traditional Masonic outfitworn during rituals (Майкл Бредли 2007: 14). As a continuation of the idea, a mason is buried in a white apron, which again conveys the archetypal symbol of resurrection (God's lamb- one's ewe – Jesus Saviour) (Майкл Бредли 2007: 41).

The idea of sacrifice of the best – the innocent – for the sake of others, originates in early times of humanity. Even before monotheism the *sacrifice* of girls, (virgins Vestals in Rome of pagan times), boys (child-my *ewe*- lamb) was expressed through myths, rituals and fairytales.

The archetype of sacrifice *Ewe-Eve* is reminiscent of another cultural layer of general semantic area. That is:

Agnes – Agni – агнец [agnets](Russian (ewe) – **огонь** [agon'] (Russian) (fire).

Agni is the second most repeated word in the Rig-Veda after Indra (up to 200 times), and has several functions. In the epic Indian tradition Agni, as a cosmic power, is one of the five elements forming the world; it hides in water, was born in water, and sometimes it creates itself, and sometimes it can be created by rubbing two pieces of *wood* (***odun***- in Azerbaijani) together.

Now, compare Russian *агнец,* Sanskrit *Agni*, and Russian *огонь*; in Vedic and Indian mythology ***Agni*** indicates the god of *fire* and the main element of Indian ritual sacrifice and *the place of sacrifice,* the sacred fireplace. It is believed that the flame of the sacrificial fire takes the sacrificed to Heaven (Мифы народов мира 1980: 35, 36).

The word cluster as a carrier of semantic meaning

Belle [bel] (English from French) – *beauty*, the most attractive girl or woman, the beautiful adorable girl

Belle (Latin) – nice, fine, good looking

Bel as *incə**bel*** (Azerb.) [injabel] – *slim-waisted* an epithet describing a beautiful girl and her 40 maids in Turkic fairy tales and epics

Belly [beli] (English) – abdomen, as in belly dance – an Oriental dance

Taliş – ethnicity in south of Azerbaijan, whose language is closed to Persian

Talliss (Hebrew) – a Jewis prayer shawl for morning

Laçər (Azerb.) [lachar] – impudent, obscene, indecent, foulmouthed (mostly women)

Lecher – (English)- profligate, a lascivious or licentious person (mostly men)

Bad (English) – not good in any manner or degree, poor quality

Bəd (Azerb.) – bad

Search (English) – to look for something, to examine

Seç (Azerb.) [ç – ch] – *seçmək*, to choose something. In order to choose something, one should first search for it.

Genus *(*English) – **a** kind, sort, class

Gins *(*Azerb) [gins] – a sort, a type

Goy – (English from Yiddish- from Hebrew ***goi;*** adj – ***goy****ish*) non-Jewish person often deragatory as opposed to its synonym *gentile*; person, contrasted with a Jew; realting to the same tribe;

Göy adam (Azerb.) – (figurately: a blue or green man), ignoramus (compare: person, who is not a Jew), an ignorant person

Изгой [iz**goy**] (Russian) – [izgoy] (Russsian) – pariah, cast-away, person rejected by a society

Göyüsh (Hebrew) – (Azerb from Hebrew) – male name in Muslim population, probably originating from ***göyish*** (plural for *goy),* with the same meaning *gentile*, which previously referred to pagans, the non-Jewish population.

Mahram ***Bilquis*** – The ruins of the legendary *kingdom* of the Queen of Sheba, contemporary of King Solomon Malika Bilquis

Builquis – female *name* given in Islamic countries

Alp *Ər Tunqa* (Ancient Turkic) – *high*; the *highest* rank in Turkic tribe

Alp (English) – *high* mountain; top of mountain

Alp *Arslan* – the second sultan (1063-1072) of the Turkic Seljuk Dynasty, who ruled by the laws of Turkic tribes based on division into ulus in a huge empire with its center of contemporary Iraq.

Oğuz ***Alp*** – [Oghuz Alp] – "The first Oghuz rulers originated form Diuz ***Alp*** [Dyuz Alp] from the tribe of Oghuz. His son and the ruler of Oghuzes Oghuz Alp (known also as Suleyman) fought with the Greeks and in a short time became an influential ruler (H.F. von Dietz 2011: 29)

Launch – to start something, to start out or forth; push out or put forth on the *water*

Launch*er* (English) – starting position; a device designed to launch a missile in position for firing; a device for a wave-transition (*waiveguide launcher)*

Lonch*or* (Azerbaijani, local) – a small hole, or pit gathering water in aryk (narrow ditch for conveying water), for further distribution of water.

Mars*i* – exonym for the people of ancient Italy (with centre of Marruvium)

Marc*ia* (Italian) – a march, a walk

March (English) – musical genre for the same reason, for military formation

Марш*рут* (Russian) – [marshroot] (Russian) – the route, from French *marche* (walk ahead)+*route* (way), to walk with regular steps

Alla ***Marc****ia* (Musical) – a tempo repeating the rhythm and style of a march

Mərs*iyə* (common for Azerb. and other Islamic population) – lament genre, rhythmically repeated lament

*Philo****soph****er* (English. From Greek) – main principles

Soph*istikate* (англ.) – one of the meanings is to *improve*

Sof*u* (азерб., диалектн.) – person, who philosophizes; also Muslim saints

*Me****shuga*** (via Yiddish, from Hebrew) – crazy, insane (compare, the archetypal image of *Majnun* has the same meaning – crazy from love, related to a *man*)

Meshuga (English, derivative of Hebrew) – cranky, mad, insane (compare: archetypal hero *Majnun* in the same value – the *madman* from love)

Məşuqə (Azerb., from Arabic) – beloved (*female*), in colloquial language usually used as disparaging and offensive

Aşiq – məşuq (Azerb., from Arabic) – a loving pair

Eşq (Azerb, from Arabic) – love (elevated, high style)

Aşiq (lover) – sometimes is replaced with the word cin (genie) especially as the part of the complex word. So the protagonist of the Arabic legend in the medieval archetypal plot of *Leyla and Majnun*, Qays goes *mad* for love, which causes people call him *Majnun* (possessed by *genie;* paronym with a word *jinni* (*genie* – supernatural creature, by the way, as well as *genius*, which is a paronym; *me* is the prefix). The name of aşıq [ashik] (bard) of the Azerbaijani epic Koroğlu [Koroghlu] is *Junun* (compare with *genie* and *Majnun*). The interesting fact that the expression "to be *madly in love*" is common to many languages and regarded nowadays as metaphorical.

Thus, "mad, crazy" and "love" join in the same semantic line.

Man – man, human

Woman – The etymology of the prefix *wo-* suggests the derivation from "a *woe*", which somehow explains the belief, that a woman on board a ship is bad luck, although boats with male crews also could be shipwrecked.

Insan (Azerbaijani) – a human in a more positive sense, as a humane human.

Insan (Korean) – ginseng, the root of which is believed to have a form of a human; *in-* in Korean means a human.

Insane (English, from Latin) – out of mind, mad

Spirutas **San**ctus (Latin) – Holy Spirit

Sanitation – hygiene

Compare: a mad person is sometimes considered to be close to god, (a god's fool).

Sanskrit – the root *san* means pure (if we take into account that Arian tribes occupying the Indian valley in the third millennium considered themselves as well as their language and writing pure, the meaning is plausible)

Sun: The suggestion that ***son*** in the culture of Sanskrit carriers was linked with fire is probable.

The root *san* in two word clusters is quite common and they are connected to each other by the archetypal meaning *become clean, pure*, with physical, psychological and mental implications.

Son – a male offspring

Sonne (German) – Sun
Sohn (German) – son
*Sam**son*** (son of the Sun?) (Latin), in Hebrew – Simson or Shimshon
Seme – semes – son (Мифы народов мира. т. 2,1982: 402.)
S(h)em –in **the** Bible and Koran one of the sons of Noah with the meaning *name, prosperity,* which gave the name of the ***Semi**tic* languages. Take into account that the family name, even in the starting of XXI century, is traditionally and preferably the *father's (*"son of" in Arabic is "aby").

This cluster is connected with the last variation ***seme***, and also can be continued with *water* (English) – *ata* (Azerbaijani) – *father.*

Water **–** clear liquid
Vater (German) – father
Father – a male parent

German vater sounds like [*f*]. The suffix –er, is lost in some languages, as for example in Russian ***вода*** *[vada]* – water, *мать* [*mat'*] – mother, but appears in genitive form *мат**ери*** *[materi*], but not in ***воды*** *[vadi*]. Taking into account these points, we can suggest that the word ***father*** used to relate to o ris a derivative of ***water.***

Pater (Latin) – father,ansector
***Pat**res* conscripti (Latin) – lawmakers, патриции (сословие в древнем Риме)
***Pat**ronym* – component of a given name, based of father or *male ansector*, still in use, equivalent of family name
***Pat**ron* **–** promoter, sample for imitation[16]
***Patter**n* – imitation
***Frat**er* (Latin) – ***broth**er* – ***brud**er* (German)
Bərad**ər* (Persian) – ***брат (Russian) brother – ***bərab**ər* (Azerbaijani) together, same.

The last word (a semantic translation from Persian that can also be an inaccurate variation of ***bərad**ər*) was placed deliberately in the cluster, as it is synonymous with ***broth**erhood* and can be translated as a ***broth**erhood*, ***frat**ernity*. Here the archetype of ***broth**erhood* and ***frat**ernity* is expressed.

*As**gard*** – ***город*** [gorod] – the dwelling place, the *city* of the Norse gods.

---

16 Online Etymology Dictionary. http://www.etymonline.com /index.php.: "The difference in form and sense between patron and pattern wasn't firm till 1700s. Meaning "model or design in dressmaking" (especially one of paper) is first recorded 1792, in Jane Austen. Verb phrase pattern after "take as a model" is from 1878. »

Ace (French) [as] – ace, a very skilled person, an expert. Semantically can be associated with the *As* – Norse gods, who advocated order and law according to *Prose Edda*, Icelandic epic poetry containing tales of Norse mythology (М. И. Стеблин-Каменский, Web)

*As**garor*** – in Icelandic variation. *Gorod* or *grad* – in Slavic, means city; in Russian – *gorodit'* – to border, to enclose; *gare* (French) – station, as a place enclosed for a crowd, *garage* – the same meaning.

Gara (Turkic) – [ga:ra:], *black* and also *mighty, great, abundant;* also as the part of expression "gonaq-*garalı*" (with *many* guests)

Woden, Wodin (Norse) or ***Odin*** (German) – Norse god, ***Oth**in* in Old High German

Wodin – Wodn**es* (Old English) – ***Woden's** day* – ***Wednes**day* – Holy ***Wednes-*day* in Passion or Maundy week (strong fast week before Easter)

Wood (English) – the trunks of trees

***Od**un* (Azerbaijani) [odun] – wood

Od (Azerbaijani) – fire

Wotan **(Odin, Wod**en, **Woutan)**[17] (German) – counterpart Odin;

This comparative word cluster, relating to the concept of tree and fire, the supreme god, surprisingly can be an added as a comment to the theory of Thor Heyerdahl, Norwegian traveler and archaeologist, according to whom Azerbaijanis, particularly those from the Absheron peninsula, moved to Scandinavia in primeval times.

On the other hand, the Russian ***один*** [odin] (one) could be an echoe of the ancient belief in sacred fire. The assumption can be built on the premises of, on the one hand, related Russian and Ancient Persian languages, and the geographical proximity with Azerbaijanis where ancient Zoroastrian temples of sacred *fire* were used until 19th century.

The latter two word clusters reflect the archaic mythological type of words, *ace – gorod* (city) – *od* (fire).

Ведать [***vedat'***] (Russian) – ***bil**mək* (Azerbaijani) – to know

***Ведь**ма [ved'ma]* (Russian) – a witch (female, who deals with devil)

***Вед**унья, **вед**ун* [*vedunya, vedun*] (Russian) – a witch, a wisard, a seer: compare with Russian *зна*харь [*zna*xar'] from *знать* [znat'] with the same semantic root – to know

Vedas (from Sanskrit *knowledge*) – a sacred Hindu text

Videvdat (compare Russian *videt'* – to see) – the part of *Avesta,* allegedly written by Maga (A Midian tribe of priests)

17 Woutan-Watan (in some Turkic languages and Arabic) means native land. Usually high style.

*Veni-**Vid**i-Vici* – The famous phrase by Julius Cesar (came – saw – won)
***Vid**eo* – of or pertaining to *television*, esp. the *visual* elements.
***Vid**et'* (Russian) – to see – from the same Latin word family
Stavit' na ***vid*** (Literally – to put on sight) – to notify
Ved- vid denote the archetype of *to know, to see, to foresee*. Russian words *быль [byl]* – an real, actual story*, быть [*byt'] – to *be,* Azerbaijani *bil*ği – to know, Avesytian ***Vid**evdat*, and the Latin root ***vid***- all are rooted in archetypal verbal line.
*До **свид**ания* (Russian) – goodbye literally "until we *see* again"
*Auf **Wied**ersehen* (German) – goodbye, literally "until we *see* again"
***Ви**деть [videt']- **вид** [vid]* (Russian) – to see; although in the German ***Wied**ersehen* – see again, *sehen* translates as *to see, and **wied**er* as *again*, the latter entering in the same orthographic and phonetic row with Azerbaijani ***vid**a (farewell), əl**vid**a (goodbye), **vid**alaşmaq (to say goodbye)* is brought to our attention. Moreover the suffix "*-er"* here can be considered as a later addition athat was lost in some words, for example, in the multilingual (Latin, English, German, Russian) verbal row mat**er**-moth**er**-mutt**er**-мат**ер**(и), daugth**er**-tocht**er**-доч**ер**(и), wat**er**-vat**er**-вод(а), frat**er**-broth**er**-brud**er**-berad**er**-брат-bərab**ər**.

***Bəl**li* (Azerbaijani)- known, acknowledged,
***Bəl**i* (Spanish – from Arabic) – *yes*
Bil (Azerbaijani) – know
Быль [bıl']- a story based on a real event.
***Бы**лина* [*bylina*] – a heroic epic, specific to Russian folklore, combining myth and real historic events.
*Para**ble*** (English) – short story for illustration of religious idea; one of the meanings is *ино**сказание*** [inoskazaniye] in Russian; *skazaniye* is synonym to bylina, *ino-* is *para-* .

Folk – people
Volk (German) – people

Considering the rule v=[f] I would suggest the etymological study of the connection between the Russian *волк* [*volk*] – a wolf, and German *volk*. We should also take into a consideration the totem of *wolf* from the myths of Turkic Oguz tribes, who regarded the totem as thier ancestor; compare also with the founders of Rome Romul and Rem , who were nursed by a she-*wolf*.

Kofta (Azerbaijani, Russian) – a blouse, a shirt

Kaftan (Turkish, Azerbaijani, Russian) – a medieval overcoat, mostly for men, although described as a dress worn by a woman, Selcan-khatun, in the Azerbaijani epic *Kitabi Dədə Gorqud* (*The Book of Dada Gorgud*).

Turk – ***Turk*** – the first historical mention is from Chinese records, the tribes originated there and in neibouring Mongolia in the first millennium BC (Ə. Rəcəbov, J. Məmmədov 1993: 5-6). The Chinese ideograph sounds like tyu-ke and considered not semantic but phonetic (Курбан Саид 2009: 69). It is known that ***-yu*** in ***tyuk-yu*** is a plural suffix in Mongolian (Ə. Rəcəbov, J. Məmmədov 1993: 5-6).

Род (Russian) [rod] – a family, a lineage, a gender, tribe

Rod – a stick, a new shoot, a branch, a shoot, a stem

Plough, plow – implement with sharp blades for turning over the earth

Плуг (Russian)[plough] – a plough

Plow (Persian, Azerbaijani) – a main dish prepared from rice

Plowman – ***əkinçi*** (Azerbaijani) *[**ekin**chi]* – *plough*man, *plow*man
The word ***əkinçi*** identifies the person, who mostly sows and plants wheat. Here there is an interesting connection between:

Əkmək (Azerb.) [ekmek] – to sow, to *plant*

Ekmek (Turkish) – a bread

Əppək (Azerb.) [eppek] –a *bread*, the word is used mostly in the Zagatala – Balaken region of Azerbaijan.

Continuing with semiotics, it would be reasonable to examine the word ***seme***.

Seme-seme gəzmək (Azerbaijani) [seme seme gazmak] – to meander, ramble, a dialectic expression used in Ilisu and Ujar regions of Azerbaijan. *Filankəs* ***səm****ədir [**sem**edir]* – someone is aimless, primitive.

Seme – one of the main terms in structuralism and semiotics, identified as "an elementary unit of meaning, usually a defining feature or characteristic of something" (Chris Baldick 1990: 201.).
Semantics and *semiology* derives from the same root.

Seme – ***səm****ən****i*** [samani] – a grain of *wheat* as an elementary unit is a symbol of a new year, signifying the sun, and good fortune in Zoroastrianism. Here – *ən* is a suffix (like in English wat*er*, Russian доч*ери* [docheri], мат*ери* [mat***er***i]).

Семя [**sem'**a] (Russian) – a seed

Семья [**sem**ya] (Russian) – a family

Семь [**sem**'] (Russian) – seven. Seven is related in the *seme* line of creation. Compare: The world was created in 6 days, on the **seven**th God rested. Thus a week consists of seven days. Accordingly, Muslims rests on Friday, Jews on Saturday (Sabbath in Hebrew) and Christians on Sunday (Russian воскресенье for Sunday [voskresen'e] – also means 'resurrection'; compare with Tolstoy's novel with the same name)

***Dom**e* (English) – a hemispherical roof
***Dom**a* (Latin) – roof
Дом (Russian) [dom] – home, house,
Dam (Azerb) – roof; living area for domestic animals
***Dom**estic* – accustomed to family life
Домашний (Russian)[domashniy] – domestic, family
***Dome**sday Book – a record book commissioned in December 1085 by William the Conqueror.

Cavan (Azerbaijani and some Muslim languages) – young
Joven (Spanish) – young
Young: the letter *J* in some cases pronounces as [*j*] (January) and sometimes [*y*] (Jadwiga, Maja).

Təriqət (Azerbaijani and some eastern languages) [tarigat] – way, path, method, an Islamic religious order, especially associated with Sufism.
Target – an aim, a goal to be reached.

Some words have a clear transformation route:
Tea – tee (German) – ***te*** (Spanish and Italian) from ***te*** – in Chinese dialect with minor variation.
Chay [chai] – [cha] – in Portuguese, Russian, Turkish, Azerbaijani etc. Both variants derives from Chinese, with one of the words being a dialectal variation.

An archetypisation of the adopted words did not occur here, since the period of time was not extensive and the etymological path stayed clear. Another cultural dimension expressed in the language is the *tea* ceremony which can be observed in Eastern and from the XVIIth century on in European civilization. The tradition of mixing tea with milk is observed in Indian, Mongolian, Bashkir, Kazakh (both Turkic nations), and some Caucasian (partly Turkic) population. The British continue with the tradition, and created a new dimension with a customary 5 o'clock, or afternoon tea.

Not – denial, refusal
Naught – zero
Notte (Italian) – ***Nacht*** (German) – ***Nuit*** (French) – ***night***

Mockery **–** a derisive, mocking action
Maskara *etmək* (Azerbaijani) – (literally to make mockery), to mock
Massacre- maliciosly killing
Məzhəkə (Azerbaijani) – jest, joke for asmusement

The last word is phonetically and semantically close to the first two words, and the word *massacre* is not accidental in the series. The verbal chain is connected to a negative sense, with mocking at, and massacre being the most derogatory and tragic.

Porta (Latin) – gate
Port (English)- harbour; town alongside of navigable water
Portal (English) – an entrance, access to a place
Porta (Spanish) – gate
Puerto (Spanish) – door, entrance
Pass***port*** – document, which allows to pass the border (*port* as the *gate* of the country)
Passage – combination with the suffix *age*
Passport – created by combination of ***pass*** and ***port***, this document is required for entrance into another country.
Пассажир (Russian) [pasajir] – ***passenger***
Passager (French), ***passagier*** (German) – passenger

Duchy (English) – a territory of a *duke* , a nobleman
Дача [dacha] (Russian) – country house, usually affordable to the well off

Penj (*Persian*) [pəndg]– five
Pancatantra (Sanskrit) – five books; a collection of Indian animal fables; *panj* + tantra (system, integrity, continuity)
Pəncə (Azerbaijani, from Persian) [pəndjə] – a paw

The name of an *archetypal genre* in medieval times, later known as "*Hamsa*" (collection of five books), mostly connected on regional basis and with the meaning of *tantra*, integrity of didactic function (see: *mirror for princes*)

Linguistic expression of a semantic field or the naming of "other" nations

Sometimes several minor ethnic groups living among a majority of another ethnos have a general name: Tartar/Tatar. Mogul/Mongol, Catyayan/Kityayan, Chin/Tsin/ Ch'I are some of them.

Tartar – has several meanings: Tatar ethnos, Tartarus of Greek myths, and a wild person. There is enough evidence of the same negative semantics being applied on the verbal level to the "Dutch" (Stereotypes in literatures and cultures 2010: 88-89). Even in modern times, Tatars and Azerbaijanis ARE sometimes called *tartars*. So, what unites all these different meanings to the word *Tartar*?

Information about the word as a negative label of a nation by another nation is discovered in the most book of ancient warfare tactics, written about 500 BC, called *The Art of War* by Sun-Tzu. Here we come across references concerning the word *tartar* alongside with *Cathayans* (Chinese), *China* and *Khan (*Sun Tzu 2002*)*.

"Tartars" was the general term applied to the barbarians who lived to the north and west of China. There were of many distinct tribes. As these tribes, one after the other gained the ascendancy among the Tartars, the name of that particular tribe was applied to the whole *race*. They were first called Hiung-nu (Huns), then Sien-Pi, and later Turks, Uigers, Cathayans, and Mongols. Their characterctics were very similar. They lived on horseback and moved from place to place with their flocks and herds in search of fresh pasture. Having no homes for their enemies to destroy and possessing greater mobility than the Chinese, who were mostly infrantry, they retreated before the expeditions sent against them until the supplies of the Chinese were exhausted and they had to return to China.

The Tartars frequently raided Chinese territory in search of plunder. They preferred silk cloth and wine, but carried off almost anything that was easily portable. They were noted for their cruelty and frequently massacred the inhabitants of Chinese cities. About the year 700 A.D., a Tartar leader named Mercho captured two cities in Shensi province and killed 90,000 inhabitants." (Sun Tzu 2002: 23)

Thus, *tartars* as well as **Cathyans** (Chinese) were a tribe neighbouring China. The same work narrates the event that after the promotion of Sun-Tzu by king Ho Lu of the state of *Wu* (now in the east of China) to the post of general, his army terrified the states of **China** and **Ch'i** (Sun Tzu 2002: 12). The name of the Chinese emperor **Chin** Hvang-Ti (Sun Tzu 2002: 22) of the **Zin** (**Tsin**) dynasty who built the Kochin Chin road and played an important role in the unification of China and built the Great Wall of China resembles the words Chin (Sun Tzu 2002: 15) and Zin.

The (name of Chinese general Ve Tsing (Sun Tzu 2002: 26) founder of Han dynasty Kaotsou (202-194 BC) is said to have built many strategically important roads (Sun Tzu 2002: 21). The succeeding rulers adopted the title of Khan as Genghis- khan (1162-1227), Kublai-khan(1216-1294).

The lexical cluster Chin-Tsin-Ch'i turns our attention to other word well known to me from my childhood – ***moghol***. The [***NG***] diphthong in Azerbaijani differentiates two ethnicities: *Mo**ng**ols* and *Moghols*. In northern parts of Azerbaijan where the local population consists of Avar and Turk (Tatar) ethnic groups, the latter is called Moghol just as the Chinese called all their northern neighbours *Tartars*. To be precise, the tribes named by the Chinese as Tartars in the mentioned areas are called Moghols (in correlation with Mongols), that is neighbours of the Chinese.

Thus, *moghol* as well as *tartar* is are exonyms denoting denoting the name of an ethnos on the lexical level. The regional characteristic of cuisine of not only *Moghols*, but local Avars brings in evidence that once the latter were also bordering *Tartars*.

Conclusions

At times the *archetypisation of lexical roots, prefixes and suffixes* is an archaic process, and, coming from ancient myths and thinking, which progressively pervades monotheistic religions and forms into archaic types. Although we should mention that some other words, being a type in the process of formation, do not turn into archetypes. Occasionally lexical similarities are evidences of *variants – archetypes emerging from temporal layers* onto the surface of the cultural stratum. The study of this process is no less important than the research of ethnogenetic parallels in language as it reveals the inetrsection of the common cultural elements of distant, at the first sight, ethnoses in different circumstances.

We believe that in spite of the legacy of a rich theory of comparative linguistics, such as nostratic theory, the theory of linguistic reconstruction, etc., sometimes it is valuable to research non-stereotypical and non-conventional material. The archetypisation of a motif, plot, or situation is considered to include an etymon which is an archetypisation of semantic spaces, a primary word in related languages as well as in non-related ones.

In the process of development etymons (a root word, a primary variant) evolve from a semiotic sign into a signification, or vice versa, from signification to a sign. Semantic areas pervade primordial as well as modern symbols. This process is impelled by new ideologies and religions. An original thought, even one contrary and critical to its predecessors, is not created in a vacuum, but from a source of inspiration and formation, using earlier thoughts. Semantic signs and symbols migrate from one language and religion to another. These semantic migrations allow for the study of a *language* not as a mere function on the lexical, morphological or syntactic levels, but as a *historical source*. Language becomes a significant factor in the research of historical aspects of cultural formation, and further, in a study of the migration of beliefs, of peoples. The identification of analogous symbols through comparison from different angles (for example, *debil* (Spanish and Russian)/ *zibil* (Azeri and Kurdish)) is similar to archaeological digs that permit penetration deep down into the layers of ethnic histories and cultural deposits. These intersections in history and culture and language it is possible to name "multiculturalism with culture," in memory of the name of Anne Philips' book, *Multiculturalism without Culture*.

Layers of semantic typology in words, being simultaneously cultural layers, draw attention on the one hand as reflexions of archetypal plots and symbols. And secondly, they draw attention as a result of the migration of words with newly acquired local features and traditions.

References

ABBYY Lingvo (12 version) electronic dictionary.

Online Etymology Dictionary. http://www.etymonline.com /index.php.:"The difference in form and sense between patron and pattern wasn't firm till 1700s. Meaning "model or design in dressmaking" (especially one of paper) is first recorded 1792, in Jane Austen. Verb phrase pattern after "take as a model" is from 1878.»

About stereotypes without stereotypes?- Stereotypes in literatures and cultures. – Peter Lang, Frankfurt, 2010

Anne Philips. *Multiculturalism without Culture*. Princeton, Princeton University Press, 2009.

Bjarke Frellesvig. *A History of the Japanese Language* – Cambridge UniversityPress. – http://www.hf.uio.no/ikos/forskning/publikasjoner/boker/history-of-the-japanese-language.html.

Chris Baldick. *The Concise Oxford dictionary of literary terms.* – New York-Oxford, Oxford University Press – 1990.

Francis Edward Jackson Valpy, An etymological dictionary of the Latin language, Vlapy, 1838.

Harrison, Charles *Art in theory, 1900-2000: an anthology of changing ideas.* Blackwell Publishing. 2003.

Ruth H. Sanders. German: Biography of a Language. OUP, 2010.

Sun Tzu. *The Art of War.*Translated from the Chinese by Lionel Giles – Dover Publications, Mineola, New York, 2002.

Qurani-Kərim. Azərbaycan dilinə tərcüməsi [Mətn] /Ərəb dilindən tərcüməedənlər: Z.M.Bünyadov, V.M.Məmmədəliyev (ön söz).- B.: Qismət, 2006

Ə. Rəcəbov, J. Məmmədov . Orxon-Yenisy yazıları (abidə mətnlərin əsli və tərcüməsi) – Bakı: Yazıçı,1993.

H.F. fon Ditz/ *Homerin Siklopu ilə müqayisədə yeni aşkar edilmiş oğuz* (Gizli missiyanın məsləhətçisi və prelatı Hayniz Fridrix fon Ditz tərəfindən). Halle və Berlin, 1815// – BSU Elmi Əsərləri, Dil və Ədəbiyyat seriyası, Bakı-Frankfurt am Main – 2011, S. 29.

(H. von Diez. New discovered Oguz version comparaible with Cyclop by Homer. Proceeding of Baku Slavic University, Baku -Frankfurt am Main 2011, p. 29).

Курбан Саид. *Девушка из Золотого Рога.* – Москва: Ad Marginen Press, 2009.

(Kurban Said. *Devushka iz Zolotogo Roga.* –Moskva: Ad Marginen Press, 2009).

А.Е. Крымский. *Низами и его современники.* Баку: Эльм, 1981.

(A.E. Krymski. Nizami I yevo sovremenniki. Baku: Elm, 1981).

Мифы народов мира. Энциклопедия, т.1. – Главный редактор С.А. Токарев. – М.: Советская энциклопедия, (второе издание) 1987.

(Mify narodov mira. Enciklopedija, t.1. – Glavnyj redaktor S.A. Tokarev. – M.: Sovetskaja Enciklopediya, (vtoroe izdanie) 1987.

Мифы народов мира. Энциклопедия, т.2. – М.: Советская энциклопедия, т. 2, 1982.

(Mify narodov mira. Enciklopediya, t.2. – M.: Sovetskaja Ensiklopediya, t. 2, 1982.

М. И. Стеблин-Каменский. *Снорри Стурлусон и его «Эдда".* Web. – Snorra Edda. Младшая Эдда. – Norrœn Dýrð (Северная Слава).Web. http://norse.ulver.com /src/snorra /stk.html.

Similarities in World Literature: Azerbaijani and Greek Epics (toward Invariants)

Kamal Abdullayev
(Azerbaijan)

This paper deals with invariant and distinct features of archetypes in Ancient Greek and Azerbaijani epics. Most plots, events, and characters in these epics have much in common, sometimes obviously, and sometimes not, with other mythological epics of world literature. The number of features they have in common increases, until finally we can see that these features appear in one form penetrating the whole structure of the epic.

The endless mystery of the *Kitabi Dada Gorgoud* epic is undeniable. There is a way leading from the implicit Dada Gorgud to the explicit Dada Gorgud. On the surface are variants based on opposites, such as "nature-culture," "norm-abnormal," "old-modern," "happiness-misery," "old-tyoung," "challenge through ordeal." The forms of the realization of these things are the matter of separate research. However, in this paper we will consider the genetic line leading primarily from Greek myths.

At the beginning of the 19th century the German scholar, Diet, conducted comparative analysis of the myth of *Cyclops* and *Polyphemous,* based on the variants of Greek and Turkic monuments. An increasing number of variants were the focus of research in the middle of the 20th century. The Azerbaijani scholar, Ali Soultanly's, in his profound research of the Greek and Turkic epic systems, provided a number of new and distinct variants (Sultanlı Ə. 1971: 11-101). Step by step the epic has revealed lines of comparison, new deeply lying variants, as well as showing ways for connecting these variants to the core of the epic, the primary source, i.e. the invariant, stable.

How are the invariants built up? Clearly, parallels exist among plot lines or characters in the mythological systems of different nations. These similarities show a number of variants. Each of them opens ways for comparisons. Finally, similar variants in different epics tend to dissolve and disappear into universal plots. The ways leading to universalization could be many or few, just like rivers flowing into the sea. This generalization is just the invariant covering those specific variants.

What do the Greek and Turkic myths present as patterns? Can we be satisfied with these archetypes, or can we add to the comparative line another variant of archaic types from other mythological systems, such as those of the Sumerian, Chinese, Indian, or Egyptian myths?

In this context we would like to reflect on the Greek and Turkic mythological lines, which are like rivers flowing into one sea, and thus shaping an invariant, we shall dip into their depth and compare them with each other. It should be noted that we have another less explicit purpose as well, which is to disclose the *Kitabi-Dada Gorgoud* epic as an integral part of the common ancient mythological system of the Turkic world view.

Similarities determine lines as variants, while differences clearly show the national peculiarities of each. Similarities and differences set conditions for the emergence of two cases.

The first case: If there are more differing features and relatively few similarities between the variants we can conclude that the line (it can be both a plot and a character) is a literary product of more ancient times. On the contrary, if there are more similarities and fewer differences between the variants, the line is relatively new.

The second case: if there are more differences and fewer similarities between the variants, the line is relatively new and rich in specific peculiarities. On the contrary, if there are more similarities and fewer differences, the line is more ancient. Maybe, it has not yet parted from the invariant core to a great extent, and here no differentiation is felt.

These cases appeared as a result of the variants' relation to each other, and at the same time in some ways, show their level of antiquity. For example, similarities between the *Cyclop* and *Polyphemous* variants or similarities between *Beyrak* and *Odysseus* are much greater than the similarities between *Agamemnon* and *Salour Gazan*, or between *Hercules*, *Admetus* and *Dali Domroul*.[1] The last ones have sufficiently differing features as well as similarities. These differences appear in the most various directions. It is clear that distribution of the same function among different characters (*Odysseus*, *Bassat*, *Beyrak*), combinations (*Admetus*, *Hercules*, *Dali Domroul*), even opposites (*Antigone*, *Beyrak*), morals and ways of behaving related to national attributes (*Gantouraly*, *Paris*), etc. are issues creating specificity, preserving the originality of the each national Epic, polishing up its artistic thinking and keeping a plot tense.

The purpose of this paper is to show that as a whole the *Kitabi-Dada Gorgoud* epic is a bridge, transferring human society from ancient times to another age. It is a transit bridge from nature to culture. Finally, it is a transit bridge from

---

1 All unfamiliar names are from the epic Dada-Gorgoud, which consists of several books with different protagonists, uniting the figures of the story-teller Dada Gorgoud and the king of Oghuz Salur-Kazan.

oral literature to written. In this context, in my view, many points can be clarified, and find their solution. Function is shown both in plot lines, deep and broad branching of characters, as well as on the level of a language and a style. The way leading from variants to the invariant is a step to the great *Gorgoud* bridge.

Let us start analyzing the similarities and differences reflected in a number of separate variants.

Similarities: Odysseus, Bassat, and Beyrak. Multi-colored and multi-branching Greek myths are divided into certain cycles. It is known that Odysseus and legends about his adventures are included in the Trojan cycle. In the imagination of the ancient Greek, the Trojan War was an event where notions like valour and cowardice, manliness and betrayal, strength and weakness, slyness and innocence, beauty and ugliness conflict with each other, and where gods pay no heed to men according to these important criteria. The historicity of the Trojan war was proved by facts indicating the destruction of the city of Troy discovered by German archaeologist Schliemann in Asia Minor in the 19th century. Schliemann based his research on the information in the Homeric epics (Г.Шталь [G. Shtal]. 1991:196-218; Рахман Бадалов 1973: 9-10).

The scientific world is well aware of a number of wars waged among different Greek cities in the historic period. The difference between these accounts and the Trojan War is that the reason, the beginning, the course, and the result of this war were not shown in any historical document, but are known as a result of artistic and mythological creativity. In the remote past Homer, a blind legendary poet, , wrote two poems: *the Iliad* and *the Odyssey* perpetuating this war in people's memory. Many Greek gods, demi-gods, commanders, rulers of cities and islands became immortalized in the poems.

Though it belongs to an author's pen, both works originated from Greek myths. And one of the main personages of both of the myths and poems was Odysseus, the ruler of the island of Ithaca in ancient Greece.

Odysseus' role, one distinguished for keen intellect, slyness and fighting ability among the Greeks, in winning the Trojan War is outstanding. Namely the courage he displayed in the Trojan War brought him both immortal fame and much trouble and sorrow.

Everything happens for this reason. The sea god, Poseidon, the brother of the chief god, Zeus, was Odysseus' enemy and kept his ships from returning from Troy in the sea, misleading them from one island to another and preventing him from sailing to his native Ithaca. There was only one reason for this. Poseidon was the father of one-eyed (also Goggle-Eyed) giant Cyclopes, named Polyphemous, and Odysseus blinded him with a trick.

Slyness was Odysseus' most salient characteristic. He was known only as a capable and sly commander. For the Greeks, who could not gain victory in the bloody fights for ten years, he devised the stratagem of offering Trojans a giant horse, where he and his men were hiding. After the destruction of Troy the Greeks returned to their lands and the sea adventures of Odysseus started. Polyphemous stands at the beginning of these adventures and Poseidon became the architect of Odysseus' troubles.

Fate brought Odysseus' ship to the island of the one-eyed giant Polyphemous. And from this point on the parallelism between Odysseus – Polyphemous and Bassat – the One-eyed (Tepe-Gyoz) takes place. Although Odysseus is Greek, and Bassat is Oghuz, they act the same way. They blind Polyphemous and the One-eyed, deceiving them, and escape from the Giants' caves in similar ways, hiding under ram's belly. It is true that there are different, even quite different features between these parallels. However, the method of battle and victory over the monster bear a very close resemblance.

Odysseus is a personage who had his place and significance among characters in the Greek mythological system even before Homer. Homer took this personage from mythology. The conflict with Polyphemous is a single episode from Odysseus' life. His rich and adventurous life is demonstrated by his desire to marry beautiful Helen, his desire to evade the Trojan War by tricking different characters whose participation was important in war, his, mostly tangled, relations with Agamemnon and Achilles, and finally, after the war, his wandering from one island to another, his fight with Polyphemous, his capture by magicians and witches, his descent to the underworld and his talk with the ghosts of the dead, his return home after softening the gods with his tears and entreaties, are all moments of a rich, at the same time, adventurous life.

Odysseus' adventures do not end when he reaches Ithaca. Reaching home, he faces new tests. His conflict with young lords asking for his wife Penelope in marriage, his meeting with his son Telemachus, his victory over his enemies, end of all his troubles and sorrow, and finally, in fact – absolutely pure mythological destiny – he is killed by his son Telegonus, whose mother was the enchantress, Circe, living on one of the islands where Odysseus had been wandering. He is killed unpremeditatedly.

To compare with the Oghuz variant, Bassat is the most informative personage of *Kitabi-Dada Gorgoud.* Using the Bassat character, it is possible to restore different developmental stages through which Oghuz society passed. There are two different times facing each other: the time when the ancient Oghuz intermingles with nature, and the time when new human relations and intersocietal relations are formed. The transition from the first to the second found its artistic expression in the Bassat character from the mythological point of view. I would say that apart from being an artistic character, Bassat is a research-oriented character having a certain function. His fight against the One-eyed is a very important part of the function he fulfills. Bassat's fight and victory shows once again that the way leading from the society backward cannot be even supposed. The way leading backward would also mean return to that chaotic, disordered and unknown nature represented by the One-eyed.

Bassat also came out of nature's lap. He grew up in the lions' den and even after being taken into human society, he wanted more than once to return to Nature, where he grew up. As if the fetters in the society were confining to him, as if his soul was being stretched taut, longing for freedom ... And this freedom was to be found in Nature.

Victory by the force representing Culture over the force representing Nature, the Cyclopes, blinding him and cutting his head off in spite of the monster's begging "we are brothers, don't kill me," shows that the way back is closed once and for all. There is no way from Culture to Nature. It is necessary to close the way leading from order to chaos for good and all. So says the Dada Gorgoud.

In comparison, Odysseus only blinds Polyphemous and escapes by rescuing himself. It is enough for him. He has no other duty as a mythological figure. Unlike Odysseus, however, Bassat kills the One-eyed. A struggle against abnormal and chaotic disorder is carried on by slaying of the One-eyed. Cutting of the head from the body with a special sword, however, leads to more ancient mythological notions. The separation of the head from the body can be the symbol of the establishing order in the universe – as in the cosmological myths about the separation of the Sky from the Earth. As a result, there would be an order in the land of the Oghuz.

The variants approach each other as well as move away from each other in this way. Maybe the meaning of the two characters will grow clearer by comparison between the One-eyed and Polyphemous. It is very difficult to differentiate antagonists in both epics– Polyphemous from Odysseus, and the One-eyed from Bassat. In fact, the variants are fraternal ones. The Greek Odysseus and the Oghuz Bassat each draw one of these variants to our times. But the Odysseus and the Bassat characters part from each other after solving the problem with Polyphemous and the One-eyed.

Among the Oghuz, Odysseus' mythological function is also fulfilled by Beyrak. Beyrak is a personage with a rich inner world, whom we distinguish as one of the young and new types of characters of the epic. In Odysseus' narrative both lines, the Bassat and the Beyrak lines, seems to be united. The Bassat-Odysseus variant clashes with the Beyrak-Odysseus one in the Greek myth. And in fact, this clash of the mythological characters turns a key for understanding the Beyrak-Bassat confrontation in the Oghuz myth.

After 16-years of absence Beyrak hears that his fiancée is going to be given in marriage to another man and escapes from captivity. After 20-years of wonderings, Odysseus returns to the island of Ithaca, and unrecognized, faces young lords who seek his wife, Penelope, in marriage. Similarly, the Oghuz beys do not recognize Beyrak either. Beyrak offers Yalynjyg, the son of Yalanchy, who was going to marry his fiancee to bend Beyrak's bow and throw his arrow.

Along with these obvious lines on the top of the variants, there are some features uniting Beyrak and Odysseus at a very deep layer. These features have remained hidden in the deep because the parallelism is not complete, the lines sometimes break, and only associations give grounds for accepting these lines as branches of a variant. The disclosed features we are talking about are related to the death of both personages.

Beyrak is punished according to the laws of the mythological system for going beyond the laws. While he was in captivity, he loved and was loved by an infidel girl. He took an oath, but broke it. Some similarity can be found in Odisseus' fate as well. There is his captivity, his relation with an enchantress (infidel girl), his forgetting the past, and his breaking the oath and final escape.

Breaking of oaths, efforts to deceive the past, as well as passion for freeing oneself from obedience to the Creator, makes it so that neither of the characters goes unpunished.

The past takes its revenge on Odysseus in the person of Telegonus, and on Beyrak, in the person of Old Arouz.

Kindred fates, kindred destinies, unite the courageous and sly Odysseus with the proud and unrivaled Beyrak like two brothers. Distinguished from the other mythological characters for their complicated inner world, these two brother characters do not part in our imagination and confirm the longevity of the variants once again.

References

Əli Sultanlı. *"Dədə Qorqud" dastanı haqqında qeydlər*. Məqalələr, Baku, 1971.
Г.Шталь. *Генрих Шлиман*. М, 1991
G.Shtal'. *Genrih Shliman*. M, 1991
Рахман Бадалов. Правда и вымысел героического эпоса. Baku, 1973
Rahman Badalov. Pravda i vymysel geroicheskogo jeposa. Baku, 1973

Eurasian Folksong Texts as Carriers of Poetic Archetype

Izabella Horvath
(China – USA)

The Turkic, Mongolian and Sino-Tibetan language speaking populations who live in the northern and western provinces of China today have a rich cultural heritage that is relatively little known to the rest of the world, even in scholarly circles. The reason for this is their isolation due to various historical and geographic factors and events. The influence of these cultures throughout Central Eurasia have been strong and lasting, reaching from the Orchon Steppes to the Carpathian Basin.

Ten years of ethnographic fieldwork in China has given me a unique opportunity to become more familiar with the music and oral tradition of the Turkic and other Altaic language speaking peoples who live in Inner Mongolia, Gansu, and Xinjiang provinces. The many cultural threads lead as far west as to Hungary leading to historical connections between the ancestors of Hungarians and those of the Turkic and Mongol peoples who live in Central Asia and the north China today. These connections can be found in the areas of art (Horvath 1992), ethnography (Horvath 1993), music Horvath (1994), as well as physical anthropology (Du/Horvath, 1995; Henkey /Horvath, 1999).

In this study a new area will be explored: the particular images that occur in folksong texts of Chinese Turks (notably Kazakhs, Kyrgyz, Uigurs, and Salars), Mongolians, and consequently Hungarians folksongs. These data will be compared, examined, and their roots traced back in history to an ancient archetype recorded in some of the earilest Chinese historical documents.

My own previous work in this area (Horvath, 1994, in Chinese) discussed the parallels found in the rhyme and syllabic construction of north Chinese and Hungarian folksong lyrics. The conclusion was that the ancient stratum of Mongolian, Turkic, as well as Hungarian folksongs share a special rhythmic arrangement: stanzas with four lines have four, six, and eight syllables per line, as well as initial, medial, and final alliteration (Horvath 1994). Thus, research shows that there are many features found in folksongs which are shared by the Hungarians and other Altaic language speaking peoples living in north China today.

Bartók already noted that the ancient stratum of Hungarian folksongs have the same melodic construction as a certain group of Turkic folksongs. This construction exhibits the descending La-pentatonic quintine shift (Bartók 1985 121). His study was ignored by Hungarian musicologists for various political reasons for over 40 years (Du 2001). Then, in the early 1980's the in-depth study by a Chinese musicologist, Du Yaxiong, compared Hungarian folksongs with those of the Yugurs, a Turkic nationality living in Gansu province in north China (Du, 1982). His findings bore out Bartok's conclusions that the structural similarity between the Turkic and Hungarian folksong suggested that the ancestors of these two peoples shared a common ancient tradition in Asia, and were subject to cultural exchanges in the remote past. Du's further research proves that the descending quintine-shift melodic construction, coupled with the very special La- pentatone can be found in the music inventory of only those peoples who live in north China, Mongolia, some parts of Central Asia, and Hungary, and can not be found anywhere else in Eurasia (Du 1993).

Du also mentions another singularity of some Chinese[1] folksongs, specifically love songs, which are germane to our study. This peculiarity is that of the typical four-line folksong stanza, the first two lines of which deal with nature while the last two deal with love (Du 1982).

The folk music of Hungary can justifiably look back upon a rich tradition, which today is unfortunately being lost by leaps and bounds in the wake of globalization. Among the many types of Hungarian folksongs, the most voluminous are the love songs among which are the "*virágénekek*" = "flower songs." These bear a very striking resemblance in content and construction to love songs found in north China, called *shaonian*, "songs of young men," and others which, incidentally are also called "*hua-er* ", that is, "flower songs." The Hungarian love folksongs also have the description of nature in the beginning lines, and descriptions of human love in the last lines of the stanza arrangement.

Demonstrating the parallels among the images and their meaning in the North Chinese, Turkic, Mongolian, and Hungarian love lyrics and tracing them back to the earliest such examples that emanate from a philsosphical arechetye will be the subject of this study.

Social environment of love songs

The north Chinese folksongs, which also include the folksongs of the Altaic lanugage speakers, are sung during courting and weddings and flower festivals, held especially for young people for the purpose of finding mates and lovers (Du, 1998). Similarly, Hungarian love songs are also sung during times of courting, as

1 *** The term *Chinese* refer to people who reside within the political boundaries of the People's Republic of China today. This includes the 65 minority nationalities, among them various Turkic peoples.

teasing songs aimed at pairing young men and women at social gatherings, and consequently at weddings (Kodály 1996).

The music tradition in the north of China is incredibly rich and also of great antiquity. There exist many kinds of music genre, and the one concerning us mostly – the love songs – are widespread all over north China even today.

Early Chinese music collection

In China the collection of folk songs and popular music had already begun as early as the Zhou Dynasty (1112-256 BC). Zhou rulers believed that because the common people would sing folk songs about their troubles and their aspirations, this information would aid the emperor in his policy-making efforts. To this end the emperors sent out musicology specialists to collect folk songs throughout the empire. Folk songs were called *feng (*wind), so doing folksong collection in the field was called *caifeng*, that is "picking up folksongs." (Even today, Chinese ethnomusicologists who collect folksongs are doing *caifeng)*. This material in turn was sent to an office higher up until the final report reached the imperial court. Consequently, a lot of folk lyrics were deposited into the imperial palace libraries and archives.

To train his students in music, one of the most important subjects in ancient China, Confucius selected 305 poems, odes, and songs from the imperial archival materials among which 160 were folk songs. He then incorporated these into a book which today is known as the "Book of Songs" (Waley 1996).

These folk songs compiled in the Book of Songs had a great impact on future generations. Not only can we enjoy them today, 2400 years later, as excellent examples of folk literature, but they represent an emphasis on folk songs and the importance of folk music in the ancient literary tradition of China.

In the Qin and Han dynasties, China has also set up a so-called "verse agency" that specialized in collecting "yue," that is, folk songs and folk music. Although the dynasty eventually fell, the work of collecting folk songs continued.

Sinologist know that the Book of Songs is considered a classic. Among the 160 folksong texts appear the first instances of texts that consist of four lines, of which the first part describe nature, or actions of nature, and the last lines describe human love, or descriptions of love. In China his particular archetype in folksongs and love poems the images of nature and human love between the opposite sex can be shown to have existed from the Zhou (1112-246 BC) though to the Qing Dynasty (1644-1671) (Xu 1994), and they survive today as folk songs, as will be demonstrated below. This pattern forms the archetype of love songs which has also survived in the cultures of the grassland peoples of Central

Asia and north China can be traced to the Carpathian Basin in the ancent stratum of the Hungarian folksongs. This archetype is the verbal imaging of the eternal existence of opposites and celebration of change, renewal, and continuity of life that was formulated in writing in the Taoist teachings (Lin Yutang 1948) and the Yi Jing (Wilhelm and Baynes 1950).

Mohammed Kashgari's collection of Turkic folk poetry from the 11th century (Geng, 1982) also contains love poems of four lines with two lines describing nature, and the last two discussing human activities:

> Let the young man shake the tree
> The fruit will fall down.
> Let them get a sheep
> Let 's celebrate the festival.
> (Geng 1982, 122)

This same style can also be found among Mongolian folk songs (Du, 1984). Clearly this stanza construction looks back upon a long tradition shared by northern Chinese ethnic groups.

The first time I heard the lyrics of these love songs in north China was during dinner parties with my Mongol and Turkic friends. I was immediately struck by their similarity to the many Hungarian folk songs of exactly this specific construction. In popular Hungarian folk song publications (*Rezeda;, Viola; Tiszán innen Dunán túl,* 1971-2) songs generally appear under the category of *szerelmi dalok* (love songs) and *párositó, házasitók és lakodalmas dalok,* (pairing off, marrying off, and wedding songs). They are by far the most numerous of the archival collections, so they comprise an important part of the folk music tradition and are worthy of detailed research.

Early research on love song texts

An early reference to Hungarian folk songs comes from János Sylvester who first translated the New Testament into Hungarian in 1541. In the addenda to the translation he writes:

> ...it is easy for our people to get used to [the parables of Jesus] because such [symbolic] speech is not strange to them. They use such speech daily, and use it in songs, especially the *flowersongs*, and all people can marvel at the sharpness of the mind of the Hungarians in [these verses], which are nothing but sheer poetry (Balassa-Ortutay 1979 460).

This special construction – two lines nature, two lines love – was noted by the well known Hungarian ethnographer Gábor Lükő in the 40's. In his book, *A magyar lélek formái* (*The Forms of the Hungarian Spirit* 1942, republished in 1987), Lükő makes an attempt to analyze this construction and explain that the first two lines of description of nature actually symbolize physical love. He gives many examples and draws parallels between Hungarian and Kazak, Tatar, Chuvas, as well as Uralic folk song lyrics. However, in some instances he has difficulties. He mentions that unfortunately, he had no access to Chinese, Mongolian, or more easterly located Turkic folk art and folk song collections to follow these parallels farther east. Neither did he have access to Chinese research materials nor Chinese historical chronicles to help him in his comparative research work. Nevertheless, his pioneering work is of extreme importance, since there exists no other such detailed comparative study on this subject.

It is also important to mention here the volume of Béla Bernáth entitled *A szerelem titkos nyelvén* (*In the Secret Language of Love*, 1986), which is a work of immense value. He analyzes the erotic meaning of Hungarian sayings, folkloric oral material, including many love songs, beliefs, superstitions, and proverbs. The present study would like to humbly follow in the footsteps and spirit of G. Lükő, Bernáth, and other Hungarian ethnographers and augment their findings with examples from ancient Chinese and Turkic literature, as well as the work of Chinese scholars.

Patterns of images as encoded message

Lükő (1942) mentions that Hungarian scholars tended to ignore or misunderstand the meaning of these love stanzas that describe two-lines of nature two lines of love, considering them naive and simple-minded poetry, and content-wise having little more merit than the descriptions of the immediate environment of the singer. Balassa-Ortutay (1979 460-63), devote but three pages to folksongs in the big volume of *Magyar Náprajz (Hungarian Ethnography),* but focus only on the feelings, sadness, and happiness of love, and choose not to deal with the first two lines that describe images of nature. In one flower song example they give, the young man yearning to "walk into the garden of the girl" is interpreted as the young man admiring the well-tended garden of his beloved (Balassa-Ortutay 1979 462). We will see below that this is a mistaken interpretation.

It is not only the Hungarian scholars who either do not understand the meaning behind the lines but the translator of the *Book of Songs*, Arthur Waley, similarly gives various erroneous explanations for the verses. In one of the many folksong texts that descirbe the wedding of the grand daughter of King Ping (ca 770 BC) of the Zhou Dynasty, there is a mistranslation:

> Gorgeous in their beauty
> Are the flowers of the cherry.
> Are they not magnificent in their dignity,
> The carriages of the bride?

Gorgeous in her beauty
As flower of peach or plum,
Granddaughter of King Ping
Child of the Lord of Qi.

Wherever does SHE angle?
Of silk is HER[2] fishing line,
This child of Lord of Qi,
Granddaughter of King Ping.
(Song 24 Gorgeous in Thier Beauty)

The bride is both a "peach or plum flower" and a "fish" who got caught. Waley regognizes that fish is the symbol of fertility, but does not understand that the "angling" is done by the groom, who has "cought " the "fish", that is to say, the bride. Waley places the pronoun "she" for the person who "angles" whereas the original Chinese has no pronoun reference either male of felmale. The correct translation should be: "What a great catch with a silken line! The groom has caught the child of Lord Qi, and the Granddaughter of King Ping." Knowing this, the entire poem makes sense, since it it not logical for the bride to go fishing during a wedding procession, nor is it, as Waley suggests, is fishing with a net, the symbol of heavenly blessing. This will be detailed below.

However, upon analysis of the lyrics, with the help of ethnographic evidence, we find they reveal a deeper meaning, which is systematically encoded in an array of surface images. Once we discover the key to the code, that is, the meaning of the images and their associations with each other, and that they are actually the reflection of a wide-spread Asian world view, it is no longer possible to dismiss these songs as naive or simple-minded descriptions of the immediate nature of primitive people.

Most scholars in the past tended to shy away from deeper analysis of the love songs due to their often overt erotic content. However, we must realize that long ago people did not consider sex evil or shameful. On the contrary, reproduction was vital for the survival of the family, clan, tribe, and indeed a people. Thus, it is no surprise that art as well as the musical culture was a fertile substrate upon which the celebration of sex and sexuality grew and flourished among most peoples as the preamble to giving new life to ensure survival. It was also the case with the Turks, Mongols and Hungarians.

The imagery inventory found in the love lyrics of these people is very rich, and to deal with all of them is beyond the scope of this study. For this reason we will limit our analysis only to four structures listed below, which are among the most common representations of nature in the first lines of the stanzas in both the north

2 Capitalization is mine.

Chinese minority's and Hungarian love song lyrics. That these images are to be found in both the Hungarian and North Chinese folk songs is in itself remarkable.

Not only are the images systematically encoded in the love songs, but actual illustrations of the images can be found in the decorative art of these peoples. Embroidery, carving, leather work, applique are but a few of the techniques used to decorate everyday objects as well as objects for special occasions and festivals with the image patterns discussed in this study. These images further demonstrate the important functions of the love songs in their lives.

The image patterns found in the Turkic, Mongolian, and Hungarian love songs discussed in this study are the following:

1. Fish in river or water + bird, fishing eagle, or fisherman. *Action*: fishing, catching, frying, or eating fish.
2. Tree or garden + bird. *Action*: nesting, perching, or alighting on a tree.
3. Tree, grass + horse. *Action*: running, feeding, grazing, or being tether to a tree.
4. Field, house + cloud, rain, wind, dragon, lightening. *Action:* falling, hitting, raining on.
5. Flower + stem, rain. *Action*: attachment, admiration.

Analysis:

Let us examine the meaning of the five sets of image pairs one by one .

1. *Association: fish in river or water* ***with*** *waterfowl or fisherman. Action: fishing, catching, or eating fish.*

The following lyrics show the various associations between fish and other aquatic animals. Sometimes fishermen catch fish. Eating of fish is also a motif. The first example is from the 2,500 year old Chinese poetic collection, the *Book of Songs.*

> *By the yellow river side*
> *A fish hawk is singing,*
> There is a good maiden fair,
> Whom a man is wooing.
> *(Song of the Immortals, Zhou Dynasty, 1994 1)*

Such images are continuously present in Chinese poetry. A Tang dynasty poem goes thusly:

> *He comes to fish by lakeside green,*
> *Late apricot blossoms run riot.*
> *The pool seems shallow, for it's clean;*
> *Fish go and leave lotus unquiet.*

He waits for her by parting day;
And moors his boat at Willow Bay.
(Song of the Immortals, Tang Dynasty poet Chu Guangshi, 1994 80)

The similarity of ancient song to the modern Turkic folk song below, collected by Yaxiong Du, Chinese ethnomusicologist, is remarkable:

A fish is swimming in the water
A swan goes down on the water,
Our love is so beautiful,
We live in a new era.
Kazak nationality (Du 1984, 249)

Let us see the research results of other Chinese scholars, who worked independently of Lükő and Bernáth, regarding the meaning of the connection between fish and water bird. In his work entitled *The Worship of Reproduction in Culture* (1990), Zhao Guohua discusses the meaning of the fish image in north Chinese Neolithic art. Fish images are found on pottery form the Neolithic Banpo village, Xian Shaanxi province (5-4,000 BC) (fig. 1). The author concludes that since the shape of the fish resembles the female genitalia and the fish can bear many offspring (fish roe), it became the "symbol" for the female element in ancient China.

Fig. 1: Fish images on water vessel

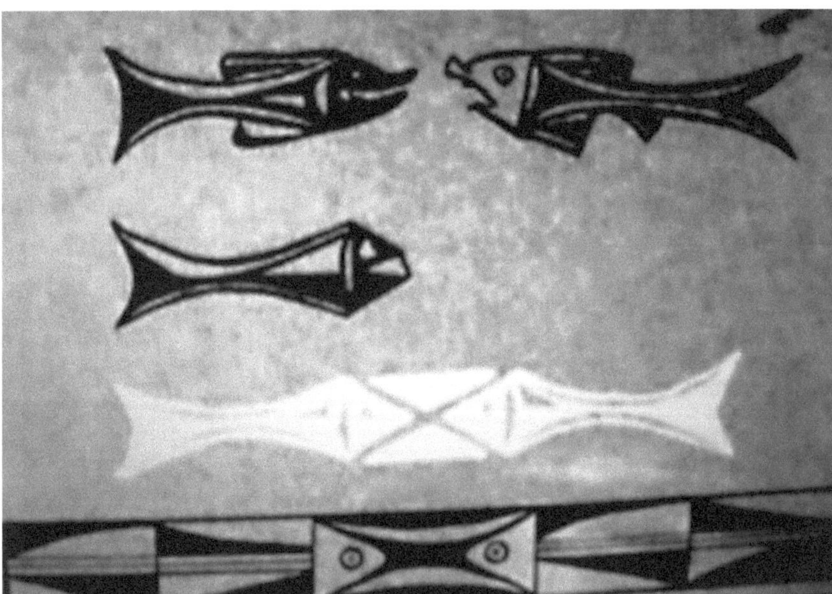

Pottery. Banpo village. Neolithic. Shanxi Provincial Museum, China.

He bases his conclusion on the common knowledge in China today, where people still associate the fish with the female sex organ (Zhao 1990, 168). Du Yaxiong, the expert on Chinese traditional music, notes that when people in China say "the fish and wild goose are together" they are referring to the act of sexual intercourse (personal communication). I myself had occasion to ascertain the meaning of this expression by asking several Chinese informants in China what this saying means. Invariably the answer was, "making love".

C.A.S Williams also writes in *The Outlines of Chinese Symbolism and Art Motives* that the fish is the symbol of connubial bliss, and specially symbolizes physical love (Williams 1976, 185).

Fig. 2: Bird holding a fish

Neolithic funerary urn. Yangshao culture. North China. In Ancient China

According to Taoist philosophy (whose roots reach back 2,800 years BC), water, the female element of softness, yielding, moisture, movement, and the lower regions (and by extension animals living in water – IH) belong to the *yin* category (*Tao Te Ching* 1972, Chapter 78).

The image of the bird in Chinese Neolithic art is also discussed by Zhao (1990 256). He writes that the bird represents the male element – sky, warmth, heat – and by extension the male sex organ. There is an urn from the Neolithic Yangshao culture site at Miaodigou, Henan province (fig. 2) that depicts a bird with a fish in its beak. The popular Chinese legend tells of Yi the Archer who lived during the Xia Dynasty (second millenium BC). He shot down nine of the 10 sun-birds from the sky for having destoryed people's lives. The famous Mawangdui banner (Han dynasty, ca. 200 BC-200 AD) also shows the moon to thel left and and the sun on the right side, and inside the sun disk there is the image of a (in the original banner, a black) bird (fig. 3).

Fig. 3: Bird in the sun disc

Silk banner of Western Han dynasty tomb of Marquis of Dai. Mawangdui, Hunan province, China. In Ancient China, p. 101.

The Chinese language also comes to our aid to further support this view. The Chinese written character is the same for "bird" 鸟 (*niao*), and "penis" (*diao*), the difference being only in the pronunciation (Contemporary Chinese Dictionary, 1998 288). A further interesting piece of evidence comes by way of a brick that was discovered in a tomb of the Eastern Han dynasty (200 BC – 200 AD), which illustrates the relationship between the fish and bird (Zhao 1990 260) (fig. 4.1).

Fig. 4.1: Bird and fish, standing for fertility and fortune

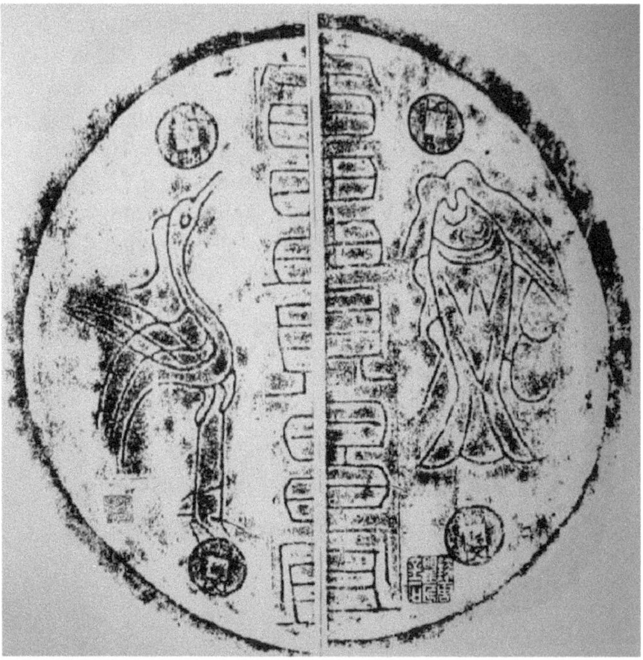

Han dynasty roof tile. In Han Hua Xuan.

Now, the first two lines of the lyrics from the *Book of Songs* become clear:

- By the yellow riverside, = near a girl (the presence of the fish in the river is implied)
- A fish hawk is singing. = a man is planning on catching her (make love to her).

Then, if we look at the last two lines, we find that they clearly state the meaning of the first two:

> There is a good maiden fair
> Whom a man is wooing.

In other words, the last part of the song decodes the encoded first lines. These encoded parts of folksongs, as well as various other more complex constructions in China are still understood today by farmers in the countryside, though somewhat less so by the city people (Du 1998).

Today the encoding is still understood among at least some Hungarian villagers. In 1993, I attended a Csángo Hungarian camp[3] in Szeghalom (Hungary). There were about twenty Csángos from various villages in Moldva (Transylvania). They came to Hungary to teach the Csángo songs and dances to young Hungarians who were interested in traditional music and dance. As they danced around the campfire, they sang a number of "pairing songs" which were followed by songs that graphically descirbed coitus. This shows that the singers still actively knew the meaning of the songs in the first round of songs as recently as 1993.

But it seems this knowledge is also retained by some in the Hungarian diaspora. In 2000, I happened to discuss folk songs with some Hungarian friends in Chicago. I mentioned the beauty of some folk songs, and I happened to mention the one below. I asked one of my friends if she understood the meaning of the words. She started smiling slyly and said, "It is obvious that the girls are trying to entice the boys to ..., you know .... play around ... make love."[4] Clearly, she understood the message of the song's text.

Here are three Hungarian love songs where the entire text is encoded, yet my friend had no problem with the decoding:

A szegedi halastó, halastó,
Beleestem kocsistól, lovastól.

The fishpond of Szeged,
I fell into it with my carriage and my horse,

Várom ugyan ki fog ki, ki fog ki.
Lesz -e olyan jószivű valaki.

I'm waiting for someone to pull me out,
I wonder if someone will be so kind.

Tiszán Innen Dunán túl (1972)

A szegedi hid alatt, hid alatt
Lányok sütik a halat, a halat.
Fehér tányérra rakják, rárakják.
A legéynek úgy adják, úgy adják.

Under the bridge of Szeged city,
Girls are frying fish, fish
They place it on a white plate
And give it to the boys.

Tiszán innen Dunán túl (1972)

---

3 I must thank Mr. Gábor Szilágyi, his wife Julia of Törökbálint and her family in Szeghalom, Hungary for their hospitality while attending the Csángó Camp in the summer of 1993 in Szeghalom.

4 Maria Molnár, nee Pongrácz, member of the St Stephan Hungarian Church in Chicago, 2000.

Hej halászok, halászok
Mit fogott a hálótok?
Nem fogott az egyebet,
Vörös szárnyú keszeget.
Hey, fishermen, fishermen
What have your nets caught?
It did not catch anything else,
Except a red-winged bream

Hát a keszeg mit eszik
Ha a bárkába teszik?
Nem eszik az egyebet,
Csak szerelem gyökeret.
And what does the bream eat
Once put into the barge?
It eats nothing else
But love-root.
Tiszán innen Dunán túl (1972)

The Hungarian ethnographer, Lűkő is correct in concluding, rather intuitively, that the verbal images of the fish and water symbolize the female, while the fisherman or bird is the symbol for the male (Lükő 1987, 8-9). However, he carries his ideas no further. But it is in Bernáth's work that we find more specific and systematically organized support for this view. Bernáth cites the following folksong:

Könnyű apró halat fogni,
De nehéz azt megtartani.
It is easy to catch a small fish
But it's difficult to keep one.

A variation of this lyric is,
Könnyű szeretőt találni
De nehéz azt megtartani.
It is easy to find a lover
But it's difficult to keep one.
(Bernáth, 1987 56-57)

The Hungarian ballad of *Görög Ilona* has the most clear references to fish as being in the female category. The ballad is about a girl and a boy who are in love, but the girl's mother will not allow her to see him. He is at wit's end as to how to procure permission, and he and his mother come up with a number of schemes. One scheme is for him to pretend to be dead so she would be allowed to go with the other girls to lament at his bier. The girl hears of his death and asks her mother for permission to see him:

Eresszen el anyám, anyám édesanyám,
Csudahalott látni, csudahalott látni

Ki érettem meghólt, halállá változott,

Let me go mother, mother my dear mother,
To see the marvelous corpse,
Who died for me, for me was done to death.

The mother's reply is:

Nem eresztlek lányom, lányom édes lányom,
Megvetik a halat, megfogják a márnát.

I will not let you go, my dear, dear daughter.
They will cast the net and catch the barbel
(a fish in the order Cyprinidae).
(Kodály 1971 240)

The meaning of the mother's warning is clear: I will not let you go, since you will be the subject of amorous overtures, which is precisely the design of the young man. The cheerful ballad ends with exactly what the mother is afraid of: the young people get together, hugging and kissing.

Bernáth brings in further evidence about the clear meaning of fish. He quotes popular expressions known even today, such as "the happiest girl is the one between whose legs you can catch a fish (or goldfish [red in color]) at night" (Bernáth 1986 57). Old women are often referred to as "*száraz keszeg*", that is "dry bream" (Bernáth 1986, 288). The *veres szárnyú keszeg (red-winged bream)* is an especially beautiful red fish, its color – and shape – most suggestive of the female vulva.

The examination of the fish names in the Hungarian lyrics, *keszeg*, *márna, aranyhal*, – that is, bream, barbel, and goldfish – also betray further parallels with the Chinese in meaning. Chinese ponds in the gardens are stocked with goldfish and carp, popular fish all ovear the country. Interestingly enough, all three kinds of fish, along with the carp, belong to the taxonomic suborder *Cyprinidae.* While all fish are prolific, the bream seems to be especially so (*Encyclopedia Britannica*, 1943 Vol. 17, 501). The carp is known to be the symbol of fertility in China, and we find the names of fish of just this suborder in the love songs. Even today in the Chinese countryside, the bride receives a jacket decorated with a baby sitting on a carp or goldfish, symbolizing fecundity (fig. 4.2) (Zazzle September 3, 2010) .

The Hungarian meaning for fish, and the fish in the Chinese saying ("the fish and wild goose are together," above) are strikingly and unmistakably the same. The expression "dry bream" for an old woman also gains meaning: she has dried up, that is, she can no longer bear offsprings (roe).

Obviously then, the bird hunting for the fish can only mean a young man is in pursuit of a girl.

Let us deal with the image of the bird in Hungarian folklore in this next section.

Fig. 4.2: Baby on a carp

Chinese pupular poster for good luck and prosperity.

2. Association: Tree/garden/flower, vegetation ***with*** *bird. Action: nesting, or alighting on a tree, being a gardener, picking fruit/ flowers*

The motif of the tree or a garden in which a bird sings or nests is the encoding for lovemaking. We have already discussed the Chinese concept of a bird representing the phallus. It is common knowledge in China that trees represent the female element. Zhao's reason is that since the tree bears leaves and fruit, as a woman bears offsprings, it is another ideal representation for the female (Zhao, 1990 225).

Not only the common folk, but the Chinese poets, when feeling amorous, also followed the assication of trees and gardens representing the female, concepts steamming from the Taoist idea of opposites. The poet Zhang Ju (768-830) wrote a poem, entitled *Reply of a Chaste Wife:*

> You know I love my husand best,
> Yet, two bright pearls are sent me still.
> I hung them in my red silk vest,
> So grateful I am for your good will.
> You see, my house o'erlooking gardens and
> My husband guards the palace, halberd in hand.
> I know your heart as noble as the sun in the skies,
> But I have sworn to serve my husband all my life.
> With your twin pearls I send back two tears from my eyes.
> Would we had met before I was a wife!
> (Song of the Immortals 1994 107)

Here is a poem by Cheng Hao (1032-1085), called *Impromptu Lines on a Spring Day:*

> Towards noon 'neath fleecy coulds and gentle breeze
> *I crossed the stream 'mid blooms and willow trees*
> Some worldlings who don't know my heart's deep pleasure
> Would say I'm like a truant fond of pleasure.
> (Song of the Immortals 194 196)

Here are two contemporary folksongs from the Salar and Uygur nationalities living in China:

> I passed my gate
> *I looked at the tree,*
> *The magpie is making its nest*
> I miss my Big Eyes (pet name for a girl).
>
> I opened the curtain door,
> I looked into the room,
> White peony is sleeping (peony is synonym for a girl)
> I miss my Big Eyes.
> Salar nationality (Du, 1984, 257)

The sun has set but tomorrow it will rise.
The flower is gone but it will bloom next year.
The beautiful little bird went away, never to return,
My youthful vigor has also left with the bird, never to return.
Uygur nationality (Du 1984, 212)

In this Uygur song above, there is a clear connection between a man's sexual prowess and a bird. Another Turkic song is below:

You are like a fish living in the free crystal palace,
my sweetheart,
I am a lark singing in the beautiful free garden,
my sweetheart.
Kazakh nationality (Du 1984, 230-231)

In the above Kazakh song, the first two and last two lines seem to have collapsed into each other, the singer clearly identifying himself as the bird in the "garden," the girl as the fish. We can compare this entirely encoded stanza with the Hungarian examples in Pattern 1 above, *Tiszán innen, Dunán túl,* 1972.

We can find the same structure in Mongol folksongs as well:

Little yellow oriole, do you know,
(girl talking to the young man, "little oriole")
There are two flowers embroidered on a boot?
There are four flowers on a pair of boots.
You and I together will have eight flowers.
Mongol nationality (Du 1984, 259)

Here are the Hungarian equivalents (the first three lines are said by the girl, the last three by the boy):

Elszállott a fecske,
Majd hazatér este a fészkére,
Én is beleülök babám ülebe.
Én is odazállnék,rózsám tehozzád!
Szólj még egyet hozzám,
Szeretsz-e még engem igazán.
The swallow has flown away,
But will return to its nest at night,
I, too will sit in my lover's lap,
I, too want to fly to you my love,
Speak but once to me,
Do you still truly love me?
(Tulipán 1971 12)

Kisétálok kiskertembe
Virágot látni.
Hát leütte őszi harmat
Virágom szinét.

I walk out into my small garden,
To look at the flowers.
Autumn dew knocked down
The loveliest of my petals.

Rajta sétál kis gerlice
Sárga lábával.
Sárga lába, zöld a szárnya,
Jaj de gyengén jár.

A little dove is walking on it
With its yellow feet,
It's feet are yellow, it's wings are green
Oh, how carefully it walks.
(Rezeda, 1971)

Such love songs can be found in abundance and are sung all over the countryside in North China and Hungary and can be found in any popular folksong books. I am sure the Turkic and Mongol readers of this study also know such songs themselves, as does this author.

Bernáth quotes a less cryptic example to explain the meaning of the tree, which is the symbol of womanhood as well as the female sex organ. The first two lines are clearly explained by the last ones:

Én ültettem az almafát,
Más köti hozzá a lovát.

I planted the apple tree
Someone else ties his horse to it.

Én szerettem meg a szép lányt,
Más éli vele világát.

I loved the beautiful girl,
Someone else is having a good time with her.
(Bernáth 1986, 9)

Note how lines 3-4 clearly reiterate lines 1-2.

According to the Altaic language speakers' oral tradition, it is the tree of life on which the unborn spirits of children dwell in the form of small birds. Many Hungarian folk art examples have images of a tree surrounded or flanked by birds, or birds sitting on its branches (Domanovszky 1981 II, 172). These images are painted on furniture and embroidered onto linen bedding and other textiles which make up the trousseau of a girl (fig. 5.1). We can see similar arrangement of bird on a tree (even a fish at the bottom!) on a pair of embroidered Mongol boots (fig. 5.2).

According to Yakut belief, the Old Ancestress lives in a tree, and among the Evenki, like among the Hungarians, she lives in the wooden pillar that holds up the yurta and the house respectively. People pray to this pillar (Bernáth 1986 109).

Fig. 5.1: Horse under a tree with birds perched on the branches

Hand made Hungarian embroidery by Eniko Filetoth, professional embroiderer. From: http://www.filetoth.com/index-3_en.html. Sept 2, 2010.

Fig. 5.2: Fish, and bird on treetop

Mongolian embroidered boots. In Mongolian Costume, Chapter 2, fig. 21.

The concept of birds as life-givers, or life itself, is found in Asian myths. The creation myth of the Altaic peoples tell of the Crow who asks the god Kuday for spirits to put into people. Then Crow drops the spirits onto the branches of the pine trees. The Hungarians seem also to have known this tale long ago. The Hungarian saying "God only knows whence the crow brought him in his beak" is used to describe a person whose parentage is not known (Bernáth 1986 109), in other words, he is a stranger.

In the Altaic cultures the tree of life of the netherworld, on top of which dwell the spirit of the unborn, is considered to exist up-side-down, (as are all things which are not of the material world). According to this concept, the crown of the tree is on the bottom (the roots are on top) and when children are born they "fly" off it into this, the matearial world. This means the crown of the tree represents the mouth of the uterus (cervix) whence the children emerge, head first, up-side-down (Bernáth 1986 109). He gives the following Hungarian folk song which bears this out:

Ezt a kislányt nem az anyja szülte,
Rózsafának teteje költötte.

This young girl was not born of a mother,
She was hatched on the crown of a rose tree.
(Bernáth 1986 109)

In the wedding song below, the "bird" of the groom alights on the "treetop" of the bride during the wedding night. Again, the first line is clarified by the second. There is not much doubt as to the resultant activity of the wedding night:

Madár száll a fatetore, A bird alights on the treetop
Most megyünk az esküvöre. We are going to be wed.
(Bernáth 1986, 109)

A logical extension of the tree is the garden, in which the tree grows. It must be mentioned that the process of love is equated to growth as is observable in the development of plants and animals in nature. First, the tree is planted, then it grows, eventually it bears fruit. Planting the tree is equated with arousing the love of a woman (Bernáth 1983 108). When it grows, and the garden flourishes, the love affair is in full bloom, and when it bears fruit is when lovers unite sexually. Below is the illustration:

Hey, rózsa viola, *Oh, rose, viola,*
Most érik az alma, The apples are ripening now,
Szedjük le hajnalba. Let us harvest at dawn.
(Bernáth 1986 318)

Another example with the garden image is a *virágének (flower song)* from the 18th century:

Ej, haj, gyöngyvirág	Oh, lily- of- the-valley,
Teljes szegfü, szarkaláb	Carnation in bloom, larkspur,
Bimbós majoránna,	Budding marjoram.
Ha kertedbe mehetnék,	If I could go into your garden
Piros rozsát szedhetnék,	*And pick red roses,*
Szivem megújulna.	My heart would be rejuvenated.
Ej, haj, gyöngyvirág,	Oh, lily- of- the-valley,
Teljes szegfü, szarkaláb,	Carnation in bloom, larkspur,
Levendula virág.	Lavender flower.
Ha kertekbe mehetnék,	If I could go into your garden,
Ha ott kertész lehetnék,	If I could be a gardener there,
Midjárt meggyógyulnék.	I would be cured immediately.
(Jácéntos Virágom nd. 9)	

Bernáth writes (1989 318) that it is common knowledge in Hungary that traditionally dawn is the time for making love, and this is born out in many folk-song lyrics, starting with the ones in the Book of Songs.

Wind and rain, chill, chill,
But the cock crowed, kikeriki.
Now that I have seen my lord,
How can I fail to be at peace?
(Book of Songs 1996 # 80)

Here is the Hungarian folksong:

Hajnallik már, hajnallik már,
Majd meg is virrad már.
Fordulj hozzám kedves kisangyalom
Majd magad maradsz már.

Dawn is coming, dawn is coming
Daybreak will be here soon.
Turn toward me, my darling,
Soon you will be alone.
(Nefelejts 1971 140)

In the popular Hungarian folk tale, *Prince Argyélus and the Fairy Ilona*, the hero Argyélus is also visited after midnight by the beautiful enchanted fairy lover, Ilona, and they are together until dawn (Illyés 1972 163-169). The further examination of other folk tales would no doubt be very rewarding in this respect.

One aspect of the bird as the male symbol, is extended to a cutting object: the knife. Bernáth notes that to "cut bread" to "have knives in the pod" (pod=vagina), as illustrated in a number of Hungarian sayings and expressions, carries the meaning of intercourse. In all of these expressions the *knife* is the male element the *bread* and *pod* the female (Bernáth 1986 221). Thus, it is not surprising that we find Turkic and Hungarian knife handles that are decorated with the images of birds (fig. 6.1 and 6.2).

Fig. 6.1: Hungarian pocket knife decorated with bird image

County of Somogy, 19th c. In A Magyar nép diszitöművészete.

Fig. 6.2: Uygur knife with bird image on handle

In Weiwu'erzu zhuangshi to'an:

3. Association: tree ***with*** *Horse .Action: run, feed, graze, or tether to a tree.*

In China, because of the sheer size of the horse's reproductive organ, its speed and power, it is often associated with male sexual prowess (Zhao 1990 322). A number of Mongolian and Turkic lyrics tell of the man riding, feeding, or cutting grass for his horse, but from the Book of Songs comes the earliest instance of such descriptions. Notice how the second stanza is the repetition of the first. The song is a lament of twarted love, using a variety of symbols:

(There is a) tall tree in the south[5]
One cannot rest under it.
(There is) a maiden on the Han River
I cannot pay court to her.

For me the HanRriver is too wide
To swim across it.
For me the Yangtze River is too long
To cross its strong current.

There is grass,
I would like to cut it,
If she marries me,
I would like to feed the horse

For me the Han River is too wide
To swim across it.
For me the Yangtze River is too long
To cross its strong current.

There is grass,
I would like to mow it.
If she marries me,
I'd like to feed the colt.

For me the Han River is too wide
To swim across it.
For me the Yangtze River is too long
To cross its strong current.
(trans. Y. Du *Book of Songs*, "The Han is Broad" (Zhou dynasty), #9)[6]

Notice the parallel images between the above stanzas from the *Book of Songs* and the Mongol folk songs below. Note also how the last lines explain the first two:

The Uli Mountain is so high
The horse cannot climb it,
I would like to meet you tonight,
But my wish cannot come true
Mongol nationality (*Chinse Folk Songs*, 1985 314).

5 Compare Chinese *south* to Hungarian "*down under* " which refers to the lower part of the female body, i.e., the genitalia (Bernáth, 1986 57).

6 A. Waley who translated the Book of Songs mistranslates these types of lines. Waley (Waley 1998 10) translates "feed her horse" whereas the pronoun "she" does not occur in the Chinese text, because, obviously, it is not "her horse" that needs "feeding."

How can the black horse
Leave the green grass land?
How can beloved Normen Dala (name of a young man)
Leave me, his sweetheart.
Oh, Normen Dala, let us live together.
Mongol nationality (Du 1984 260)

The horse is clearly the euphemistic expression for the male reproductive organ in an old humorous Hungarian folk song below:

A jó lovam, paripám a gatyában vagyon,
Abrakos tarisznyám szép asszonynál vagyon.
My good horse is in my pants,
My feedbag is with a beautiful woman.
(Bernáth 1986 9)

Bernáth explains that the feedbag represents the female genitalia, the "head" of the horse fitting into the "bag" for "feeding" (=coitus) (Bernáth 1986 9).

Other evidence for the image of a horse as part of the male category can be found among common expressions in Hungary even today. The expression "even the horse whinnies at beautiful things", means men love to look at beautiful women, or " Even the old horse guffaws at the oats" means that even an old man likes to flirt with women, though he may not have other intentions (Nagy 1982, #710, and #719).

Domanovsky, the noted Hungarian ethnographer, notes that in the rich Hungarian woodcarving tradition the majority of items are ones made by men for women as love-tokens or gifts of love. There is an example in his book of a mirror case on which the carving depicts a man riding a horse in a background of trees and bushes with roses and tulips growing on it (Domanovsky 1981, II. 309/#103) (fig. 7). The gift giver even wrote a message on the bottom, like a caption: "Bogár Imre (name of man and gift-giver) is traveling here." It looks as if the carver illustrated the 18th century flower-song cited above (*Jácéntos virágom, nd. # 9)*, "If I could but go into your garden, how happy I would be ...".

A *shaonian (young men songs)* from Gansu province, north China, mentions the horse, gun, and hunting, where the last two lines leave no doubt as to the intention of the first two:

I rode a little horse and took my gun,
I fired into the forest twice,
The bullets hit a peony
I cried twice for that peony.
(Ji Zhengzhu, Gansu singer 1998)

Fig. 7: Man riding a horse among flowers, with inscription "here travels Imre Bogár"

Reverse side of a Hungarian mirror. Somogy county, first part of 20th c. In A Magyar nép diszitöművészete

Tethering the horse to a tree is a very ancient encoding for lovemaking. The well known Siberian gold belt buckle from the collection of Peter the Great (Hermitage, St Petersburg) (fig. 8.1) depicts a man with his head in the lap of a woman, which represents aposition immediately following coitus. Behind them are two horses next to a tree, clear allegories for the amorous scene. The same motif also appears in frescos in medieval Hungarian churches, illustrating the *St. László Legenda,(Legend of St Laszlo)* as well as a number of folk tales, such as Molnár Anna (Hoppal, 1990 65-66) (fig. 8.2).

Fig. 8.1: Horse tethered to tree with man's head resting in a woman's lap

Siberian Gold plaque. From the treasure of Peter the Great. Hermitage Museum, St. Petersburg. In A Népvádorláskor műveszete Magyarországon (The art of the Migration Period in Hungary)

Fig. 8.2: Horse tethered to tree with man's head resting in a woman's lap

Legend of St. Laszlo. Fresco from Bantornya In A Népvádorláskor műveszete Magyarországon (The art of the Migration Period in Hungary)

Let us look at some Hungarian folksongs about tethereing a horse to a trees:

Én ültettem a cédrusfát,
Más köti hozzá a lovát,
Ne kösd hozzá a lovadat,
Elviszem kantárszijadat

I planted the cedar tree,
Someone else tethers his horse to it.
Don't tether your horse to it,
Or I will take away your reins.
(Tulipán 1971 42)

Also the stanza below from Bernáth (1986 107) illustrates the horse tethered to a tree.

Tisza mellett van egy nyárfa leásva
Ahho van a babám lova pányvázva.

By the River Tisza there is a poplar planted
My lover's horse is tatered to it.

3.1 Association: Barley/oats ***with*** *horse – Action: feeding on*

A horse feeding on oats, (explanation see below) is another encoding for the sexual act (Bernáth 1986, 47-58). Bernáth cites many expressions and sayings which clarify that *oat* and *barley* represent the clitoris. By extension, a faithful lover was *barley*, but a loose girl was described as *oat* (Bernáth 1986 54). The two stanzas become clear now that we know the meaning for horses eating oats, and wading in water (extension: mud), refer to parts of the female reproductive organ as well as vaginal fluid (=water) (Bernáth 1986 9).

A koppányi hegyek alatt
Barna legény zabot arat,
Zabot arat a fekete lovának,
Szeretőt keres magának.

Under the mountains of Koppány (a village)
A dark-haired young man is harvesting oats.
He is harvesting oats for his black horse,
He is looking for a lover.
(Viola 1971 34)

Kiöntött a Tisza a partjára,
Kispej lovam térdig jár a sárba,
Sáros kantárszára a kezembe,
Gyere kis angyalom az ölembe.

The Tisza has overflowed its banks
My small horse is wading in the mud up to its knees,
I hold its muddy reins in my hand,
Come my lover into my lap.
(Viola 1971 42)

From these we can surmise the rest of the encrypted message of the second stanza, whose last line clearly shows the human activity alluded to in the first two-three lines.

In the following examples the symbolic images are layered, one on top of the other:

Esik eső csendesen az árpa tarlóra,
Gyere kedves galambom segits fel a lóra.
It is raining quietly upon the barley field,
Come, my lovely dove, help me onto the horse.

Boros vagyok, sej-haj, nem tudok felülni,
Almás-deres a lovam, nem akar megállni.
I have drunk too much and cannot sit up,
My horse is apple-grey in color and does not
want to stand up.

Almás -deres a lovam, nem eszi a zabot,
Mert már kicsiny korában az árpára kapott.
My horse is apple-grey in color and does not eat oats.
Because since it was a colt it's been used to barley.

Kis angyalom, sek haj, szoktatta azt rája,
Engem pedig sejehaj, a csókos szájára.
My lover got him accustomed to it (barley),
And she got me used to her kissable lips.
(Muskáatli 1971 44-45,)

With a little attention, and now armed with the meaning of the images, we have no trouble interpreting the four stanzas above. The meaning of rain (discussed below), is the emission of seminal fluid, seed, and life-giving force (Bernáth 1986, 47-58, 146).

Here is one final Hungarian flower folksong from the 19th century:

Lovamat kötöttem piros almafához,
Magamat kötöttem gyenge violához,
Lovamat eloldom, amikor a hold kel,
Toled, szép violám, csak a halál old el.

I tied my horse to a red apple tree,
I tied myself to a tender viola,
I untie my horse when the moon rises,
But only death will separate me from you, my lovely viola,
(Öt évszázad magyar dalai, hi-fi record, 1972 ? song #7)

Thus, fortified with this information, the decoding of the stanzas above becomes easy and the meaning quite clear. In this song above, only the last line gives away the true meaning, physical love, because the rest of the song is encoded as "feeding and caring for the horse".

4. *Association: field, flower, or a house* ***with*** *cloud, rain, wind, dragon, thunder, lightning –. Action: falling, hitting, raining on.*

To "play the cloud and rain game", an expression in Chinese that everybody understands even today, means sexual intercourse. Emanating from the cloud, rain is the life-force. One ancient example can be found in the *Book of Songs*, alluding to sexual union at dawn (cock crowing):

> *Wind and rain, dark as night,*
> *The cock crowed and would not stop*
> Now that I have seen my lord,
> How can I any more be sad?

The common Hungarian expressions *"szerelemhideg", "kirázza a hideg"* – to have love-chills or chills – mean being in love or wanting to make love (Bernath 1986 52-53, 250). It has the same meaning in Chinese, as we see in the stanza above. The song continues:

> *Wind and rain, chill, chill,*
> *But the cock crowed, kikeriki.*
> Now that I have seen my lord,
> How can I fail to be at peace?
>
> *Wind and rain, oh the storm.*
> *But the cock crowed, kukeriku,*
> Now that I have seen my lord,
> How can I fail to rejoice?
> (Book of Songs 1996 Zhou Dynasty folksong # 90)

The last two lines, again describe the resulting feelings of passionate lovemaking (*oh, the storm*) encrypted in the first two lines. Not only do we find parallels between the Hungarian and Chinese lyrics regarding the stormy, cloudy, rainy day, (see below) but the time of day for making love is also the same: at dawn when the cock crows (Bern'th 1986 187).

Dragons in China are associated with cloud, rain, and water (fig. 9.1). C.A.S. Williams writes:

> The eastern dragon is not the gruesome monster of mediaeval (i.e. European – -I.H.) imagination, but the genius of strength and goodness. He is the spirit of change, therefore life itself...He unfolds himself in the storm clouds.....The Shou Wen dictionary (AD 200) states that of the 369 species of scaly reptiles , such as fishes, snakes, and lizards, the dragon is the chief: it wields the power of transformation, and the gift of rendering itself visible or invisible at pleasure.. In the spring it ascends the skies. (Williams 1976 132).

As the Chinese dragon, the Hungarian dragon is also closely associated with water, rain, and storm. This snake-dragon relationship was explored in a monograph by Sándor Erdész (1984).

Here is a song from the Han nationality where the dragon produces rain:

Brother is a dragon in the sky
Sister is a flower on the earth[7]
If the dragon does not turn over, it does not rain
If the rain does not water the flower, the flower
can not be red.
Han nationality, (Du 1984 10)

Dragons dwell in clouds in Hungarian folk belief as well, and cause fierce rainstorms (Ortutay 1981, Vol. 4, 400-401). In the teasing verse below, the dragon represent the male element which suggests the act of coitus,

"Szálj le sárkány, csergét adok,
Ha megeszed, megint adok".
[Descend, dragon, I give you bacon
If you eat it all, I'll give you more.]
(Bernáth 1986 141).

Bernáth elaborates, using various data showing that the bacon is the symbol of the female genitalia (140-41). The role of the dragon as the mount of the shaman (called *táltos* in Hungarian) who flies it over the clouds, is still very much alive in a number of Hungarian folktales. The drawing seen in fig. 9.2 is a *male* dragon accompanied by the *táltos* from a folk tale. Similarly, the celebration of male strength is the reason for the annual wrestling tournaments in Inner Mongolia. The wrestling outfit on fig. 9.3 was decorated with images of two fierce dragons as the symbol of male power.

In Hungarian verses the power of fertilization is associated with rain, which brings fecundity (Hoppál, 1990 68). According to universal folk belief, lightening is also considered to be the male element and the instrument of fertility (Hoppál 1990 234-5). The examples below illustrate the specific erotic association of rain and lightening (male) with meadows and the roadside inn (female). The *meadow, house, or inn*, carry the meaning of the female reproductive organ (Bernáth 1986 16-17, 28, 180, 280):

Jaj, de szépen esik az eső,
Eső után zöldel a mező.
Közepébe legel, tyuhaj, egy bárány,
Nincs szebb leány mint az én babám.
Oh, how beautifully it is raining,
After the rain, the meadows are verdant

7 The terms "brother" and "sister" between lovers is not a sign of an incestual relationship. These terms are common in both Chinese and Hungarian (szep hugom=beautiful sister), and is used as a common term by boys to refer to an unmarried girl. It is a linguistic term worthy of further research.

In the center of it, a lamb is grazing,
No girl is as beautiful girl as mine.
(Tiszán innen Dunán túl, 1972, 87)

Esik eső hull a villám, rakásra.
Ráesett a kisbodali csárdára.
Ég a csárda, nincsen aki locsolja,
Árva az én szivem mert nincs vigasztalója.
It is raining, the lightening is falling into a mound,
It hit the Kisboda's roadside inn,
The inn is on fire, but there is nobody to put it out
My lonely heart has nobody to console it.
(Muskatli l971, 43)

In other words: the singer (the inn) wants to make love (is on fire) but there is nobody to make love to her (put out the fire).

Fig. 9.1: Dragons among clouds and waves

Chinese spirit wall. Chinatown, Chicago.

Fig. 9.2: Male dragon with Hungarian *táltos (shaman)*

Drawn by Sándor Szűcs, In the 1830's. in Hungarian Electronic Library. http://mek.niif.hu/02100/02152/html/07/397.html. September 2, 2010.

Fig. 9.3: Mongolian wrestlers wearing trousers decorated with dragons

In Mongolian Costume, Chapter 3, Fig 11.

5. *Association: Flower* ***with*** *handle, rain, bird. Action: attraction or attachment to or admiration of a girl*

One very common image for the female element is the flower. A rich array of flower images exist in folksongs. These are the rose, peony, tulip, or peach or cherry blosssom. Upon examination, we gain some interesting insights. A Zhou dynasty folksong, already quoted above calls a lady peach blossom:

Gorgeous in their beauty
Are the flowers of the cherry.
Are they not magnificent in their dignity,
The carriages of the bride?

Gorgeous in her beauty
As flower of peach or plum,
Granddaughter of King Ping
Child of the Lord of Qi.

Wherever does he angle?
Of silk is his fishing line,
(he caught)This child of Lord of Qi,
Granddaughter of King Ping.
(Book of Songs "Gorgeous in Their Beauty" # 24)

Here is a Han nationality folksong:
Brother is a dragon in the sky
Sister is a flower on the earth
If the dragon does not turn over, it does not rain,
If the rain does not water the flower, the flower
can not be red.
Han nationality (Du 1984 10)

The Chinese song above clearly states in the last two lines that the flower is the girl whose "red"-ness receives the "rain", that is, when the boy (the rain-causing dragon) makes love to her. Both the color red and the flower are associated with the external part of the female reproductive organ (Bernáth 1986 186). The color red (red-winged bream), we have already discussed above.

Turkic folk songs similarly call the girl flower:

Sweetheart, you stand at the gate
Just like a blooming peony.
I would like to be with you forever,
And never be separated, my dear Mandanhan
(name of girl)
Uigur nationality (Du 1984 225)

And another song,

There are a thousand beautiful flowers
You are the most beautiful one
There are thousands of beautiful girls,
You are the one who is in my heart
Uigur nationality (Du 1984 395)

Your face is just like the spring moon
Giving light in the night sky.
You are as beautiful as a flower,
Many birds are attracted to you and sing songs
Uzbek nationality (Du 1984, 417)

From Hungarian folk art the many wooden linen presses given by young men as love tokens to their lovers, gives us more data regarding the importance and meaning of flower, especially the rose and tulip. The surfaces of these household tools are richly decorated with flowers (female symbol, flower >> fruit). What is noteworthy is that it's handle ends in a "heart-shaped' bud-like tip, with the stem and leaves of the flower running the length of the handle, resulting in a phallic-like shape (fig. 10). Another such example, (fig. 11.1) and (fig. 11.2) shows clear example of the tulip-heart connection. The Hungarian folk embroiderers, furniture decorators, and painters have a special name for the "heart" shape. They call it *tökös, or* "gourd," a common Hungarian term for "scrotum" a term used even in today (Domanovszky 1981/ II, 308 #101; also Hoppál 1990, 240-41; Kocsis/Csomor nd. 148). Thus, the giver and the receiver of the linen press; and the occasion for which it was given, leaves little doubt as to the iconography of the decoration: physical love is represented by the "heart" fused to the "red rose". Similarly, this very same association of images of tulip with the "heart" can be found on various articles in the decorative folk art of Uygur Turks of north China (fig. 11.3) bearing out the meaning in the folksongs from the region.

The meaning of the decoration on the Hungarian linen-press seems to be underlined by the *shaonian* folk song from Gansu, China. This song is sung at the flower festival held annually in many areas in Gansu province. The purpose of the festival is for young men and women to meet, and choose partners. There is lot of free love-making that night, some leading to marriage. The songs are sung by the participants, and good singers are sought after by the opposite sex (Du 1998). This text below sounds as if the singer was describing exactly the Hungarian linen-press, decorated with flowers and having a bud- or "heart"-shaped handle.

The penis hangs just like a bud,
The pubes look like leaves.
Little sister's vagina looks like a morning lily flower
The penis can be the stem of the flower.
(sung by Li Guizhou, a Gansu folk singer, 1998)

Fig. 10: Linen flattener with flower image, handle ending in a phallic shape, from Veszprem and Vas counties, Hungary. End of the 19th c.

In A Magyar nép diszitöművészete, p. 308, fig. 100, 101.

Fig. 11.1: Tulip and heart shapes, forming the female sex organ and scrotum

Woodcarving on a Hungarian washing mallet. Magyarvalko, Transylvania. In Jelképtár, p. 225 fig. 918.

Fig. 11.2: Tulip and heart carving on a Hungarian linen stretcher (center)

Kolozs county, Transylvania, mid-19th c. In A Magyar nép diszitöművészete, p. 281, fig. 32.

Fig. 11.3: Tulip and heart embroidery on an Uygur pillow

Turfan, Xinjiang, China. In Weiwu'erzu zhuangshi to'an, p. 34.

The linen press from Hungary which is a love token form a boy to a girl he is courting seems to illustrate this very lyric above. The press is richly decorated with flowers and leaves and ends in a phallic-shaped handle (fig. 10).

Conclusions

In the above analysis we found the images in Chinese, Turkic, Mongolian and Hungarian folk song texts constructed in the following way:

1. male=bird, horse, dragon, rain, lightning,
2. female=water, fish, tree, flower,
3. special verbs as symbols of the union of the two opposites – male and female: catch, eat, hunt, enter, fall into, ride, tether, rain upon, reap, run, feed, cut.

The images of nature, representing the opposing elements of male and female are brought together in the Turkic, Mongolian, and the Hungarian folk song texts, and according to the examples, there can be little doubt as to their encoded meaning.

The lyrics examined above function in a system and have the following features:

1. Love songs are sung at weddings or at occasions or festivals when young men and women are brought together for purposes of physical love;
2. The beginning lines describe nature, and to the uninitiated have no relationship with the last part of the stanza;
3. The ending lines (or subsequent stanzas) generally explain the cryptic encoding of the first lines; the decoded message is physical love. Often the entire stanza is "encoded" with natural images, juxtaposed on the actions of the humans involved.
4. The natural images bring the male-female symbols into direct association or contact;
5. The symbols fall into a pattern for pairing up the male-female images and elements with each other, i.e., bird/fish, horse/tree, dragon /field;
6. There are no male-male, female-female image associations in any of the love lyrics, thus further proving the sexual connotations of the covert content.

Reflections of an archetype

Not only are these images and their associations rich in their poetic variety and subtlety, but as we can see, they also form a pattern, which leads us to suspect the existence of a much larger system in the Asian folksong and folk art tradition because we are not dealing with random and isolated images. The system underlying these images is the philosophy of Daoism.

According to this philosophy all things fall into tow opposite groups: Yang (male) and Yin (female) (fig. 12). Therefore, a rose is not only a symbol of Yin, flowers themselves fall into the female category, as do the earth, vegetation, trees, water, moon, and darkness – just to name a few. To the Yang (male) element belong the things of the sky, brightness, warmth, creatures of the sky such as birds, dragons, and swift powerful (flying) horses. Thus a horse is not only a symbol of maleness but is male by nature, as is a human male. Therefore the Daoist mindset can be said to be the underlying archetype to these folksongs and poems in the oral tradition and images in the visual arts of the peoples whose culture is distributed thoughout Eurasia, from north China to the Carpathian Basin.

Fig. 12: Common Daoist Yin-Yang symbol with the 8 hexagrams

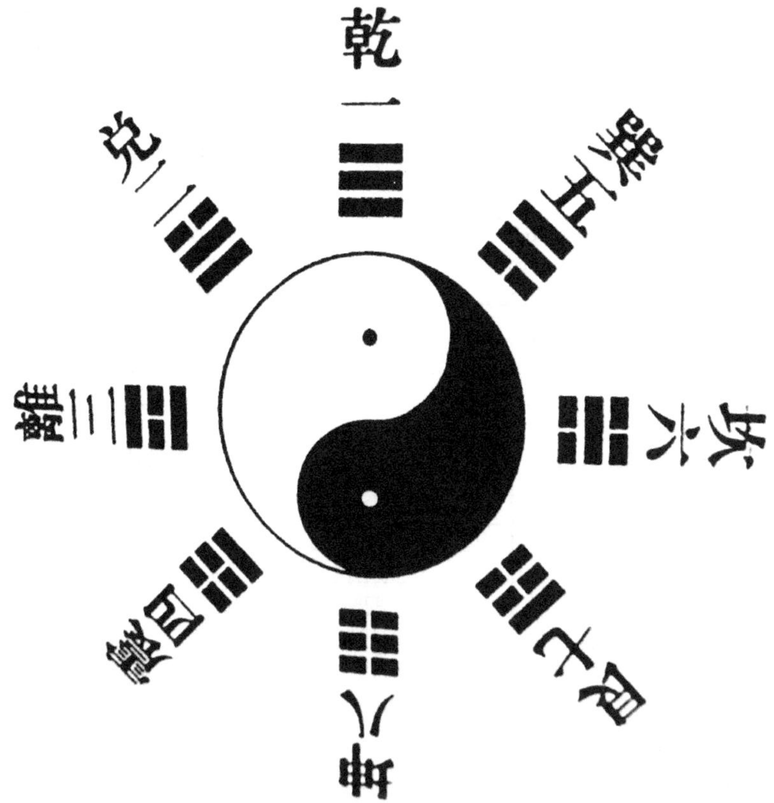

Examples from visual arts and oral tradition from Turkic, Mongolian, and Hungarian cultures support the patterns which underlie the categories and associations apparent in these lyrics.

Though images of flowers, birds and other natural scenes also exist in the art and music of other non-Altaic language speaking cultures, this system of associations discussed above can not be found. This pattern of associations formes a whole, and when we understand that they reflect the ancient philosophy of Dao, they carry clear and specific meaning: the celebration of physical love, fertility, life, and the dependence on and balance of the two opposites. The act of sexual union is paramount to the contiunation of a family, a clan, or a nation. It is this very pattern rooted in the Daoist world view found in the Turkic, Mongolian, and Hungarian love songs that sets them apart from the possible different meanings for the same images found in the art of other cultures.

The above examinations and conclusions also leave little possibility to suppose that these image associations and their peculiar encoding in exactly the same social circumstances – love festivals, marriage, courtship – in the Turkic, Mongolian and Hungarian cultures could have developed independently from each other. Therefore, we can assume an ancient cultural connection among them.

Male element (yang) (hot, bright, active, high, heavens, energetic, powerful, intrusive)	**Female element (yin)** (cool, shaded, deep, passive, receiving of energy, weak, accepting, soil, earth)

Image from nature	Image from nature	Action/association
Fishing bird, hawk	Fish, water, river	Catch fish, eat fish
Bird	Tree, branch, garden	– Walk in garden – Alight on treetop
Horse	Tree	Horse tethered to tree/ feeding/ grazing
Dragon	Field, earth	Dragon causes could to rain onto field, earth, house
Stem of plant	Various flowers,	attachment
Man	Woman	

References

Ádám, Jenő. *Tulipán.* Zeneműkiadó, Budapest. 1971.

Balázs, Lajos. *Az én első tisztességes napom.* Kriterion, Bukarest. 1994.

Bernáth, Béla. *A szerelem titkos nyelvén.* Gondolat, Budapest. 1986.

Berze Nagy, János. *Az égigérő fa.* Tudományos Ismeretterjesztő Társulat Baranya megyei szervezete, Pécs. 1958.

Bonnefoy, Ives (W. Doninger, trans.) *Asian Mythologies.* University of Chicago Press, Chicago, London. 1991.

Borsi István, Rossa Ernő. *Tiszán innen, Dunán túl.* Zeneműkiadó, Budapest. 1972.

Contemporary Chinese Dictionary. Beijing. 1998.

Culture Bureau of Inner Mongolia. *Mongolian Costume.* Mongolian Science Publishers. Hohhot, Inner Mongolia. 1991.

Deák Bárdos, György *Muskátli.* Zeneműkiadó, Budapest. 1971.

Diószegi, Vilmos. *A sámánhit emlékei a magyar népi műveltségben.* Akadémiai Kiadó, Budapest. 1998 (reprint).
Domanovszky, György. *A magyar nép disziőművészete I, II.* Akadémiai Kiadó, Budapest. 1981.
Domokos, Pál Péter *Rezeda.* Zeneműkiadó, Budapest. 1971.
Du, Yaxiong. "Comparative research between western Yugur folksongs And related folksongs of other nationalities." Chinese Music, No. 4. Beijing (in Chinese) 1982.
Du, Yaxiong. "*Classification of Pentatonic scales and their construction*" Chinese Music 52, No. 4. Beijing (in Chinese) 1993.
Du, Yaxiong. *Selected Folk Songs of China.* Sichuan People's Press Chendu, China 1994.
Du, Yaxiong. "Ancient Hungarian Folk Songs and Shamanic Songs of the Minorities of North China" Shamanism in Performing Arts. Akadймiai Kiady, Budapest 1995.
Du, Yaxiong. "*Shaonian, courtship songs from Northwest China*" Chime No. 12-13. Leiden, The Netherlands 1999.
Encyclopaedia Britannica Volume 17. Encyclopaedia Britannica Inc. Chicago. 1942.
Erdész, Sándor. "*Kigyókultusz a magyar néphagyományban*" *Studia Folkloristica et ethnographica, 12.* Kossuth Lajos Tudományegyetem néprajzi tanszékének kiadványa. Z. Ujváry (ed.), Debrecen 1984.
Faragó, József, et. al. *Kalotaszegi Magyar Népviselet* (The Folkwear of Kalotaszeg). Krietrion Publishers, Bucharest 1977.
Filetóth, Enikő. *Website of professinal Hungarian emroiderer.* http://www.filetoth.com/index-3_en.html. Sept 2, 2010-
Gazi, Amat (ed). *Collection of Uygur Folk Designs (*in Uygur, Chinese, English) Xinjiang Art and Photography Press, Urumqi 1992.
Geng, Shemin. *Ancient Turkic Poems.* Xinjiang Pople's Press, Urumqi 1982.
Hajdu, Mihály and Kálmán Halász. *Viola.* Zeneműkiadó, Budapest 1971.
Hawley, W.M. *Chinese Folk Designs.* Dover Publications, New York 1971.
Henkey, Gyula and Izabella Horvath. "Physical anthropological field report and comparative research results on the Kazaks and Kirghiz from the Peoples republic of China" International Journal of Central Asian Studies. Soeul, Korea 1998.
Hofer, Tamás and Edith Fél. *Magyar Népművészet.* Corvina Kiadó, Budapest 1975.
Horváth, Izabella. *The Journey of the Griffins from Inner Asia to the Carpathian Basin. (Bilingual monograph).* Folklore és ethnografia, 66. Debrecen Kossuth

Lajos Tudományegyetem Néprajzi Tanszékének Kiadványa. Z. Ujváry (ed.), Debrecen 1992.

Horváth, Izabella. "Comparative researach on Hungarian and Ancient Turkish folksong lyrics" (in Chinese), Chinese Music 94.3. Beijing 1994.

Horvath, Izabella. *"A comparative study of the shamanistic motifs in Hungarian and Turkic folk tales"* Shamanism in Performing Arts. M. Hoppal (ed.) Akadémiai Kiadó, Budapest 1995.

Horvath, Izabella/Du, Yaxiong. *"Xinjiang's population of the pre-Turkic age in light of Chinese archeology and historical sources"* Eurasian Studies Yearbook. No. 67. Indiana University, Bloomington, Indiana 1995.

Hoppál, Mihály et. al. *Jelképtar.* Magyar Helikon Kiadó, Budapest 1990.

Illyes, Gyula. *Hetvenhét magyar népmese* (Seventy-seven Hungarian Folktales) Móra Könyvkiadó, Budapest 1972.

Ipolyi, Arnold. *Magyar mythologia* (facsimile of 1854 ed.) Europa Könyvkiadó, Budapest 1987.

Kazak Folk Art Design Editorial Board. (KFAEB) *A collection of the Kazak Folk Art Designs* (in Chinese and English). Xinjiang People's Publishing House, Urumqi 1983.

Kodály, Zoltán. *A magyar népzene.* Zeneműkiadó, Budapest 1971.

Kodály, Zoltán. *Folk Music of Hungary.* The Macmillan Company, New York 1960.

Kodály, Zoltán. *Ecseri lakodalmas* (Wedding at Ecser). CD, Hungaroton Classic LTD. Hungary 1996.

Kocsis, Mária and Lajos Csomor. (nd) *Festett bútorok a Székelyföldön.* (Painted Furniture in Transylvania) Népművelődési Propaganda Iroda, Budapest.

László, Gyula (nd) A népvándorlás művészete Magyarországon. Corvina. Budapest.

Lao Zi. *Tao Te Ching.* New translation by Gia-Fu Feng and Jane English. Vintage Books, a Division of Random House, New York 1972.

Li, Guizhou and Zhengzhu Zhi. *Folk singers From Gansu province, People's Republic of China*; performed at the International Festival of Arts in Wellington, New Zealand. Feb 7, 1998 (Trans. Du Yaxiong ; Book containing these songs are in press by Jack Body, Wellington, New Zealand).

Lin, Yutang. ed. *The Wisdom of Laotse.* Modern Library, New York 1948.

Luko, Gábor. *A magyar lélek formái.* Pannonia Könyvek, Budapest 1987.

Magyar Records. *Öt évszázad magyar dalai.* New Brunswick, New Jersey1972(?).

Mathia, Károly. *Nefelejcs.* Zeneműkiadó, Budapest 1971.

Minority Affairs Bureau of Inner Mongolia ed. *Mongolian Costume.* Mongolian Science Publishers, Chifeng, Inner Mongolia 1991.

Meothy, Mihály and Ernő Hetényi. *Ji csing, a változás könyve*. Hatter Lap és Könyvkiadó, Budapest 1989.
O. Nagy, Gábor. *Magyar szólások és közmondások (*3. Kiadás). Gondolat, Budapest 1982.
Ortutay, Gyula (ed). *Magyar Neprajzi Lexikon I-V.* (MNL) Akadémiai Kiadó. Budapest 1981.
Rózsavölgyi és Társa. (?) *Jácéntos Virágom* (song book). Rózsavölgyi és Társa, Budapest 1943.
Tianjin Meishu Chubanshe (Tianjin Art Publishers) (ed.), *Han Hua Xuan*. Tianjin, China 1982.
Waley, Arthur (trans). *The Book of Songs*. Grove Press, New York 1996.
Willhelm, Richard. *The I Ching* (24th printing). Bollingen Series XIX. Princeton Universtiy, Princeton, New Jersey 1990.
Williams, C.A.S. *Outlines of Chinee Symbolism and Art Motives*. Dover Publications, New York 1976.
Xie, Kai. *A Collection of the Khalkhas (Kyrgyz) Folk Designs* (in Khalkhas, Chinese, and English). Xinjiang People's Publishing House. Urumqi 1985.
Xu, Yuan Zhong. *Song of the Immortals*. New World Press, Beijing 1994.
Zhang, Hengde and Lianten Han ed. *Weiwu'erzu zhuangshi tu'an* (Uygur Decorative Designs). Renmin Meishu Chubanshe, Beijing 1994.
Zhao, Guohua. *The Worship of Reproduction in Culture* (in Chinese). Social Science Press of China, Beijing 1990.

Scientific Discourse of Post-Totalitarian Regimes: Fears and Hopes

Aslan Mamedly
(Azerbaijan)

In literary criticism the concept of "archetype", introduced by K. Jung, differs from the Jungian meaning. It is understood as any primary image found in any cultural context, which includes also the personal archetypes of a writer. Such an understanding of archetype deprives it of its universal psychological content and transforms it into a discourse-making constituent of creativity (compare Иваницкий А.И., «Архетипы Гоголя», 2001 [Ivanitskiy A.I. Gogol's Archetypes, 2001]). Sometimes the archetype is connected to ethnic standards, (compare Гулиев Г., «Архетипы рода Горгуда" 2000 [Guliev G., Archetypes of Gorgud).

The analysis of scientific language allows the claim that it is not at all formed irrespective of time; conditions of space and time are reflected directly in scientific discourse. However, there is a question: what level of the scientific text is affected by spatio-temporal characteristics? The answer to this question will be unequivocal: on the level of connotation. However another question immediately emerges: to what extent is it legitimate to speak about connotation in the scientific text? The answer is: the scientific text or, more widely, a scientific discourse, like any discourse, is structured in close relationship with cultural characteristics of space and time. The strictest mathematical texts have pragmatic aspects. However, they are not all expressed or not always expressed explicitly. Science in its strictest sense is supposed to be beyond national mentality. Nevertheless, if the scientific tradition or the tradition of a scientific discourse is formed in a national environment, then, in my opinion, it is quite natural to speak about the pragmatic tradition of a national scientific discourse. The first word in the phrase *a **national** scientific discourse* does not emphasize the circumstance that the law of gravity in Russia or in Azerbaijan works differently than in England or Congo, but that the reflective discourse of textbooks on physics, not only represents the laws of physics, but also has specific culturological characterictics. Meanwhile *culturology* is understood here as a reflection on the fact, in this case on the fact of gravity.

Culturological reflection, probably, is national-pragmatically designed. The given pragmatic characteristic of the scientific text is especially distinct in popular scientific books. For example, J. Perelman's popular books on physics and mathematics on which generations of the Soviet schoolchildren have been brought up, clearly has a distinctive Jewish mentality, found both in the style of language, and in presentation and connotation. Altogether these features make the book more appealing. Reading Perelman's *The Entertaining Physics* or *The Lively Mathematics* gives pleasure, a deep satisfaction received from dialogue with a really intelligent person.

Compared to the above, the pre-revolutionary textbooks for high school were written completely differently. To be more precise, I refer to textbooks written by Germans and translated into Russian. Even the translations have not lost the German spirit.[1]

The translator of the Latin textbook, S. Rozhankovsky, wrote in the foreword: «Needless to say, that the comprehension of singularities of Latin speech by means of synonymy should tell rather favorably on the native language, as the pupil, developing and forming the mind on synonymic shades of Latin, on the sample of classics starts to use Russian cautiously and consciously, distinguishing e.g. expressions like «it seems to me, I think, I am confident, I am convinced" in compliance with their logic value, that is, synonymy becomes for him, by Dr. Tegge's neat expression, practical logic (compare the Charter of gymnasium and progymnasium) (p. 4-5).

Further S.Rozhankovsky writes: «The scholars' opinion on the value of synonymy in gymnasium teaching, stated in his remarkable writing, is worth quoting entirely here. «First", Tegge says , «and the supreme principle of teaching classic languages, in particular Latin, in spite of different opinions on volume and an ultimate goal of the teaching, in formal attitude is discipline and exercise of thinking, development and education of mind» (p. 5). Further the translator specifies: «Those who have taken out such discipline and education of mind from school, has acquired the distinctness of thinking in the language most precise sense of form , has obtained such treasure of knowledge which is doubtless more valuable than knowledge on so-called formal logic" (p. 6.) S.Rozhankovsky respects the *German* spirit of the textbook, so, he points out: «The translator should add in summary, that the German original of this textbook has undergone only minor alterations which in antibarbarus are determined by differences between Russian and German phrases, and only once German phrase which doesn't have a respective equivalent in Russian had to be left out" (p. 7). The problem of

1 See: «Греческая этимология гимназического курса по учебнику Э.Коха и другим с приспособлениями к употреблению в русских гимназиях и с прибавлением отделов об образовании слов и о греческих дилаектах. Москва, издание книжного магазина В.Думнова, под фирмою наследников бр. Салаевых, 1889, [*Greek Etymology of Gymnasium Course on Textbook of E.Koch*,] or: Латинская грамматика по Штегману ,составил В.Никифоров. М.: Наследники братьев Салаевых, 1912, [Latin Grammar by Stegman], «Учебник латинской синонимики» Др.Тэгге (М.: Издание книжного магазина А. Ланга, 1889) [Latin Synonymic by Dr. Tegge]

the influence of German mentality on the Russian in the 19-20th centuries via the translation of educational and academic literature is a special subject of research.

Thus, scientific discourse is not deprived of connotation. Considering this idea as the first thesis, the second can be formulated as follows: «the connotation of a scientific discourse has national-specific features". And lastly, the third thesis could be expressed as such: if the connotation of a scientific discourse has national-specific features, then within the space of these national-specific features it is quite admissible to search for archetypes.

In this context the concept "archetype" has in a certain sense *an intermediate* content, intermediate in terms of its realization between the Jungian and philological understanding. In other words, the archetype in this case is formed as "universal", not in relation to all mankind, but the mankind framed by "national-specific features". As such the archetype represents ethnic psychology, ethnic thinking and outlook.

For example, in the work entitled "One-Storeyed America" Ilf and Petrov wrote that the American workers had agreed that the idea that expropriating the millionaires' properties is fair. However, they added that the law should allow a person to own wealth up to 5 million dollars, and no more. In my opinion, such an attitude of the working class to wealth is archetypical, has national-specific feature, and characterizes the American mentality. Russian literature exhibits the same archetypical features. They can be detected in modern Russian scientific discourse. For example, modernity actualised people's distrust to the wealthy and hatred for the rich in Russia. Today such a concept as «bloodsucker» is popular in scientific literature more than ever before. It is impossible to say that the actualization of this concept is devoid of motivation.

Modern Russian scientific discourse reflects, despite scientific characteristics, the fears of post-totalitarian time. In the words of one Russian politician "The state does not care about the citizens, «(it) does not keep them on a short leash,» which seems to strengthen the general uneasiness of the time."

As the object of the research A. Nikiforov's book is selected: Никифоров А.Л. Логика и теория аргументации. – М.: Современный гуманитарный университет, 2005. (A.Nikiforov. The Logic and Theory of Argumentation, Moscow: Modern University of Humanities, 2005) The analysis of the book's language suggests that all fears of the time are reflected in it. Thus, the philological analysis of such scientific discourse can be conducted in two directions. The first is focused on the definition of fears and their motives. The second reveals the existential information behind these fears.

In the foreword to his book the scientist-philosopher, A. Nikiforov, writes the following:

> The biological species to which we belong, is referred to as Homo sapiens – "the person reasonable". The reason is considered to be the major distinctive feature of the person in comparison with other animals. But how little we care about the development of our own reason! Looking at our politicians, reading periodicals, finding out about absurd economic or political decisions of government officials, sometimes one starts to doubt, whether these people are reasonable, whether they use reason. Observing disputes in the State Duma [The lower-house of theRussian Parliament], at various meetings or in ordinary life it is easy to notice that there is a lack of reason in these disputes, and abundance of emotions and aggression. In whatever activity you are engaged, whatever life you live you cannot do without reason. And it is logic that teaches how effectively we use and develop it. Therefore an acquaintance with logic is necessary for any person» (Никифоров А. 2005: 7).

The beginning is quite emotionally charged, by the way, and is also connotatively understood and can be referred to as *straight to the point*. The ending of the foreword is also significant:

> I want to warn the reader: without your own efforts nothing will work! It is impossible to become an educated and thinking person without putting forth one's best effort. It is possible to purchase books, it is possible to employ the most skilful teachers who will do all hard work and spoon-feed you, but it is you who should swallow! Indeed, in this world each person should do something himself, including studying, to make efforts to become an educated person. One can buy educational diploma, but not education. "The pig remains a pig though shower it with stars!", as a poet has said. (Никифоров А. 2005:9).

In the passage above, negative connotation is realized at the explicit level in the sense that all essential signs of a discourse are presented. The only requirement to such discourses is a transformation of judgement. For example, the first sentence *The biological kind to which we belong is called Homo sapiens – "reasoning man"* means «I doubt that the biological category to which we belong, refers to Homo sapiens – "the person reasonable". In other words, «I doubt that the people surrounding me are reasonable". The objects of doubt are obvious and designated in the discourse. The persons referred to are politicians, the editors of periodicals, the makers of economic and political decisions, government officials, and members of the State Duma. After these designations there is a phrase: *Whatever activity you are engaged in, whatever life you live, you cannot do without reason*, it is quite clear that for A.Nikiforov all these people, *politicians, the editors of periodicals, the makers of economic and political decisions, government officials, and the members of the State Duma*, are deprived of even a hint of reason.

The symbolic role in the text is carried out also by the word *looking* (*looking at our politicians)* – if *looking*, hence, there is nothing worth to look at.

In my view, in this introduction not an intellectual arrogance but a philistine fear of the intolerable present and unknown future is expressed. The ending of *the Foreword* is just as easily understood. Frankly connotation is expressed here in a lowered key again. The transformation of judgement demonstrates that «if you have money, it does not mean that you can purchase a mind and an education. He alleges that, «it is a usual phenomenon to buy a diploma» and, certainly, «you, gentlemen, are pigs!»

In the section 1.4. of the book entitled *The Development Stages of of Logic* explaining the term sophism as such:A.Nikiforov states:

> You feel, that you are being slightly duped but it is difficult to say what the matter is. Aren't reasoning of our modern statesmen similar to these sophisms? For example, we have spoken a lot about voucher privatization? We were persuaded that the voucher is a check for receiving a decent piece from the public pie! Well, what is the result? – my voucher lies in the drawer, it is enough just to get Chubays's autograph on it and then after ten years it will be possible to sell it to collectors of curiosities" (Никифоров А. 2005)

And in the section 3.4, Methods Similar to Definition he continues: «Poets sometimes find such similarities which simply amaze with their unexpectedness: "As the horse with horse cloth is dressed a forgotten grand piano" (I. Anennsky); "Blood drips, as roses, from a mouth" (A. Ahmatova); "The grass breathed as a skin of the sweated lion" (N. Gumilyov). But also scientists are sometimes able to please us with amusing comparisons. Once I have asked the friend economist to explain me what "recession", "depression" and "panic" mean – "Well, they are simple things, – he has answered. "Recession" is the period when people tighten their belts. During "depression" it is difficult to buy a belt to hold trousers. And when the person remains without trousers, "panic" begins.Obviously, it is necessary to be able to use descriptions, characteristics, comparisons" (citation1, 50).

Despite the playful tone and the comic effect of the text, it certainly frankly expresses fears of our times. In the examined text in general and in its whole connotation, fear is directly presented. Connotation and its lowered character are created by the constituents of the text, that is, words and phrases, the understanding of which does not suppose hermeneutical analysis. However, modern scientific discourse is till in waiting for analysis and particularly, it waits for analysis of implicit meanings. Such research should have complex and systematic character. Hence, scientific discourse is able to substantially supplement to the image of a time.

References

Никифоров А. *Логика и теория аргументации.* М.: Современный гуманита рный университет, 2005.

Nikiforov A. *Logika i teorija argumentacii.* M.: Sovremennyj gumanitarnyj universitet, 2005.

Part 2
Eastern Archetypes in the West: Rumi, Ashik-Kerib, Qurriat Al-Ayn

Renditions of Rumi in Europe and North America

Simon Sorgenfrei
(Sweden)

Introduction

In a famous essay published in 1977 the French literary theorist and philosopher Roland Barthes declared "the death of the author", and simultaneously the vivacity and independence of the text. By shifting focus from author to text, the constructive agency of the reader is advocated. The meaning of a text, according to Barthes, is created when a reader interprets it (Barthes 1977).

The Sufi poet Moulana Rumi has been dead for more than 700 years, but his texts are as vibrant and influential as ever. Written in Persian in thirteenth century Turkey, the poems of Rumi have been read and interpreted as words of spiritual wisdom for seven hundred years in what we sometimes carelessly call "the Muslim World". And for more than a hundred years now, his popularity has been on the rise in Euro-America. This has presented us with a great diversity of interpretations, some of which I will reflect upon in this chapter.

Inspired by Barthes' shift of focus from the authors' intentions to the reader's interpretation, as well as by the sociological study of religions bestowing more attention to individual religiosity than to normative or essentialist theological abstractions – I will consider three contemporary interpretations and presentations of the poetry and teachings of Moulana Rumi. The interpretations, all done in a Euro-American context, are made by, respectively, the Chishti Sheikh Inayat Khan, the American poet Coleman Barks, and the self-help guru Deepak Chopra.

As soon as a text is written, according to Barthes, it begins a multitude of lives of its own – independent of its author's intentions. A text is not, he says, pregnant with a single 'theological' meaning, which he compares to the 'message' of the Author-God. Rather, he says, it is the reader who bestows a text with multiple meanings. "Every text is eternally written here and now," (Barthes 1977) says Barthes, and therefore there is no such thing as an ultimate meaning to a literary text.

In a way somewhat similar to Barthes treatment of text and meaning, the sociological study of religion has shaped its view on religion. "The sociologist of religion is concerned with religion only insofar as it relates to the context in which it inevitably exists, writes Meredith McGuire in an acknowledged introduction to the field (McGuire 2008). This has resulted in a paradigmatic shift of focus from the metaphysical to the mundane and social dimensions of religious activities. Not taking positions on the existence or non-existence of religious "truth" or "essence," sociologists of religion have focused on religion as a social construction and on individual interpretations of religious texts and traditions.

I argue that this theoretical framework will allow me to analyze how Inayat Khan, Coleman Barks, and Deepak Chopra all in different, but similar, ways can be understood to present what they define as the "essence" or Rumi. It will help me understand how these "essences" all are to be understood as *individual* truths which then are translated to English. Rather, therefore, than linguistic translations, I believe we can understand the above mentioned translations as theological. The above mentioned theoretical positions will help me to do so without having to take a stand on whether their interpretations can be said to be correct or not. Whatever Rumi wanted to say in his poems – or what is to be the correct way to translate and interpret these is not my interest here.

Background

Rumi is one of the most popular poets of Muslim cultural and religious origin of all times, and has been called the world's foremost mystical writer. He was a Muslim Scholar and a Sufi Sheikh, and has until fairly recently chiefly been read as a Muslim Sufi poet. In the mid nineteenth century he was introduced into German by Joseph von Hammer-Purgstall and later by Johann Wolfgang von Goethe. The first substantial translations into English were made in the late nineteenth century by James Redhouse and E.H. Whinfield, and in the early twentieth century all the six volumes of his *Masnavi-ye Ma'navi* was translated to English by Reynold Nicholson. Since then his popularity has significantly increased in Euro-America.

During the 1990s American magazines talked about the "Rumi phenomenon," as Rumi was then claimed to be the best selling poet in North America. But it was not Nicholson's or other scholarly translations that attracted readers of different walks of life, but rather versions of these made by the poet Coleman Barks. Barks has received a lot of criticism, especially from academia, as well as from some Muslim readers, for ignoring the religious, historical, and biographical context of the poems in presenting them as expressing a perennial Universalist wisdom rather than a Muslim-Sufi creed.

Inayat Khan and the Hand of Poetry

But Barks was not the first to "un-read" Muslim or Islamic theology and terminology from Rumi's poems. In the early twentieth century the Chishtiyya Sheikh

Inayat Khan came from India to North America and Europe as a musician and Sufi missionary. The popularity of Khan's mission has been explained by him introducing Sufi teachings without an Islamic vocabulary, presenting them as a universal spirituality unfettered by any institutional religion. In a book entitled "The Hand of Poetry," Khan lectured on a handful of Persian poets – amongst them of course Moulana Rumi. Rumi, he say, is:

> the greatest poet the world has ever known: a poet whose message, in his life and work both, marks a distinct line as a new era, a new step in Sufism, which was the most ancient school of Mystics and Philosophers, and which originated from the ancient mystic school of Egypt. The first and best known initiate of that particular school was Abraham, the father of the three great religions of the World: Judaism, the Christian religion and the Islamic religion. (Khan 1993: 64)

Here Khan does two things. First he "liberates" Sufism from any single religious tradition in presenting it as a primordial mysticism of unclear origin. Egypt, in the early twentieth century indicated age old mysteries and wisdom. Sufism is not, says Khan, exclusively Islamic. If connected to any religion, Sufism belongs to Judaism, Christianity, and Islam.

Rumi, as presented by Khan, preaches an individualized religiosity according to which one must make a God within oneself, to attain the "real God." In *The Hand of Poetry*, Khan explains Rumi's message as follows:

> It is only seeing your self in its perfection which is the vision of God. All revelation, the whole secret, can be found in the heart of man. [...] In order to attain to that God, we must make a God within ourselves. Therefore, the God of each one is different. [...] This is the fulfillment of all religion, all philosophy, all mysticism. (Khan 1993: 71f, 73)

> Inayat Khan's take on Sufism and Rumi has become tremendously influential in the Euro-American context. As the quote above suggests he presents a very individualized religion, set free from the cages of ritual, doctrine and the hierarchy of institutional religions. Every individual is free to find, or create, her own truth within. This has been a very prominent way of being religious in Euro-America during the 20th century (Roof: 1999, McGuire 2008: 292-295).

Khan gives no mention to Rumi ever being Muslim. He says he was a "statesman, politician, at the head of the law in his country [...]" (Khan 1993: 64) In individualizing spirituality, Khan makes it universal. In Khan's interpretation, Rumi's poems express a religious truth which cannot be limited to one religion, such as Islam, but rather transcends religion or is to be understood as the *essence* of all religions.

Inayat Khan's Sufism has attracted hundreds of thousands of Americans and Europeans on the look out for a universal, non institutionalized or dogmatic religion. One of these seekers is the poet Coleman Barks.

Coleman Barks, the Essential Rumi

Coleman Barks was studying Literature at Berkeley University in California in the 1970s, when he first was introduced to the Poems of Rumi by his colleague Robert Bly. As the story goes Bly gave him a copy of Rumi's poems translated by A. J. Arberry, saying: "These poems need to be released from their cages." (Barks 1997: 290) What Barks, who doesn't know Persian, has done ever since is to re-work others translations of Rumi's poems into modern English poetry. He says that he tries to be "faithful to the images, the tone as we hear it, and the spiritual information coming through." He says he wants to place Rumi in the strong tradition of American free verse, and that his are "free translations" but that he hopes they remain "true to the essence." (Barks 1997: 292)

The most debated method of Barks', besides calling himself a translator of Rumi not mastering Persian, is eradicating from the poems words and terms associated with Islam. Discussing his method of interpretation, Barks once said he: "took Islam out of it". (Curiel 2002) If Khan neglected to mention that Rumi was a Muslim Scholar and Sheikh in presenting him for an American audience in the early twentieth century, Bark's openly states he is removing what he considers to be Islamic in the poems eighty years later.

The best selling of Bark's many books of Rumi poems is the compilation "The Essential Rumi". I believe the title of Bark's collection can be understood in two ways. The most obvious way to read the title is that Barks wants to say he has collected the most important of Rumi's writings and here presents a volume in which the central themes and thoughts are presented. However, we can also understand the title, I argue, as a presentation of what Barks finds to be the *essence* in Rumi's poems and teachings – unfettered of its religious context. That he presents the perennial wisdom of Rumi released from the contextual cages.

In a biographical introductory chapter, Barks briefly describes Rumi's life. Just as in Khan's book this is done without any mention of Islam or of Rumi being Muslim. Rather he is described as a learned professor and religious scholar becoming a mystic after meeting the wandering dervish Shems-e Tabrizi. Barks explain that Rumis' poems are "a fluid, continuously self-revising, self-interrupting medium. They are not so much *about* anything as spoken from *within* something. Call it enlightenment, ecstatic love, spirit, soul, truth, the ocean of *ilm* (divine luminous love), or the covenant of *alast* (the original agreement with God). Names do not matter." He tells us he has done his "versions or translations or renderings or imitations as homage" (Barks 1997: 291) to his spiritual teacher, the Sufi Sheikh Bawa Muhaiyaddeen. Bawa's work, he says, is beyond religion. "Love is the religion, and universe is the book." (Barks 1997: 291)

I believe this is important, even though it is not often discussed, for understanding Barks versions of Rumi's poetry. The renditions of the poems are means in his own spiritual quest. Just as Khan was using Rumi in presenting his own spiritual teachings, Barks' renditions of Rumi can be read as expressions of his own spiritual conviction and therefore be understood as translations of his subjective spiritual experience into modern English rather than from Persian to English.

Deepak Chopra and Rumi beyond Rumi

My last example comes from a small book of poems called "The Love Poems of Rumi" which is edited by self-help guru Deepak Chopra. Just as Bark, I argue, Chopra's notion of Rumi and Sufism can be understood as a result of Inayat Khan's mission. But if Barks freed Rumi's poems from their metrical and religious cages – Chopra takes it a step further and separates Rumi from Rumi altogether. Whatever the title might promise, reading the fine print we soon understand these are not love poems of Rumi, but love poems by Deepak Chopra and someone called Fereydoun Kia, which were inspired by Rumi's poetry.

In the introduction to the volume Chopra lets us know how he met Kia in 1996 on a course he gave called "Seduction of the Soul". And "during that week of spiritual rhapsody," he says, "we spent many moments exulting in the ravishing ecstasy that the passion of Rumi evoked in both of us." (Chopra 1998: 11) This led them to produce their own poems, while dancing and listening to music. Chopra writes:

> "These poems reflect the deepest longings of the human heart as it searches for the divine. They celebrate love. Each poetic whisper is urgent, expressing the desire that penetrates human relationships and inspires intimacy with the self, silently nurturing an affinity for the Beloved. They are not direct translations, but 'moods'", he continues, "that we have captured as certain phrases radiated from the original Farsi, giving life to a new creation but retaining the essence of its source." (Chopra 1998: 11f)

Just as Barks, Chopra and Kia say they have found what they call the essence of Rumi's poems, and this essence, then, is found through the deepest longing and in the most intimate of the self. This echo of Inayat Khan's teaching that the way to the "real God" goes through the making of an individual god within one's self.

Conclusion

All three of these renditions of Rumi's poetry focus on what they regard to be the essence or Rumi's teachings. This essence is experienced through separating, to different degrees, the text from its religious, historical, and biographical context. Inayat Khan, Coleman Barks, and Deepak Chopra claim to have experienced the essence of the teachings, understood as an archetypal spiritual truth. This archetypal essence is evoked in the heart of the reader, rather than found in the text. The essence of Rumi is, as understood by the three interpreters focused upon in this chapter, multi-locative. It is simultaneously comprehended as universal and deeply individual – or universal just because it is individualized.

All three interpreters are in this way, consciously or non-consciously, declaring the death of the author in celebrating the autonomous life of the text. In unreading what Barthes called the "single theological truth" of the text, they simultaneously offer their own, individual, theological truths in presenting what they consider to be the essence of the poem's meaning. Claiming access to the essence of a tradition is, I argue, a way to legitimize a highly individual understanding or experience of tradition, and an illustration of what Charles Taylor called the subjective turn of contemporary religion (Taylor 1991). *The individual experience understood as the essence of a teaching is made an archetypal religious truth.*

References

Barks, Coleman. *The Essential Rumi*. New Jersey, Castel Books. 1997

Chopra, Deepak. *The Love Poems of Rumi*. New York, Harmony Books1998

Curiel, Jonathan. *Poet follows his own Muse*, San Francisco Chronicle 2002-04-04.

Barthes, Roland. *Death of the Author*. Aspen No. 5-6,1969.

Khan, Inayat. *The Hand of Poetry. Five Mystic Poets of India*. Omega Publishing, New Lebanon 1993.

McGuire, Meredith. *Religion. The Social Context*. Long Grove, Waveland Press 2008.

Roof, Wade Clark. Spiritual Marketplace. Baby Boomers and the Remaking of American Religion. New Jersey, Princeton University Press1999.

Taylor, Charles *The Ethics of authenticity*. Cambridge, Harvard University Press1991

Archetype of the Creator: the Semantics of Cultural Universals of the East (Mikhail Lermontov's "Ashik- Kerib")

Tatiana Megrelishvili
(Georgia)

M.Y. Lermontov's tale "Ashik Kerib"[1] has been studied mostly from the standpoint of language and style, as well as in comparison[2] with Dastan "Koroghlu"[3] – an ancient legend about the poet-singer and the warrior. Lermontov's tale has also been considered as a romantic narrative,[4] as the East seemed to be an exotic location for Lermontov, being one of the components of his so-called Byronism. Lotman identified the geographical East as a separate component of Lermontov's work: "The

---

1 About the directions of development of Lermontov's tale "Ashik Kerib" in conjunction with the legend of "Koroghlu": Enikolopov, I.K., A fairy tale "Ashik Kerib" Lermontov, M.Y., L., Ashik Kerib. Turkish tale, Tb., 1941; Manuilov V.A., M.Y. L., and his record of tale of Ashik Kerib. – Ashik Kerib. Coll.for perfoming ballet in Leningrad. State. Acad. Maly Opera Theatre, L. 1941, p. 5-41, A.V Popov, M. Lermontov. in the first link. – Stavropol, 1949, p. 70-78, M.S. Mikhailov, On the lessons M. Y. L. "Tatar" language. – Tyurkologic. Coll., 1, Moscow – Leningrad, 1951, p. 127-35, S. Yakubov, Azerbaijani folk legend "Ashig-Gharib" – Baku, 1968; Murzaev E.M., Years of searching in Asia. – M., 1973, p. 54

2 Oriental folklore genre resembling the Romance of heroic literature, usually with a hero of ordinary descent.

3 Kor-oghlu", "Koroglu" – folk-epic monument, popular in the Middle East and Central Asia; formed in about 17th century. Version of "Koroghlu" conditionally divided into two groups: the western (Armenian, Georgian, Kurdish, Azerbaijani, Turkish version, dating back to the Azerbaijani epic "Koroghlu") and eastern (Turkmen "Gerogly", Uzbek and Kazakh "Gorogly" Tajik "Gurugli" or "Gurguli"). In western versions the hero is the people's avenger and the poet-improviser, whose goal in life – to pay back the despot, who blinded his father (hence the name of the hero from Turkic – son of the blind). For more about this: Ker-oglu, oriental poet and horseman, Tiflis, 1856; Koroglu, B., 1959; Gorogly, Ashgabat, 1958; Zhirmunsky V.M., Zarifov H.T., Uzbek people's heroic epic, M., 1947; Karryev BA, Epic tales of Koroghlu, a Turkic-speaking peoples, M., 1968; Koroglu H., A new version of "Koroglu" – Theoretical Issues of Oriental literature, M., 1969.

4 On the refinement of Lermontov's Caucasus works into the European and Russian romantic narrative pattern: "... the action of his romantic works developed on the background of the phenomena of reality, denoting social evil as universal (prison, inquisition, masquerade, cruel life of the fortress) and transferred to an environment far removed from modern everyday life possibly less similar to those – in Russia the era of Ivan Terrible or Pugachev, to Spain, to Caucasus ... "[LE 1981: 475]" Lermontov's image of the Caucasus was formed under the influence of freedom-loving motives of Russian poetry of the 20-ies." [LE 1981 213]

theme of the East, images of the Oriental culture accompanied Lermontov throughout his creation" [Lotman 1985:115]. This feature of the narrative and artistic creative layer of Lermontov's legacy, rightly pointed by Y.M.Lotman, is based on two factors: the first is cultural and paradigmatic, that is the oriental direction common to romanticism and the "Eastern Problem" in Russia's socio-political discourse between 1830–1840. The second factor is related to the typological system of images characteristic for the mature phase of Lermontov's creativity. Thus "Ashik Kerib" has been studied in parrallel with such layers of Lermontov's artistic heritage as his "Caucasian" lyrics and lyric-epic. More recently, an attempt was made to read Lermontov's tale through the prism of Islamic esoteric tradition.[5]

Despite of the wide range of analysis, answers on several questions are still not found. What interested Lermontov in the story of Ashik Kerib? Was it only an ethnographic "oriental" flavoured fairy-tale, which he might have heard from his friend M.F.Akhundov in Tiflis?[6] Could Lermontov with his poetic talent and philosophical tendency of the mind have been drawn to "Ashik Kerib" just because of his romanticism or because of the desire to capture the elements of Islamic esotericism in his work, as P.V. Alekseev suggests?

Exploring Lermontov's poetic legacy is not an easy task. In a letter to the author of these lines one of the greatest lermontoveds of XXth century V.E. Vatsuro wrote: "Lermontov is a "closed" poet, highly individual. <...> Special – for many reasons, he is like a creature in isolation: he did not write critical essays, literary letters <...> his environment is restored bit by bit, and almost the only material of the study is his work, and the method of study is intra-reading and analysis of anarrative" (Vatsuro2008: 689).

For this reason, any interpretation of Lermontov's works is nearly always speculative. One interpretation of the text of "Ashik Kerib" examins the genre of the text, a fairy-tale. This way the last two questions posed can be answered negatively: he did not consider it an romantic, ethnographic oriental tale, nor was he interested in Islamic esotericism. Regarding the first question, the answer can be found hypothetically by analyzing the components of the text.

5 Alekseev, P.V., A turkish tale of M.Y. Lermontov's "Ashik Kerib" in the context of Islamic esoteric tradition – Mode of access: http://ec-dejavu.ru/l/Lermontov.html.

6 At the end of 1837, Lermontov wrote to S.A. Rayevsky from Tiflis: "Started learning Tatar, a language which here, and generally in Asia, is as necessary as French in Europe – pity, I will not finish, but it could be useful." [Lermontov, 1976:404]. I.L. Andronicov assumed, and till now this hypothesis is not refused, that Lermontov's teacher was Mirza Fatali Akhundov – an Azerbaijani poet and educator, who lived in Tiflis from 1834 and was a translator of Oriental Languages at the office of Baron Rosen, chief administrator in the Caucasus [LE 1981:27]. (In the time of the Tsars Azerbaijani were called Tatar by Russians).

A fairy tale most clearly manifests itself through the "collective unconscious," the most abstracted elements of which are translated into archetypes [Jung 1922]. The importance of fairy tales for the development of the person's inner world is apparent. The representative of the Jungian psychoanalytic school H.Dikman proved that many people follow fairy tales in their lives and its motifs strongly influence self-esteem and outlook [Dieckmann 2000]. In other words, the tale can affect the behavior of adults and their psychological life. The individual consciousness, interacting with the unconscious mind through a transcendental function, breaking the border between unconscious and conscious, is able to connect to the collective consciousness,[7] In our case, by the collective consciousness, we mean the Russian artistic consciousness, captured by Russian literature during the period between 1800-1840-s, at the peak of romanticism, the pinnacle Lermontov's work.

One of the components of fairy-tales are archetypes. Analysis of Lermontov's "Turkish tale" seen through the prism of the archetypes can contribute to the reconstruction of some of the philosophical and artistic landmarks of the poet's work during 1837 and 1838, the time when his creativity saw significant change.[8]

It was between 1828 and 1836 that Lermontov, a romantic by nature, described and perceived the world, reflecting his mood of longing and passion. His works reflected deep feelings of love and hatred, pride and humility, exploits and deeds. For him, "a wave and the solitary sail", the "winding road", "a lonely cliff", "a leaf", detached from the "native branches" are the symbolic images that express inner anxiety and loneliness, painful experiences of a forlorn human swimming against the stream, "the crowd", "our generation, expressions Lermontov became famous for." The desire to escape from the stereotypes imposed by the "crowd" was formulated in a poetic formula: "And he, the rebel, asks for the storm, / As if in storms there is peace."

Lermontov understanding of the poet's role and mission in society for that period is in a line with romantic trends of the poet's image.

A period spent in the Caucasus in 1837 was vital for Lermontov's life and deeply influenced his work. His profound interest toeastern culture is a significant factor in understanding his oriental works, commonly referred to as "Caucasian works." Simultaneously, the fact that they are not homogeneous is somehow overlooked.

---

7 "The collective consciousness, expressed in forms of collective ideas about collective feelings, and attitudes in the individual consciousness are reflected as a neotype – unchanging from generation to generation the values revealed, and perceived by man in his individual existence" [Seyidov 2009: 264].

8 The nature of this change has been discussed many times in studies on Lermontov, Different version sof events has been offered, but mostly it was a question on the movement of Lermontov's works from Romanticism to Realism [Megrelishvili 2000:10-24].

His Caucasian poems described at least two cultural layers. One was the formation of a Christian culture in Georgia ("Demon", "Georgia's Song", "Dagger", "Tamara"), and the other was a development of an Islamic culture in the Caucasus ("Complaints of a Turk" "Dispute", "Ismail Bey", "Aul Bastundzhi", "Haji Abrek", "Two Slaves", "Valerik"). In some Caucasioan works both layers interact ("Gifts of the Terek River," "Three Palms", "Rendezvous", "Mtsyri," "The Poet", and "Caucasus").

Apart from modern academic studies of Lermontov's Caucasia, there is the possibility of the comparison of these layers within the creative consciousness of Lermontov. This process should be considered within the boundaries of the artistic search which led to the change and became the the subject of his work at the turn of 1837.

Lermontov, whose extraordinary intelligence and tremendous poetic talent was aknowledged in his lifetime, even by enemies, came to the Caucasus in 1837, with indirect knowledge of the region.[9] His actual experience in the Cau-

9 About the history of Lermontov's personal acquaintance with the Caucasus: "The motives and images of Caucasian folklore in the works of Lermontov's are significant and diverse. [...] The original source of direct information, the place of meeting, was Shelkozavodskoe estate or "earthly paradise", near Kizlyar on the Terek and the estate of Goryachevodsk (Pyatigorsk), where together with his grandmother E.A.Arsenevoy, Lermontov came in 1820 and 1825 to visit the Hastatovs, relatives on the maternal side. The third time he visited Shelkozavodskoe in 1837, returning from his first Caucasian exile to Russia. The "family traditions" of Hastatovs's were connected with the Russian-Caucasian war. The head of the family, A.V.Hastatov (1756-1809) General-major, participated in the Russian-Turkish war, where he met with Ismail Atazhukin, the famous Circassian prince. He deserted the Russian Army, returned home, and fought on the side of his people in rebellion against the colonization of the Caucasus. The fate of the semi-legendary hero inspired Lermontov to create his early poem "Ismail Bey" (1833). Besides these impressions in the first trip to the Caucasus, Lermontov certainly was acquainted with the songs, legends, traditions, as well as some national customs of the highlanders.
In Shelkozavodskoe estate together with the Russian serfs lived Georgians and Armenians, descendants of Persian prisoners who were released by Peter I. Perhaps the later autograph postscript to "Georgian Song" (1829): "I have heard something similar in the Caucasus." was added in association with these memories. The plot of the adolescent poem "Cally" [corrupt Turkic "bloody"], presumably dating from 1830-1831 is associated with custom of blood revenge – typical for the life of the highlanders. There is evidence that Lermontov presented at one of the folk festivals around the Hot Waters and listened to songs of the famous kubanian singer Karim Sultan Giray. Some researchers have suggested a personal acquaintance with the poet Shora Nogmov, a translator of Circassian folklore and mythology, the author of "Stories of Adyg people, sketches from legends of Kabardins." The book was completed in 1843 and submitted to the Russian Academy of Sciences. During his study at Moscow University and at cadet school, Lermontov's connection with the Caucasus was not interrupted. Along with new meetings and acquaintances, Caucasian literature became available. Travels of Russian and foreign authors, memoirs and notes by Caucasian officers in a variety of ethnographic descriptions

casus has generated massive interest to the general culture of the Caucasus. A Russian "Wanderer"[10] – "an officer travelling on government business" – Lermontov arrives in Tiflis for the government service. At the time of his arrival the urban culture of Tiflis (modern Tbilisi) was dee fined by ethnic diversity.[11]On the one hand "Ashik Kerib" in this regard demonstrates Lermontov's attitude to the spirit of diverse people, such as the Turks, Arabs, and Persians. On the other hand, the similarity of the tale to the epic "Koroghlu" in its different variants allowed Lermontov to touch a "creative product" (the term A.Losev) of the Muslim culture of the Caucasus, which combines significant things for the East with basic cultural archetypes.

Lermontov himself seemed to be aware of the Caucasus as an cultural crossroads, and it has remained so until today. And if, prior to a personal acquaintance with the Caucasus, in the narrative typology of his works antithetical space is defined by a few speculative and abstract categories of like "East-West", his meeting with the Caucasus cultures prompted the poet to cspeak more specifically, introducing a genre with signifying adjectives ("The Demon"An Oriental tale, "Ashik Kerib"A Turkish tale). In the works that do not contain such direct references in the title, cultural space marked in the text (the names of heroes, places, peoples etc.).

It is known that Lermontov's works are very subjective: unlike his predecessors, the Romantics of the 1810s and 1820'ies, "the contradictions of social reality take on an abstract character, the absolute opposititon of isolated abstract entities: good and evil, innocence and sin, beauty and ugliness "[Mikhailova 1957: 114-114]. This philosophical essence defines the outlook of Lermontov, aiming not only to understand the world, but to be an active player in life ("I need to act ..."). Active life is clearly evidenced in the culture of the Mountain Peoples of the Caucasus and Transcaucasia,[12] which could not be unnoticed by Lermontov.

---

were published in magazines, or in separate editions. Revival of Russian oriental studies, the establishment of the Institute of Oriental Languages, appearance of oriental courses by professor M.A. Korkunova A.V. Boldyreva at Moscow University contributed to the development of interest to history and culture of the Caucasus" (1990:32 Hodanen).

10 On pilgrimage as an element of Russian cultural code, see: T.G. Megrelishvili, Narratology of romantic poem in Russian literature. – Problems of Modern Literature. Coll.of materials from II International Symposium. Tbilisi, 2009, p. 35-46; Problems of poetics of memoirs of the Russian emigration (1920-1960). – Tbilisi, 2005, 168 p., p. 72-81, "Petersburg Dreams" Georgi Ivanov. – Our St. Petersburg. C. The scientific papers. Tbilisi, Publishing House of Tbilisi State University, 2006, p. 96-127.

11 More about this: Kartlis Tskhovreba,. Ed. Kaukhchishvili S.G. – "Sabchota Sakartvelo"Tbilisi, 1973, p. 7-8 (in Georgian).

12 The nature of the land itself determined the formation of active and emotional characters, since, in contrast to the plains of Russia, with its long winters, where the activity of life is reduced, in

The motives of human action were familiar. A Russian person in his motivations is directed toward infinity (compare with Dostoevsky: "Russian people are wide, I would have narrowed"). The breadth of spaces of Russia, as well as the space of the East as was understood in Lermontov's period, defined this mental unity, which is directly opposed to the Western mentality, in which the motive of human action is inherently rational. Certainly, in the close geo-political boundaries of the major Western cultures, desire to acquire power over the limited scope of the physical world is able to fully satisfy a man, while the personality type of oriental culture is aimed toward infinity, which includes areas such as the human spirit, his "earthly" and "heavenly" existence.

Thus, Lermontov discovered "at the ridge of the Caucasus" forms of mentality, which were initially attractive to him. This thesis is supported by a well-known fragment of Lermontov's conversation with A.A.Kraevsky (1841), where the poet expresses his attitude to Eastern culture: "Why do we all follow the Europe and the French? I learned a lot from Asia, and I would like to go inside the mysteries of the Asian worldview, the foundations of which for us and for them are still poorly understood "[Gerstein 1941:123]. It can be assumed that the fairy-tale "Ashik Kerib" was interesting for the poet because of the elements of the "Asian outlook" and the "mystery" which the poet tried to penetrate.

Following this logic, one could argue that the plot lines (M.Azadovsky)[13] of this fairy-tale suddenly connected to Lermontov's internal philosophical reflections

---

the Caucasus (Caucasus mountain range) the climate is much milder, the number of warm sunny days increases together with the activity of the population in winter. Moreover, mountainous terrain does not imply easy and careless, but always active movement. All these features are reflected in such well-known cultural components of the peoples living on both sides of the Caucasus Mountains as dances, songs and folklore. In Georgian folklore, for example, a passive personality is understood as a tragedy (hence the tragic theme of one "chained" Amirani) [Dzhagodnishvili 2004: The chapter "Epic of Amirani"].

13 M.Azadovsky also considered this story: "The husband leaves (often forcedly) his wife (or groom – the bride) she makes a promise to wait a certain number of years ... The wife (bride) is brought false news about the death of her husband or fiancé, and she is forced into marriage. The hero finds out one way or another about the upcoming wedding and rushes home, often with the help of magical power. Upon returning home, disguised as a beggar, a pilgrim or a musician, he gets into the wedding feast, where the recognition takes place. His wife recognizes her husband's voice, or finds the ring, which he throws into the cup of wine. "The oldest classic example of this story – the story of Odysseus' return. It also includes Russian tales of Nikitich and Alyosha and a number of Rus. fairytales. In fiction this subject is found in the story of the "Decameron" by Boccaccio, in the stories G. de Maupassant in "The Return", M. Prevo ("De sire"), P. Fevalya ("La chanson de Poirier"), etc. The story was written by L. in autumn 1837, possibly in Tbilisi according to M.F. Akhundov. Wandering through the Caucasus and Transcaucasia, L. took a special interest to the folk creativity [L.E. 1981: 42].23].

and quests. Some archetypes[14] of fairy-tales became extremely relevant to Lermontov, were successfully "laid" on the basis of his mentality, differentiating him from the identity of the western mental values ("No, I'm not Byron, / I am the other").

When a person raised in one culture is met with the creative product of a completely different culture, the interest of the first for the second can increase at the unconscious level by inclusion in the cognitive process of archetypes, elements of the "collective unconscious" [Jung 1922]. At the same time a reflection of these archetypes on the person should be somehow close and familiar.

There are both archetypes of "collective unconscious" and literary archetypes in the tale of "Ashik Kerib". Apart from this, archetypal characters (the mother, Kurshud-Bey (the enemy), teacher / coach) present in the text, perform a specific function: their task is to help the protagonist to understand the rules of life and achieve his goals. Thus, in the centre of the system of characters stands an image of ashug "Garip" (which can be translated as the bard "Stranger"; another meaning of ashug is "fallen in love"). The main character also bears the features of one central archetype – the archetype of the creator.

Lermontov constructed the story of Ashik Kerib in a following way. The young poet, a poor but talented man, wants to marry the beautiful Magul-Megeri, but is not ready to do so because of his excessive pride, which urges him to search for glory through recognition of his genius as ashug ("I vow to my soul: I promise to wander over the world seven years and either win wealth or die in distant deserts "[Lermontov in 1976: 325]). Prompted by this feeling, he decides to travel to earn some money for the marriage, becomes "garip" in foreign lands. The initial position of the hero, seeking wealth and thus, motivated by false values, cannot give him happiness. On the roads of wandering, he finds himself in a variety of situations and could lose his way if he were not given certain "signs" that help him choose his way. At the same time he finds a mentor ("a rider on a white horse"), who helps him to find the path to the goal ("... well sit back on my horse and tell the whole truth, where you need to go" [Lermontov in 1976: 327]). Returning to his hometown, the hero, because of the changed spiritual and moral priorities, achieves his goal, finds happiness.

---

14 The image-archetype embodies the most robust and ubiquitous "schemes" or "formulas" of the human imagination, manifested both in mythology and in the arts at all stages of its historical development. Penetrating the whole of fiction from its mythological origins to its modern manifestations, archetypes constitute a permanent fund of stories and situations that passes from writer to writer" [Borisov, 2009: 23]. Modern researchers M.E.Fillips and K.Hantli identified seven different archetypes according to their characteristics of "Action" and "decisions" [M.E.Fillips, K.Hantli 2004].

The motive of happiness in Lermontov's lyrics reflects a complex set of poet's own problems. As a rule, happiness for Lermontov's hero is unattainable. It is unattainable also for Pechorin (the protagonist Lermontov's work "The Hero of Our Time"). The reason for this is the protagonist himself. However, the search for happiness is perhaps the main spring of all action for Lermontov's lyrical hero and Pechorin, the central character of his prose – (Belinsky felt the characteristic of Pechorin's emotions to be: "wildly chasing" for happiness, searching for it everywhere). The archetype of happiness in the Russian mentality is closely linked with such concepts as the soul-a particularly important world-and adoption of a life following the right principle of "what to do" (comparing the "The Hero of Our Time" Pechorin's response to Maxim Maksimych in "Maxim Maximovich": "Well, what to do, everyone has his own path ..."), whose semantics A.Vezhbitska considers unique, special to the Russian language [Wierzbicka 1997:17-21]. In terms of human qualities this archetype refers to such features of Russian national mentality, as humility, selflessness, faith, merging with the world, nature and (passive) expectation of a miracle.

Analysing the socio-cultural typology, shaped by Lermontov's creative mind, Lotman mentions that happiness belongs both to the area of "western philosophy" and "eastern philosophy" [Lotman, 1985]. At the same time the main features of western psychology are greatness, glory, genius, and "according to Lermontov, the defining feature of eastern philosophy is fatalism" [Lotman 1985: 8]. While agreeing in general with this statement, the following can be noted. After the first encounter with the culture of the East Lermontov got a real opportunity to closely observe it in 1837 in the Caucasus. The strength of his impressions may be observed in the following lines:

To Fate, like a Turk or Tartar,
I am equally grateful for all ....
[Lermontov in 1976 a: 167].

This position is completely contrary to the earlier one coupled with Byronic protest, rejection of reality and one's own destiny up until the angry reproaches of God. The position of the "I am greatful for all" relates the mental characteristics of Russian Christian culture and the Muslim cultures of the East, while at the same time contradicting the romantic concept of the West, with its atheistic approach. In this case the phrase "equally grateful" is read in the context of Lermontov's general thoughts about happiness in conjunction with the concept of "rest", which already formed a central component of happiness (see: "I'd like the freedom and peace," "Then humbled my soul's anxiety /Then disperse the wrinkles on his brow, – / And I'm ready to grasp happiness on earth, / And in heaven, I see God ... /" [Lermontov, 1976: 33]). It is interesting to compare the dates of writing of

"Ashik Kerib" and the poem "When the Yellowing Cornfield Worried." The second poem, according to A.P. Shan-Giray, was written in February 1837, the first – during his stay in Tiflis, from October to the end of November 1837. Therefore, we can assume that around the time of 1837 a qualitatively different characteristic of the mature period of Lermontov's work was formed, the principle ofunderstanding happiness.

Happiness in the story of "Ashik Kerib" serves as the archetype, fitting into the mainstream of the traditional oriental mentality of identifying happiness with the comprehension of the true path in life, which helps one to understand chance: Destiny and Chance (a kind of miracle) are used as synonyms here. This understanding was not entirely alien to Lermontov (compare to the understanding of happiness in "Let the poet be accused" (1830-1831) and "When the yellowing cornfield worried" (1838): in both works, happiness is perceieved as a miracle) [Megrelishvili 2000:123]. The drama "Masquerade" will be a repetition of the scene of conflict

> I watched with dumb excitement
> As the wheel of happiness spins.
> One was lifted, the other crushed by it.
> [Lermontov 1976 a: 281].

The symbolism of the archetype appears in a Western form. "The wheel ... of happiness" is the Wheel of Fortune. In "Ashik Kerib" this conflict can be seen in episodes of random meeting with Kurshud-bey at the beginning of his wandering, the arrival of Ashik Kerib at pasha Khalaf, and meeting with a white rider.

Chance, presented in a tale as a synonym for Destiny, should be considered in close connection with the intended topic of the text. There is an opposite understanding of the role of mind in Eastern and in the Western mentality. In Western consciousness the mind is perceived as rational. "The faustian spirit" (O. Spengler) of West based on the primacy of rationality over feelings is thought as one of the main advantages of an individual. However, the mind is considered to be responsible for creating personal characteristics in the eastern philosophy, and is opposed to rationality.. It is also synonymous with sense perception, beyond which is established the prerogative to gain insight in life, and hence to achieve happiness. Man, endowed with a rational mind, does not go beyond formal logic, and is perceived as "silly" ("Kurshud-bey's brother, a silly person, took his dagger, claiming:" You lie, how it is possible to come here in three days from Khalaf?" [Lermontov 1976 в: 330]). In the Russian mentality, the hero of folk tales known as Ivan-fool hits the road in search of happiness, and commits irrational acts on his way (saves a gray wolf, a bear etc.). Not accidently the Russian word for "mind" is derived from the Indo-European root aw / aus, meaning "the perception of the senses" (cf. also the Russian word mouth, ear and Latin audio «to listen», as well as reality – all perceivable by human in sensual way, "manifest" for feelings). Thus, understanding the mind in the Russian and Eastern mentalities finds a common cognitive element – the mind is a human ability to commit an irrational act.

Th closed triangle "Chance-Destiny-Mind" formed Kurshud-bek's statement, which is similar to a "Fatalist"'s (1839) ("What is written on the forehead at birth is not possible to avoid", "[Lermontov 1976 в: 330]). In this interpretation, the idea of predestination may be read as a verbal formulation of the archetype of Happiness, which being announced in the eastern form, fits the Russian mentality well, which will be demonstrated in the "Fatalist", where the bearers of "Eastern beliefs" are three characters: Vulich with his desire to "try his luck," a Cossack captain ("... is not possible to escape the fate" [Lermontov in 1976: 103]) and Maxim Maximovich ("Впрочем, видно, уж так у него на роду написано", "However, we see, one is preordained like that") [Lermontov in 1976: 111] .) At the same time the understanding of fatalism in its Western sense as a rock in human destiny (Fata Morgana) is not synonymous with the Eastern understanding of destiny. Happiness, as demonstrated in "Ashik Kerib", is finding true destiny through man's wise (if irrational) behavior.

In favor of this interpretation of the text is the collision of Ashik Kerib with Kurshud-bek, as protagonist and antagonist. Happiness is impossible without justice, which in the mentality of the Russian people is inextricably linked with the concept of morality (In Russian folklore and literature the winnerof the fight is the hero who stands on the side of truth, a righteous Warrior, a righteous Christian. Unrighteous actions are always punished – the fates of Raskolnikov, Ivan Karamazov, Smerdyakov in Dostoevsky, Anna Karenina's and Vronsky's fate in Tolstoy etc). As a result, Ashik Kerib marries Magul Megeri and Kurshud bek is married to Ashik Kerib's sister. The triumph of truth resolves the moral conflict.

A protagonist of a fairy tale is the central figure, to which all other characters are related. He the focus of all the motives and conflicts of the work. At the same time the whole story, read from the position of the present archetypes, demonstrates the story of person's way to the "truth", the acquisition of which is not a gift from God possessed at birth, but is a necessary lesson learned in the process of life. In this regard, Ashik Kerib's answer to Kurshud-bey's question about the name "Shinde Gerursez (know soon)," fits into the overall scheme of work as a story about the path to truth. It is not accidental the protagonist continues his answer to Kurshud-bek with a song, which talks about all the stages he passed on the way to the truth. In this case the form chosen also seems natural for the hero of this story – a symbolic song, the deep subtext of which Kurshud-Bey, a wise man, is able to understand.

The fact that Ashik Kerib is a poet is very important. In the beginning of tale, he seeks recognition of his talent, as well as happiness with his beloved. After many trials and difficulties in the way, he naturally achieves happiness. Wealth is given to him deservedly for his actions. For Lermontov this tale with a central image of the poet was of particular interest.

In Lermontov's work the image of the poet passed through a serious evolution. If in the poem "The Poet" (1828) the interpretation of the image of the poet, "is close to that which was entrenched in mass romantic lyrics of the 20-ies, varied, and simplified, in particular, the concept of Pushkin's "The Poet" ("While still Apollo isn't demanding"1827)" [LE 1981: 441], in the poem "The Poet" ("With trimming of gold is sparkling my dagger" 1838) he deployed a comprehensive understanding of the role and the image of the poet in society,. At the same time the character of the poem is to represent the wise truths, "the mighty words," which catches the people (cf. the reaction of characters to Ashik Kerib's words at the wedding of Magul-Megeri and Kurshud-bek). Apart from this the poetry itself is wider. It acts as a form of participation in all the events of a people's spiritual life and forms an absolutely necessary part for both the people and the poet himself ("Singers from four sides are usually collected in one place" [Lermontov in 1976: 330]).

Thus, the interpretation of Ashik Kerib's image, on the one side fits into Lermontov's image of poet as it appears in the writings of the late 1830s. On the other hand, the image of a young ashug relates to central motifs of Lermontov's lyric. The main character appears in two guises, as the agent of Oriental culture in Tiflis and as a component of the subject of culture, a subject of others' stories about him in which he is the protagonist. Ashik Kerib is a poet, celebrating "the ancient heroes of Turkestan", in whose behavior is presented ideas about the role and significance of the poet in society (cf. the motives of the poem "The Poet" in 1838, and conflicting images of the poet-ashug: revealing the truth to people – episode of Ashik Kerib's return).

So what is Ashik Kerib's image? Of course, we have traditional image, which appeared in many cultures of the Caucasus and the Middle and Central East. It seems possible to trace the motifs of ancient prototypes, such as Odysseus (a hero-wanderer) and Orpheus (a poet-musician). In the version presented by Lermontov this ancient folk tale image is divided into different components, since a literary archetype here is presented as the concept and a symbol. The concept of wandering is a part of an image explicitly fitting into the conceptual sphere of Russian (and world) literature. The symbol becomes the motif of the poet and poetry, which connects this image with the semiosphere of Russian culture, in which the theme of each cultural epoch, starting with the creation of a new period of Russian Literature in the XVIII century, relates to important spiritual and philosophical codes. The image of Ashik Kerib is culturally ambivalent, since the features of eastern and western cultures are presented here. For the eastern consciousness the image of the poet-ashug manifests a special type of the expression of truth, veiled by a parable form of narrative. This image becomes a component of Russian culture through G.Derzhavin's "Monument", Pushkin's "The Prophet" and "I built a monument to myself,", and Lermontov's poem "The Poet".

The literary archetype of the poet's image as it appears in "Ashik Kerib", does not only refer to classic features of an ethno-folkloric prototype, but is also supplemented by the author's personal world view, "exemplified" by his own destiny. An interesting pattern appears. The exiled poet realises the truth of life through wandering, which allows him to become the guardian of "the oath" (a little later the poet's voice, according to the Russian literary tradition, should sound "... like a bell in the tower at evening/In the days of the People's celebrations and disasters"). At the same time being in exile, he expects to return to his homeland, triumphant, for he managed to keep the spirit of the "oath". The future path is seen as progress from being righteous to becoming a Prophet (the episode of returning of vision to the mother by the protagonist), which again is consistent with the evolution of the image of the poet in Lermontov's lyric ("The Prophet" in 1841).

The process of Lermontov's creative thought should be judged by taking into account the relationship of his own thoughts with the structure of the tale, where all the archetypal symbolic and ideological dominants of Oriental culture merged, forming a complex interosculating unity. In this case the major things for Lermontov were not only these dominants, but also the definition of fate and the character of the protagonist, the poet-ashug.

"The culture [..]", wrote V.E.Vatsuro, "and every cultural epoch is an ongoing process [...] the migration of ideas, themes and poetic images, borrowing and reinterpretation, assimilation and rejection. This polyphony is the form and the norm of its existence. Genius's creativity grows on such a polyphonic substrate, it assimilates itself, integrates, transforms the "foreign" ideas and images, sometimes marked with an individual stamp, and sometimes ... become the part of the common cultural heritage" [Vatsuro 2008: 5].

The archetype of the poet-creator can be considered a cultural universal, something essentially common that unites different cultures as a specific form of human activity. This is largely the kind of activity that makes us human. Lermontov's image of the poet grew up on the "polyphonic substrate" of Eastern and Western cultures, and this image skipped through the prism of the values of the Russian culture of his time.

The tale of "Ashik Kerib" is one of the milestones towards a development important for the understanding of the creative heritage of Lermontov. For the late period of Lermontov's poetic creativity the "I" is immersed in universal being without losing its personal identity. In its final version Lermontov's image of the poet-prophet itself becomes a value, a kind of literary archetype that determines further movement of Russian literature, its special "Lermontov element." How this component developed can possibly be seen "through the crystal ball" of "Ashik Kerib".

References

Alekseev, P.V., Turkish tale M.Y. Lermontov's "Ashik Kerib" in the context of Islamic esoteric tradition – Mode of access – http://ec-dejavu.ru/l/ Lermontov.html.

Azadovsky M. *Commentary on "Ashik Kerib"* – Lermontov literature of the people of the Soviet Union. 1974.

Borisova E.B. *The content of the concepts of "artistic image" and "imagery" in literary criticism and linguistics.* – Journal of the Chelyabinsk State University, 2009, № 35 (173). Philology. Arts. No. 37. S. 20-26.

Dikman H., Legend, and allegory. Jungian analysis of fairy tales. – St. Petersburg, 2000.

Dzhagodnishvili T.*History of Georgian folklore.* Part I (XIXcentury). – Tbilisi, Publishing prose. – Tbilisi, Publishing House of Tbilisi State. University Press, 2004 (in Georgian.lang).

Fillips M.E., Chaxli K.,*Dramatica: A New Theory of Story by Four Edition*, Screenplay Systems, 2001; *Tenth Anniversary Edition*, Write Brothers, 2004, ISBN 0-918973-04-X

Gershtein EG *Lermontov and the "circle of sixteen"* // Lermontov's life and work. M., 1941.

Jung C. Collected papers on analytical psychology. – H., 1922.

Khodanen L.A.. Lermontov's poems. The poetry and folklore-mythical traditions. – Kemerovo, 1990 – ISBN 5-230-207420-X.

Seyidov S. Phenomenology of creativity. (History, paradoxes, personality) – Baku, 2009.

Vatsuro, V.E. *About Lermontov. Work over the years.* Compiled by T. Seleznev, A. Nemzer. – M.: New Publishing House (New materials and research on the history of Russian culture. Vol. 4), 2008.

Wierzbicka A. *Understanding Cultures through Their Key Words*. New York: Oxford University Press, 1997.

Лермонтов М.Ю. *Собр. соч.* в 4-х тт. Т.I. М., 1976.

Lermontov M.Ju. *Sobr. soch.* v 4-h tt. T.I. M., 1976.

Лермонтов М.Ю. *Собр. соч.* в 4-х тт. Т.II. М., 1976.

Lermontov M.Ju. *Sobr. soch.* v 4-h tt. T.II. M., 1976.
Лермонтов М.Ю. *Собр. соч.* в 4-х тт. T.III. М., 1976.
Lermontov M.Ju. *Sobr. soch.* v 4-h tt. T.III. M., 1976.
Лермонтов М.Ю. *Собр. соч.* в 4-х тт. T.IV. М., 1976.
Lermontov M.Ju. *Sobr. soch.* v 4-h tt. T.IV. M., 1976.

Desiring the Oriental "Other" in the Persian Poems of Velimir Klebnikov

Angelina Saule
(Australia)

This paper intends to explore the use of the figure Qurriat Al-Ayn in the work of the Futurist Russian poet, Velimir Khlebnikov. The following analysis proposes that the employment of this figure in the work of Khlebnikov is characteristic of the archetype of the East as personified by a female, who is pious, devout and slightly risqué in nature. Needless to say, such an analysis is influenced by certain ideas central to post-colonial theory. (Bhabha. 2008)

Before exploring Velimir Khlebnikov's use of Qurriat Al-Ayn, we must situate her historically. Associated with the Islamic radical movement Babism in 19th century Iran, Qurriat Al-Ayn is a female figure venerated for her uncompromising activism within the movement. Babism was a movement similar to the Reformation in Europe (A.P. Zabiyako, A.H. Kranikova, and E.S. Elbakya. 2008: 207), and was seen as a threat to the traditions of Shiite Islam and Sharia, and therefore many followers and teachers of the Bab (which means in Arabic 'door' or 'gateway'), were martyred for what was seen to be a heretical interpretation of Islam.

Although having grown up within an auspicious circle of religious scholars, and consequently studying theology vigorously (something quite unusual for a young girl), Al-Ayn became a leading adherent of Babism. Shocking the status quo, she divorced her conservative husband, traveled, preached (a first for women at that time), threw off the chador, and encouraged a form of prayer which was to be devotional, rather than obligatory in form.

The name Qurriat Al-Ayn is translated from Persian as 'Consolation of the Eyes.' It is generally believed that the Bab (Sayyid Ali Muhammad), also stressed her purity by not only accepting her as one of his eighteen disciples, but also naming her 'Tahira' (the 'Pure One'). In several accounts she is esteemed for her theatrical and eloquent speeches which she gave tirelessly, her captivating beauty, sharp intelligence, and the scandalous split from the traditional mores of her family and society. In one academic account her saga is given a romantic color with her horizons sinking and clouds graying on the day she is to be executed. This fictional adornment is somewhat misleading historically (N.G. Aganyats. 1910: 42). Meanwhile, in the dramatic account of a Russsian writer, Isabella Grinevskaya, the fictional love affair between the Bab and Al-Ayn depicts a lovesick child who joins a branch of religious radicalism out of faith and love. At the end of the play, the bereaved Qurriat inspires other bereaved women to remove the chador. Her own martyrdom is curiously left out (I. Grinevskaya. 1916).

Given these interpretations of Al-Ayn, she has come to represent an image of the virtuous, defiant, poised female of the East – a promotion of the familiar and the strange concurrently. This historical dimension buttresses the mythology of Asia with speculation and drama, highlighting the richness which the East can represent. It is as a given that is associated with Al-Ayn, and this is where Khlebnikov's work comes into this analysis.

As already revealed, there are several accounts of Babism in Russian literature prior to Khlebnikov's use of the figure of Qurriat Al-Ayn. For example, one writer notes the fact that Sheikh Jamal of the Bab movement lived in St. Petersburg, seeking the help of the Ministry of Foreign Affairs to fund a campaign to India (C. Umanets.1904: 45-6). Whether or not Khlebnikov was aware of this cultural exchange taking place in Russia is a mere speculation, although one critic, Ronald Vroon, assumes that Grishnevskaya's play and other sources connected to Babism or Iran in general may have heavily influenced Khlebnikov (R. Vroon.2001: 342). Another Khlebnikovian expert, Tartakovsky, states that Khlebnikov's use of this archetype is rather traditional for Russian Oriental-inspired poetry (p. I Tartakovsky. 1992:230). In the seminal work *Orientalism*, Edward Said emphasizes the notion of Orientalism as a discourse or "style of thought based upon an ontological and epistemological distinction between the Orient and the Occident", which is perceived to be exploited for aesthetic or imaginative purposes" (E. Said. 2003).Certainly, Khlebnikov's use of Al-Ayn as an archetype of the East denoting something benign, luxuriant and exotic, is a stimulating backdrop for certain ideas. This is obvious in his autobiography *October on the Neva*, where she is upheld as an image of justice and equality, at a time when Petrograd itself was hovering between revolutions:

> And if a new blackeyed Qurriat Al-Ayn devotes her silky, splendid locks to the planet, where there will be a burning, preaching equality and justice. We still don't know, we're only watching …
>
> И не новая ли черноокая Гурриэт Эль-Айн посвящает свои шелковистые чудные волосы той планете, на которой будет сожжение, проповедуя равенство и равноправие, Мы еще не знаем, мы только смотрим ….

This passage is also connected to his 'Proposals', where he suggests that a statue of Al-Ayn should be erected off the coast of La Manche:

> In the shallows of La Manche a Persian girl burning at the stake may be erected coming out of the water. Let the seagulls sit on it, as steamships full of Englishmen pass by.
>
> В мелком Ламанше может быть воздвигнут морской, выходящий из воды, памятник Гуриэт Эль Айн, сожженной на костре персианки. Пусть чайки садятся на него вблизи парохода, полного англичан.

As Vroon states, her image burning at the stake (R. Vroon: 344), also symbolize a force of resistance against British colonialism. Though special attention should be given to Khlebnikov's historical inaccuracies, this would require a deeper analysis than the paper allows. Ironically, the colonialism that Khlebnikov criticizes in terms of British-Persian relations, is similar in nature to his own scene of fantasy or colonialism in the poem 'Look Persia, I am coming', where

> We bow to the hair of Qurriat Al-Ayn
> We bow to the golden tiredness of Zarathustra –
> Persia will be a Soviet country
> As the prophet has stated.

The prophet/speaker contradicts the liberation sought out earlier in other texts, and by idolizing certain figures of Persian culture, tries to colonize them in the process of heralding them. This is important, as Qurriat Al-Ayn is never given her own voice or speaks directly: it is the speaker of various poems and essays representing her, she appearing incongruously voiceless.

She is also seen by the author as a breath of fresh air that is somehow held captive. In 'Truba Gul Mully' (*Gul-mullah's Trumpet*) this archetype is alluded to as a "girl of Iran", who is staring back at the narrator from the world of the chador, and in the poem 'Novruz Trud', where the Persian girls are also shrouded in their scarves behind to the male Adams of the poem who are rightfully celebrating the religious holiday. These girls are not unlike the images utilized in the poem 'Asia', who are personified at first. It "is always a slave girl …," herself turning the pages of her own history, which she is unable to read due to her predictable illiteracy. In another poem the voice declaims, "Oh, if only Asia could dry my face/ in her hair – her warm golden towel –". The promotion of the archetypical Eastern woman as both hero and victim, whose submissiveness and activeness can soothe the narrator, is reminiscent of other sources containing many contradictions in depicting the complexity that inhabits the image of Qurriat Al-Ayn.

Further on, in the poem 'Ladomir', the contradictory façade of beauty and liberation continues, as:

> And you, images of freedom!
> Eyelashes of secrets brightly
> Circling the grand eyes
> Of Qurriat Al-Ayn.

> И вы, свободы образа!
> Кругом венок ресницы тайн,
> Блесят громадные глаза
> Гурриэт Эль –Айн.[1]

---

1 In this context, the archetype of Helen of Troy should be considered.

In 'Truba Gul Mully' parallels are also made between the power of the eyes, the willfulness of Qurriat Al-Ayn, and the flight of liberation via death:

> The wind: a Shepard of godly eyes.
> Qurriat Al-Ayn,
> Tahira, herself tightening the rope,
> Having asked the executioner,
> Turning her head:
> "A bit more?"
> The tin and reins
> In your fiancé's chest!
> Her dead body: snowy mountaintops.
>
> Ветер – пастух божых очей.
> Гурриэт Эль- Айн,
> Тахирэ, сама
> Затянула на себе концы веревок,
> Спросив палачей, повернув голову:
> «больше ничего?" -
> Вожжи и олива
> В груд жениху!
> Это ее мертвое тело: снежные горь.

Likewise, the corpse of this figure is something akin to an ice-queen, having become untouchable and serene in choosing death.

In the poem 'Asia! I have made you my obsession", the historical image of Qurriat Al-Ayn becomes an archetype associated with an imagined Asia, a location where purity, love, and liberation can blossom. The actual Qurriat Al-Ayn as a tangible figure, is melded and re-constructed to create the Orient itself – which initiates the question: Asia as Qurriat Al-Ayn, or Qurriat Al-Ayn as Asia? Controversially, Qurriat Al-Ayn becomes an archetype of the repressed Oriental woman seeking freedom in Khlebnikov's oeuvre. She is a mythic figure of discourse who conceals the origins she ought to describe, and instead becomes a figure developed, transformed, becoming somehow synonymous with the multitude of Oriental female characters that also are made to represent the 'Orient' in Khlebnikov's work (such as Leila in *Mejlun and Leila*, Venera in *The Shaman and Venera*, the Persian Princess in *Razin*).

In one of his untitled poem, the speaker declares:

> O Asia! I torture myself with you,
> Like the girls brows I am grasping the clouds
> You Asia, could twist my knees
> And a girl could whisper a secret wail
> And quietly, happily, sobbing
> The eyes dried by braided ends.
> She loved, she suffered –
> A vague, universal soul.

О Азия! Себя тобою мучу,
Как дева бровы я постигаю тучу
....мне Азия обвила бы колени
И дева прошептала бы таинственные пена,
И тихая, счастливая, рыдала
Концами кос глаза суша.
Она любила, она страдала –
Вселенной смутная душа.

The archetype of the Eastern female as conceived in these poems and other literary oeuvre is a dream quest for an archetype (personified by Qurriat Al-Ayn), who represents both the desire for an East which should exist, and the loss of that world and the need to shape it via this archetype. A case in point is in the following poem, where only this archetype in exemplifying the East can somehow attain to representation, and in Khlebnikov's utopian manner, quite possibly save humanity:

Her passionate tongue
Subdued by shadowed eyes.
Her saintly name is whispered
The human race.

Ее очами теневыми
Был покорен страстей язык.
Ее шептать святое имя
Род человеческое язык.

Although this archetype moves fluidly throughout Velimir Khlebnikov's works, I would contend that these 'Eastern' archetypes are static, buttressing a projection that governs this archetype, rather than representing things as they are, contesting these representations. Qurriat Al-Ayn becomes a figure of elegant rebellion, an unquestioned assumption that is taken as a given.

Incidentally, it should be noted that in the modern world of mass media, this archetype has been used fairly recently, and can be crafted outside the realms of literature. During the opposition demonstrations in Teheran last year, a young chadored (covered) woman, Nada, was killed by military forces, and this image was beamed around the world to signify the pious, Oriental woman's martyrdom in the face of Eastern chaos and repression. This image has been a source of controversy, having been used by the deceased woman's fiancée to become a celebrity. The continuation of this archetype reinforced and appropriated, reminds me of these lines:

Like a tender girl of Islam,
Or, did the artist take a brush in hands
"Tell us neighbour – my Creator! –
Who is that living Mother of God?"

Как дева нежная ислама
Иль в руки кисти взял художник
«Скажи, соседка, – мой Создатель!-
Кто та живая богаматерь?" [citation]

References

Aganyats, N.G. Babism and Bahism: An academic and religious experience of research. Tbilisi: Elektropech, 1910.

Bhabha, Homi. *The Location of Culture.* London, Routledge, 2008.

Grinevskaya, Isabella. *The Bab: A dramatic poem from Persian history in Five Acts*. Petrograd: The Second Publishing House, 1916.

Khlebnikov, Velimir. Y.R Arenzon & R.V. Duganov eds., *Collected Writings – Volumes 1-6.* Moscow: The Institute of World Literature of The Russian Academy of Sciences, 2005.

Klebnikov,Velimir. *Letters and Theoretical Writings*, Paul Schmidt, trans. London: Harvard University Press, 1997.

Khlebnikov, Velimir. R.Vroon, ed., *Selected Poems*, Paul Schmidt, trans. London: Harvard University Press, 1997.

Said, Edward. *Orientalism.* London: Penguin, 2003.

Tartakovsky, P.I. *Khlebnikov's Poetry and the East.*Tashkent: Academy of Sciences of the Republic of Uzbekistan Press, 1992.

Umanets, C. *Contemporary Babism.*Tbilisi: Melik'-Karakuv Publishing, No. 5, 1904.

Vroon, Ronald. "Qurriat Al-Ayn and the Image of Asia in Velimir Chlebnikov's Post-Revolutionary Oeuvre," in Russian Literature. 2001, 335-362 www.elevier.nl/ locate/ruslit.

Zabiyako, A.P., Kranikova, A.H., and Elbakya, E.C. *The Encylopedia of Religion.* Moscow: University of Philosophy, RAN, 2008.

Part 3
Archetype as a Symbol and Image

Hamlet and Iskandar:[1] The Breakdown of the Persona Archetype as a Condition for Identity Formation

Gorkhmaz Guliyev
(Azerbaijan)

The well known and later vulgarised Shakespearian expression "all the world's a stage, and all the men and women merely players" was revitalised by the analytic psychology of Carl Gustav Jung. The phrase could be interpreted in the light of the collective unconscious, and thus enrich and determine the principle of role-making in individual relationships. The framework of the collective unconscious establishes that the person is an actor as well as a spectator in the play called life, an actor directed by a community. The role of a human being is determined as soon as he is born, and the public defines the moral taboos by which he is compelled to play and is judged.

The analysis of the theatrical metaphor based on principles of the analytic psychology of C. Jung shows that the Persona archetype, which serves the director, aka "society", as the tool of control and submission, has a special place in the arsenal of the collective unconscious, which works as a guardian of the unity of a community.

According to the Swiss psychologist, the etymology of the Persona is further evidence which demonstrates its primary meaning as a *role*. The word "Persona" came via Latin to European languages, and has an Etruscan origin meaning "a theatre mask". However it was subjected to semantic transformation which gave it a modern meaning, "a character" (Dictionnaire Petit Robert, 1967: 280). It is worth pointing out that another word of the same origin "a personage" keeps its connection with the primary meaning, which proves furthermore that the previous meaning is still present in memory.

Jung, using the primary meaning of the persona as an archetype, considered it to be the part of a collective psyche that is forced by the community onto rebellious individuals, and which is worn as a theatre mask. On the one hand the persona is a tool for the integration of a person into the community. On the other, it is also an attempt of a person to reassert the self limited by the requirements of the community. As a matter of fact the archetype is the unit of centrifugal and

1 Iskandar is a protagonist of the drama *Ölülər* (*The Dead*) written by Azerbaijani writer Jalil Mammadguluzadeh (1866-1932) in 1909.

centripetal tendencies existing in the community and complementing each other. It is necessary to consider that the community mercilessly uses the Persona archetype to adjust individual features to a social standard in order to prevent a possible danger for the collective unity.

On the other hand, the community consisting of ordinary and indistinct individuals consequently transforms into a degraded mob. The important condition of the survival of a community is the union of manifold characterful individuals as programmed by the structure of the collective unconscious in the Persona archetype. At the same time, since adaptation to standards is more important for the unity of the community, the Persona archetype does not allow the complete self-assertion of the individual in the community. The community directs the actions of individuals to its own advantage by prohibitions and a system of rules. In this case the distinctive character of individuals functions only as a display, and does not reflect their core nature.

Meanwhile C. Jung constantly reminds us that the Persona archetype creates the possibility of a transformation of a mask into true individuality, and in some sense this is what is expected. Sometimes the persona hides features that shock the community, providing for the easy integration of a person. The first years of a child are limited to the close circle of family. Later, as his intellectual and verbal capabilities grow, his potential for integration into the community increases. However, very soon the community persistently affects him via different channels of influence. The individual in the persona mask tries to solve antisocial problems under the disguise of social actions.

It should be mentioned that a personality forms and grows in society, that is to say the Persona (the mask) introduced from his early years, influences and becomes part of his worldview, values and beliefs. The process is very natural and the individual cannot comprehend the existence of the mask on him, and perceives imparted qualities as his own. Intuitively he feels the masked self, but consciously he cannot comprehend it. Moreover, via the persona archetype the community's repressing instincts impart the qualities and characteristics necessary to lead a normal life.

A human being having unalterable personal characteristics and playing a certain social role based on collective norms is split into two poles. In normal circumstances the differences do not emerge. However in times of crisis one part strives to completely socialize and the other struggles to isolate and individualize itself, thus creating the source of neurosis for the individual. Analyzing the mutual relations between the persona and the individual Jung considered society and especially the individual to be in a more or less normal moral and emotional state. However literature usually prefers to describe an unusual state of society or people. The person controlled by the collective unconscious via the Persona archetype in normal circumstances seems to be not very appealing in a narrative.

As was mentioned above the Persona is a mask that provides for the integration of the individual into the community. By wearing the persona (the mask) the individual willingly complies with the rules and regulations, ethical and moral principles, and a norm of conduct imposed by the community, and accepts them unwarily as his own. It does not resolve the tension between the inherent and the inborn, but suppresses them into the unconscious.

The persona archetype deceives the individual as well as society: they both sincerely consider the qualities and characteristics imparted into a person as inborn. This is related with the community's immanent system values for the relationships between individuals. The *other* (embodying the community in relation to *me*) evaluates me on the basis of socially approved codes and principles. *I*, wearing "social" glasses, judge myself using the *other*'s viewpoint. It constitutes one of the main conditions of the integration of the individual into the community: I can create the uncomplicated relationship with others only by being able to see myself through others' eyes, and adjusting my values to that of others'. In reality this means that in the community nobody perceives each other's genuine qualities and features. A complete appearance is substituted for reality. The system of traditions, sets of rules, prohibitions, and taboos embed individuals into the community, thus delaying the collective response to the occurring upheavals.

The community believes that by choosing a Persona-mask closely resembling the individual's genuine character, it is possible to expand his actual characteristics. However in reality the more the Persona-mask is "implanted" in the individual, the more it corrupts and obscures his genuine qualities. In fact the community accomplishes its task by skilfully covering up the inner self, hiding it from itself.

At first sight the aim of the persona archetype is to embed the individual into the community, to regulate his actions. However, at the same time it reveals the tension between him and the community: "The Persona is the complex system between individual and collective consciousness. It is supposed to create a certain image on the one hand; on the other hand it hides the real self." (Лейбин В. 2008: 220)

Thus we can conclude that both the community and the individual actively engage in the process. However the interests of the individual and the community very often do not coincide, but create a conflict. The community naturally acts as the ancient outlaw Procrustes, adjusting everybody to its own measurements. The community attempts to socialise the individual at such a high level in order to completely transform the individual into a mask. All traditions, rules, moral-ethical values and prohibitions established in the collective unconscious are arranged to ram the individual into a hole. As a matter of fact, the community behaves as an aggressor towards the individual. Using the persona archetype the collective unconscious strives to completely own the individual. The metaphoric comparison of a human being with an onion was based on exactly this: the defenders of the theory that a human being is a total social animal believed that peeling off all social layers of a personality-onion would leave nothing left of him. The supporters of the conception assumed that moral and mental world of an individual is entirely socially characterised.

However the marginal situation (a fear, a deep anxiety, a disturbance or other personal emotions) reveals precisely inner qualities. Thus during the conflict situation the individual is forced to decide between the Persona-mask and personal qualities. The essentially antagonistic conflict implicitly appears also in socially quiet situations without any visible cause, unconsciously influencing the individual, and becoming the source of a socially derived neurosis.

The human being like Proteus has to play various roles according to social situations, structure, and atmosphere. The universal and invariant archetype of the Persona-mask breaks up into multiple variants and adopts different guises according to circumstances.

On the one hand the persona archetype is "the kind of a natural vector similar to the impulse of nesting in ants or birds" (Лейбин В. 2008: 218), on the other hand, it can be modified depending on the condition of its structure. This dual representation allows it to keep its invariant core while at the same time adapting to constantly changing conditions. On the one hand, the conflict is created between the inner "self" of the individual and his acting "selves"; on the one hand, the clash occurs between the acting "selves." The community's different circumstances demand *me* to be from time to time moral or immoral, adamant or flexible, good or bad. The different images of the individual struggle against each other. As a consequence they are influenced by centrifugal tendencies and cause his moral breakdown. All the things mentioned above, undoubtedly, cannot be a source of neurosis. However, neurosis that emerges in these circumstances and involves only the upper layer of the individual's psyche and does not have an antagonistic character.

* * *

As a rule the people in the initial situations (directly represented as in *Hamlet* or implied as in *The Dead*) of a work of art or literature are positioned and act in the framework of traditions, sets of rules as well as the archetypes of the collective unconscious. However this is merely for the sake of exposition, an introduction, a preparation to the main part. It is the literary object of the representation of catastrophes and upheavals in the communal and especially personal life that is really at the bottom of things.

This situation can result in mutation of the collective unconscious which provides for communal unity within certain limits. It causes the qualitative change or even complete withdrawal of archetypes, which are the manifestation of the collective unconscious and its agents for the control of the individual. Hence literary thought prefers to describe unusual situations and periods of transformation.

A catastrophe brings to radical opposition day and night, light and darkness, positive and negative, upper and lower, which were adapted to each other in the collective unconscious for ages. It creates a psychological tension area within society and the individual, and requires a creation of new values with the revaluation of the old ones. The individuals subjected to the world thus pulled apart have to reject the system of values and the behavioural models (archetypes) controlling them before accepting the long term continuing painful process. The Persona archetype, as an integration tool of the individual to society, is subjected to an even deeper transformation.

One can observe the rejection of the traditional Persona model together with the process of the creation of a new mask. Although the new "theatre" mask resembles the Persona in many instances, it differs in its essence. That is, if the Persona originates with and imitates the individual (I articulate common things in a personalized manner), the new mask is individually derived but mimics the community (I articulate my personal thoughts in a general mode). As hard as it is to escape from the deep embrace of tradition, the rejection of a Persona and the adoption of a new mask is an important condition for the formation of a personality released from stereotypical modes of thinking.

As a rule literature depicts as its main protagonists the outcasts who refuse to adopt the images of the Persona-mask, as Mammadguluzadeh's Iskandar, or the aristocrats opposed to the existing situation, as the Shakespearean Hamlet. In this case the relations between a society and an individual in terms of their representation in literature raise theoretical interest.

We want to emphasize beforehand that society in both literary works the *Dead* and *Hamlet* is portrayed as a substance principally lacking the inner change, or activity. It is a puppet in the collective unconscious' control. It does not see the upheaval abolishing all existing values, it does not react (*Hamlet*) or comprehend the necessity of change, an act complying with the demands of modern times (*The Dead*), preferring to continue in accordance with the old values.

The social conflict in the form of providence knocks not only on the doors of the chosen ones like Hamlet or Kefli Iskandar, but at the doors of the whole society they represent. Actually the crime of Claudius, murdering his brother and succeeding to the throne, overthrows the value system of the whole of society. The crime of Claudius is an event concerning the whole society. One should bear in mind that the described events take place in a medieval society based on the principles of a rigid hierarchy. Thus if the person occupying one of the highest ranks in society and playing an exemplary role for the rest murders his brother and owns his wife, who can prevent the ordinary people from the same behaviour? In Denmark a fish has rotten from the head down, thus allowing a whole body to decay. Hamlet as the embodiment of the most perceptive member of society is able to clearly see and consider the process. The act III, scene IV where Hamlet is able to see and talk to the ghost of his father, while his mother cannot, in reality informs us of his high sensitivity, which enables him to rise above the level of the totally corrupted society.

Society in Shakespeare's portrayal is not included in the sphere of moral catastrophe. However in *The Dead* society itself becomes the object of tragedy. At first sight there is nothing extraordinarily in the fraud performed by some one from Iran. Nonetheless the deed of Sheikh Nasrullah creates distrust and devalues outdated customs and values of not only Irevan, but of a whole Islamic world. Confronting the helpless community with an antique cosmos, that is the world of dead and living, forces it to make a radical choice.

The two artists engaged with the individual-society dualism approach the problem of society differently. In the tragedy of the ancient Greek dramaturge Aeschylus *Oresteia* Clytemnestra openly in front of the whole population of Argos betrays her husband Agamemnon, planning to kill him on his arrival. The community does not perceive her plans, and the author's attitude to their neglect is neutral.

Portraying a disinterested society Shakespeare somehow continues the tradition of ancient dramaturgy; still an important matter should be taken into account. While Agamemnon and his son Orestes doesn't perceive the community at all (the community is a chorus of old men, only narrating the outward story), Hamlet is not only dissatisfied with the stance of the fellow-citizens, but he accepts as his own tragedy the situation in Denmark that has been created by their indifference. Thus the famous words of Hamlet that "Denmark is one of the worst prisons", on the one hand points to his uncle and mother, who are directly responsible for the situation, on the other hand – it points to the society which voluntarily accepts the state of affairs, authorises it.

In this case it is not a coincidence that Polonius, as the most typical member of society, repeatedly becomes the object of Hamlet's sarcastic ridicule. For Shakespeare Polonius is not only a dummy controlled by own pragmatic principles. The qualities and characteristics dictated by archetypes, especially, the persona, have penetrated into the deepest parts of his personality and have become his essence. Shakespeare felt that adaption to circumstances was an important condition for the personality's integration into the community, but it can deprive him of specific qualities and moral-ethical principles and create the danger of his transformation into the amorphous chameleon. The famous dialog of Hamlet with Polonius in Act III Scene II explicitly demonstrates this:

Hamlet: Do you see that cloud, that's almost in shape like a camel?
Polonius: By the mass, and it is like a camel, indeed.
Hamlet: Methinks, it is like a weasel.
Polonius: It is backed like a weasel.
Hamlet: Or, like a whale?
Polonius: Very like a whale.
(Шекспир 1960: 89)

The killing of Polonius by Hamlet, who only pretends to be mad, being in reality fully conscious, has symbolic meaning. By the symbolic act the protagonist demonstrates the release of a mutated individual, a rat, who negated his moral principles for the sake of conformity, from the area of influence of the collective unconscious, the ultimate liberation from the Persona fetters. Iskandar (*The Dead*) like Hamlet, rejecting the position of his community, that is the denial of enlightenment, refuses submission to the Persona archetype that would transform him into the member of the community.

At first sight the protagonists of Mammadguluzadeh and Shakespeare having different reasons for the escape from the sphere of influence of the collective unconscious and, being developed in dissimilar areas of tension, cannot be compared. In the Shakespearean tragedy the King, the person is murdered by its own brother. The murder is not an ordinary one. It is a plot against a monarch, the symbol of the moral values, the unity of the nation, the assurance of law and order. The usurpation of power by Claudius and his marriage to the wife of the late king, as accepted by the society, is the justification of the crime. This indicates the mutation of the collective unconscious, the collapse of the communal unity.

The problem facing Iskandar and society is not tragic at all at first sight: the educated young intellectual full of innocent desires wants to share his knowledge and hopes with his fellow-citizens, but the society turns its back and isolates him. The rejected youth changes into the alcoholic pessimist nicknamed Kefli Iskandar [Drunken Iskandar].

If one takes into account the principles of objective indifference there is nothing tragic in the refusal of the society to realise the hopes of Iskandar: tomorrow or in 100 years society will eventually accept the ideas of enlightenment. According to Iskandar society should take the main road to enlightenment right now, otherwise it will forever lag behind the civilised societies. Iskandar takes personally the Mirza Alakbar Sabir's phrase, that "foreigners fly on the aeroplanes, and we have not seated yet in autocars".[2] There is a huge difference in these terms between the protagonists of the English and Azerbaijani writer. The murder of his father for the Danish Prince is primarily a subjective matter and by murdering Claudius he attempts to solve his personal problem. Like Alexander the Great, with the one

2 Mirza Alakbar Sabir (1862-1911) was a famous Azerbaijani poet and satirist.

blow of a sword he wants to cut the Gordian knot. The main desire of Hamlet is to perform his moral duty. The liberation of Denmark as an objective accomplishment, naturally follows from his subjective deed. For Iskandar there is no personal gain or need, he is completely absorbed in community problems. For Mammadguluzadeh's protagonist, the rejection of the problem of enlightenment is both a social and personal tragedy. Thus if solving a personal problem brings Hamlet social gain, for Iskandar personal problems will be settled after the adoption of enlightenment ideas. Both personages were freed from the influence of the Persona archetype by travelling abroad. Hamlet is interested in the destiny of his new mask. Iskandar's worry is about the possible renewal of the content of the Persona archetype and the collective unconscious. The separation from the Persona mask does not result in the complete negation of a social mask. Both Hamlet and Iskandar, after rejecting of the persona mask connecting him with the community, immediately put a new mask, or to be precise, are forced to do so. However this cannot prevent their alienation from the community.

First of all we should admit that despite the tragedy of their alienation both personages live in a community and accordingly have to keep and create some relationships with society. In this case the narrative paradoxically combines two functions: conveying the truth and at the same time concealing it. The differing functions of the narrative are also displayed in the discourse of the person controlled by the Persona archetype. However in normal circumstances the individual employs the archetype unconsciously, and only during a cataclysm does he consciously choose.

The new social mask of the person, who rejected the Persona archetype, differs in some properties from the previous one. First of all, the person who was controlled by the Persona archetype initially perceives it not as an imparted, but his own image. Conversely the person with the newly adopted social mask not only clearly comprehends it, but takes an active part in the construction of its features. Clearly the refusal of Hamlet to obey the Persona's "advice" was partially the result of the encounter with his father's ghost. However the Shakespearean hero in the new ethical situation consciously identifies his new way of life. He adopts the mask of total satire, alienates himself from society, and attempts to prove the revelations of the ghost.

Iskandar, disobeying the rules of the Persona archetype and adopting the new social mask, also exercises his volition. He could put on the sentimental- melodramatic mask of a tragic sufferer like N.Vezirov's Fakhraddin.[3] However the protagonist, remaining the utmost realistic attitude towards the world (it can be

---

3 Fakhraddin is a protagonist of N. Vəzirov's (1854-1926) *Müsibəti – Fəxrəddin* (*The Tragedy of Fakhreddin*).

admitted that *The Dead* is written from the certain perspective where everybody is in a deep sleep except for Iskandar), chooses a completely different mask: the mask of Kefli Iskandar, who lost hope for positive changes and ridicules everybody, and first of all himself, like Hamlet.

Iskandar is surrounded by unintelligent but frank, dim-witted but honest people. Hence his hope that one day his satirical accusations will bring some changes is somehow justified. The appearance of Sheikh Nasrullah as an "aid," unexpected by Iskandar, resulted in a tragic disturbance and accelerated the process much against Iskandar's expectations. In *The Madmen Gathering*[4] the process turned the indifferent and submissive society into a moral swamp and ended in ethical corrosion. Molla-Abbas sentenced to live in a society deprived of moral-ethical norms was forced to cease all relations with people and put on the mask of madness.

The social mask adopted by Hamlet, Iskandar and other protagonists being a rejection of the Persona archetype is at the same time its confirmation in a new context. Stated otherwise it is a dialectical attitude towards the community of the individual absolutely transformed by moral upheavals and aware of the impossibility of living outside of the social milieu, which can preserve the unity of the person with the help of the Persona archetype. Hamlet, used to living, thinking and breathing in the liberal Renaissance environment of England, perceives the unbearable moral conditions of medieval Denmark. However the prince cannot even imagine leaving "one of the worst prisons" of the world. Morally abused Iskandar is addicted to alcohol and prefers rather to drink Karapet's *Smirnoff* than to breathe the air of freedom in a foreign land. Molla Abbas even more radically than Hamlet declares himself insane and embeds himself into the madmen community. He explains his actions as being for the sake of love to Sona, however in reality he has no place to go.

The rejection of the manifestation of the Persona archetype by protagonists living in different spatial, temporal and social circumstances demonstrates an interesting pattern in their relationship to society: in spite of their marginalisation inevitable after the wearing of a new mask, they become connected to the environment even more closely. In this context it is impossible to imagine Hamlet without Denmark, Iskandar without Irevan, and Molla Abbas without the madmen. The rejection of the persona archetype and the adoption of a new social mask indicates the hero's arrival at the final point where the destined mission awaits him. Thus Hamlet in order to restore the harmony and peace that existed before the crime of Claudius and his mother is forced into brutality, as Alexander the Great was to cut off the Gordian knot by the sword. The situation in *The Dead* is completely different: Sheikh Nasrullah instead of Kefli Iskandar, with an

4 Drama written by Jalil Mammadguluzadeh in 1926.

opposite aim, shakes the community by fraud and awakens it. Iskandar is just satisfied to bring it to a close. Molla Abbas, lingering in morally deprived society, understands the impossibility of changing things and prefers to communicate by esoteric signs. In spite of the different attitudes towards the mission given them by providence, the protagonists have two similar qualities: firstly, they rejected the persona mask and adopted a new social mask, and secondly, they connected even more strongly to the community by the use of the new mask.

World literature has many examples of protagonists with differing attitudes to the Persona archetype. Don Quixote rejected the Persona mask of Renaissance times, that is, its way of life and its values, and put on the Persona mask of past ages of chivalry. For this purpose Miguel Cervantes' hero even imaginarily changes a simple farm girl into his virtual lady love Dulcinea and does not refrain from declaring his love to the whole world. However, the most radical rejection of the Persona mask in world literature is found in the image of Majnun: the protagonist of Mohammed Fusuli[5] withdraws into the dessert and ceases all relations with humans.

* * *

The community consists of different social strata. The people in each stratum communicate using different language conceptions: a) among each other, b) with people from other stratum. Obviously, the archetype of Persona controls the highly complex and dynamic process of the integration of an individual into society. The individual exposed to moral catastrophe and thus forced to reject the Persona has to build relations with society based on new principles. The person detached from society by objective reasons, at the same time not willing to leave the social milieu, puts on the surrogate of the Persona mask. The confrontation of different systems of values and perceptions results in a temporary separation from the traditional way of life. Both the protagonists of Shakespeare and Mammadguluzadeh were educated abroad, which results in the formation of the new Weltanschauung. Hamlet and Iskandar are dissatisfied with the state of their community. Being able to play a certain social role within the community, they consciously choose a new strategy for relating with the society. The person recognises that he is on the stage called "society" and plays a certain role. The particular feature of the consciously chosen role is that one has to communicate with people in their languages and therefore has to carefully select a strategy for various relations.

The new social mask indicates two stipulations in the process of communication: firstly, the individual has to communicate in such a way that society will

5 Mohammed Fisuli (1454-1556) is a famous Azerbaijani poet and thinker who lived in Kirkuk, modern Iraq.

overlook his outward appearance, name, family etc., and recognise him in the framework of his new way of life and Weltanschauung. Secondly, his relationship should be constructed in such a way that the community could not consider his existence outside of the society, and, on the other hand, perceives his determination for a fundamental transformation of its present state. It also brings abut a complete change to his conception of language. The person uses linguistic variations in his dialogues, that is, he speaks the language of his opponent. At the same time there emerges a different invariant of the new linguistic conception related to his new social (marginal) status. The language-mask in the discourse of Hamlet and Iskandar comes into view as a total sarcasm and scorn.

Shakespeare depicts the different stages of the rejection of the Persona archetype in the individual and the development of the intonation of total ridicule in his discourse. In his first appearance in the second scene the protagonist Hamlet is still controlled by the Persona-mask. His mood as the son who has lost his father is in a complete accordance with the traditional principles dictated by the collective unconscious. Although the quick marriage of his mother to his uncle has affected him, concern is manifested only in the form of discontent and does not have yet the power of catastrophe and contradiction. Hamlet's mode of discourse in the scene literally corresponds to his mood, which is excellently illustrated in the first monologue. His reflections of the betrayal of the memory of his father by his mother, the comparison between the idealised image of the late parent and his uncle are determined in the context of the traditional social value system. At the same time, it should be mentioned, that this monologue also shows the intonation, not actually verbalised, of Hamlet's doubts over the death (or murder?) of his father. Shakespeare prepares for the future psychological cataclysms awaiting his hero. In the same scene Hamlet talks to his friend Horatio. The content of his conversation: the present situation in Denmark, the death of his father, the hasty marriage of the mother, – proves his control by the Persona.

In the third scene, the world, or to be exact, the attitude of Hamlet to the world is abruptly changed. Although he still uses the language of the Persona in his conversation with Horatio, and the main specific feature of his new social mask – total ridicule – is not present yet, the protagonist is already confronted with the new state of the world. However, according to the law of inertia he still builds his relations with people and his communication with them in an old manner.

The rejection of the Persona, as an event related to the catastrophic state of the world and its corresponding perception by Hamlet, is represented in his second monologue. Since "the time is out of joint" and Hamlet's duty, in his understanding, is to mend it. In the second scene of the second act the protagonist has already rejected the Persona, and put on the mask of madness which allowed him express/conceal the thoughts and to use the total scorn that corresponds to his mood. The mode of speech that he uses in the dialog with Polonius fully represents his new image. The conversation with Guildenstern and Rosencrantz characterises Hamlet's transformation from one mode of discourse to another. At the beginning the protagonist asks common questions, however, realising that they were sent by his uncle, he puts on the mask of madness and chooses to talk in an abstract metaphoric manner. His comparison of the world with a prison and Denmark being the worst part of it, takes place exactly in this dialogue.

Before the change of his attitude toward society in the first scene of the third act Hamlet, being sincerely in love with Ophelia, talks with her. The new social mask demands a new mode of discourse, and the prince demonstrates its specific qualities. First, he announces that he does not love her:

> HAMLET: ... I did love you once.
> OPHELIA: Indeed, my lord, you made me believe so.
> HAMLET: You should not have believed me; for virtue cannot so inoculate our old stock but we shall relish of it: I loved you not.

The dialogue indicates that Hamlet is still in the period of change from one set of values to another.

> Iskandar is depicted as having rejected the "commands" of the Persona archetype a long time ago, having lost hopes for the transformation of the community in the way he desires. For Hamlet, tormented that his father was killed by his uncle and that his mother has hastily married to the murderer, the social problems seem abstract and uncertain, and exist only in the context of a prison Denmark as a background. The cause of Iskandar's alienation is social: his sister, brother and father in the first place are part of the community, and his communication with them is framed by this context. It is also mirrored in his communication strategy with society. Iskandar's mode of discourse, as Hamlet's, is a total scorn as an invariant of communication. Although the discourse of Hamlet, especially his monologues, demonstrates his personal tragedy, and the scorn is used to cover up his true worldview, Iskandar's speech, even his monologues, focuses on social themes. His personal feelings are concealed under the mask of a drinker which caused the community's hatred and his marginalisation.

However the total scorn of Iskandar does not keep him from expressing personal feelings towards particular members of the community. The analysis of his conversation with the sister proves it.

> Iskandar (hugs Nazly): My beautiful sister Nazly. Whole day you are sitting home learning to cook stews from your mum; but you do not come to my place, so I could tell you about the cities I have been, you could know what is going on in the world! Look, the sun is outside, if you can't see its light, what is it for then? The grass is greening on the fields, the trees are flowering: what are the flowers, the meadows for without you? (Məmmədquluzadə C. 2004: 387)

In his remark there is almost no scorn, except for the part about "the stew lessons", where ridicule is also mildly expressed. At the example of his sister Iskandar feels the pity for the destined life of the whole female population. As a result

Iskandar temporary removes his special mask and uses a moving mode of discourse differing from his usual way of talking. However, at once, feeling ashamed of his own betrayal, he returns to the usual scornful discourse:

> "Your snotty brothers go to canals and gather clover and you sit at home and chew your gum. At home with your nitty sisters you play around and say: O my jolly! Oh my jolly lover, with a long dress ... " (Məmmədquluzadə C. 2004: 387)

In the conversation with his brother Iskandar returns to the mode controlled by the Persona archetype. Jalal is in some way sentenced to repeat the destiny of the older brother. He still has hopes for his future, he does not know that following steps of his brother he will eventually become like Iskandar:

> Iskandar: Jalal, hey Jalal! Now you run off me, say I'm drunk; but I swear by the holy saint, one day when you finish your studies, you'll be sleeping near [wine] jars like your brother Iskandar. (Məmmədquluzadə C. 2004: 387)

Here Iskandar's scorn is generated by the regret and is directed to himself, first of all.

* * *

Although the collective unconscious functions mostly on the level of social interests, really it works both ways. To function normally society allows the person to act naturally, to love what he likes, to hate what he dislikes etc. In other words it has to create the conditions for the functioning of existential demands. The balance created as a result of this mutual agreement appears to be steady (since all traditions, system of values, moral principles and taboos experienced and worked out for thousand years are at the guard of it), however, it is highly unstable, and any cataclysm can bring an end to it.

As a matter of fact, the wholeness of the collective unconscious, the balance providing its influence on the person, can be affected not by outer factors only, but by the person who prefers his egoistic demands to the basic principles of the community as well. Sometimes the behaviour of the person who is satisfied to comply with his "instincts" shows some rationality and logic: Claudius murders his brother for the sake of power, Sheikh Nasrullah, to feed his lust, uses fraud. Sometimes under the influence of instinct the person acts unreasonably: the destruction of Othello at any cost is the result of irrationalism.

The decline of the influence of the collective unconscious produces an area of tension in the community; at the one end is the source of the decline, on the other end is the individual incapable of accepting morally his new (fair without but foul within!) state.

The individuals on the first pole are in the guard of the old state, thus they behave "as if nothing happened". The person chooses the mask according to intrinsic interests. Obviously, he cannot use the persona mask, since he breaks the rules of the collective unconscious, but he knows that open rejection can repel the community from him. Thus he hypocritically imitates the Persona: Claudius acts sorrowful at the loss of his brother, kind and caring for Hamlet. Sheikh Nasrullah, wearing the mask of the honourable and virtuous person in order to fulfil his plans, wants to keep the Irevan population in superstition and prejudice.

On the other pole is the person who is not willing to live in the moral chaos and absurdity created by the break of the order of the collective unconscious. Unlike the other members of the community this individual clearly sees and recognises the causes and the source of the disturbance. It is not a coincidence that the crime of Claudius and the fraud of Sheikh Nasrullah are recognised only by Hamlet and Iskandar. It should be mentioned that the sensitivity of Claudius and Sheikh is no less than that of their antagonists, since they also want to solve the hostile confrontation. Claudius attempts to send Hamlet back to Wittenberg, or even kill him, Sheikh Nasrullah is eager to marginalise Iskandar in order to minimise his influence over the community.

As far as is known Freud suggested that the person's psyche consists of three parts which are at the same time connected and antagonistically separated from each other. In this case the psychic wholeness of the person is out of the question. Jung believed that despite the influence of diverse centrifugal forces, an individual's psyche was not fractioned, but a whole. He put forward the idea of the archetype of the Self as the protector of the person's wholeness. The Swiss scholar assumed that the Self signifies the unified consciousness and unconscious, and "it is sufficiently definite to express the wholeness of the person, and is sufficiently indefinite to express the indefinable nature of the Self" {is a certain as far as it concerns the wholeness of the person and indefinite and indescribable as far as it concerns the nature of the wholeness"}. (Юнг К.Г. AION. 1997:38)

The Self and the Persona working together ensure the existence of the person's psyche. In my view this important characteristic explains their opposition: unlike the Persona conducting the integration of the individual into society, the Self mostly creates the basis for isolating him from society. "The self can be defined as the central inner regulator... It is a centre constantly controlling the growth and development of a person. However the multifaceted and total state of the psyche at early stages appears as inborn non-manifested yet possibility" (Юнг К.Г. 1997:158)

Considering, this Jung supposes that "the Self is the central archetype uniting all psychic characteristics of a person." (Лейбин В. 2008:231)

Trying to define the dialectical wholeness of the person, which on the one hand exists in a certain time and place, on the other hand represents humanity at all times and places, Jung compared it with Jesus (Christ), in the sense that a certain person Jesus is born just once, thus is carnal, but is an embodiment of God, total and timeless. "Thus the Self as the core of the person emerges in the concrete time and is unique; however as an archaic symbol it is an Imago Dei, thus is universal and eternal" (Лейбин В. 2008:230).

Therefore on the one hand the Swiss scholar tries to bring an individual into concrete time and space and on the other hand he separates it from the time and space and represents it as ultramundane. For Jung the human is a dialectical being with one foot in the immemorial past and the other in the modern world. Threatening the balance can cause upheavals in the person. "It must be reckoned a psychic catastrophe when *the ego is assimilated by the self.* The image of wholeness then remains in the unconscious, so that on the one hand it shares the archaic nature of the unconscious and on the other finds itself in the psychically relative space-time continuum that is characteristic of the unconscious as such." (Jung, Aion, CW 9, part II, 1978: 24).

Apparently, the excessive socialization of the archetype that is the discrepancy of the fragile stability between the ego and society in favor of the latter can bring bad consequences: influenced by heavy moral cataclysms even the most strong, immunised ego-personalities can fall into the slavery of the community.

The strange, alienated condition of Hamlet and Iskandar is related to the problem that they both cannot exist in the accustomed standards, and cannot define the parameters of a new personality for objective and subjective reasons. However their alienation does not result in the separation from the community. On the contrary, since his meeting with the ghost of his father, Hamlet becomes closely involved in the uncle's crime, his mother' betrayal, and the situation in Denmark. His own concerns and emotions are left behind because of the scale of the crime, forcing the released instincts. This can explain his obscure attitude towards Ophelia whom Hamlet loved so dearly once: Ophelia now is not a naive and sincere girl, but the daughter of hypocritical, obsequious, and rat-like Polonius. Hamlet is negatively socialised, completely dissolved in social problems, and consequently has lost personal feelings.

Iskandar is in the same position as Hamlet, unsurprisingly the only personal feeling which is left in him is the genuine delicate brotherly love to Nazly: the hatred to the world of the hajjis lead by Sheikh Nasrullah, the attitude of total scorn are socially characterised; his transformation into Kefli Iskandar, signifying the loss of identity, arises from the failure of his social, not personal mission. Iskandar's opposition to his brother's education can be explained also by personal feelings of failure as well. However, the vital reason for transformation of Maarifçi (Educated) Iskandar to Kefli (Drunken) Iskandar is related to his belief that Jalal will inevitably repeat his fate. The main idea of *The Dead* is defined in terms of a society unwilling to hear the voice of Iskandar and existing in the swamp of superstition and prejudice.

The explicit weakness of the actions of a strong willed Duanish prince and Azerbaijani intellectual – Hamlet's hesitation to take vengeance, the delay in execution of a human's and offspring's duties – Iskandar's indecision to disclose Sheikh Nasrullah's fraud – is related to the impotence of ego (I) in the face of society (community), and the victory on this stage of the community over the person.

According to Jung individuation is the process of transformation into a "true self". It is the realisation of unique individual characteristics. It should be mentioned that in Jung's view "the process commence when an individual starts the study of mythology directly connected with archetypes, the symbolism of alchemy, the individual and collective transformations, conscious and unconscious changes"(Лейбин В. 2008: 234). Noticeably, Jung represents individuation not in the context of actual social process but as a theoretical notion. With this perspective one can propose the idea that the harmony of human inner and outer worlds can be split and even antagonised as the result of individuation.

However real life is characterised by the contradictions between the person and society, and they rarely come to agreement. In Jung's account, the actualisation of individuation becomes impossible. Paradoxically, the periods of social upheavals "atomise" the person influenced by the irresistible centrifugal forces, on the other hand, they demand the emergence of the individual with a supreme moral potential to solve the existing problems. The study of *Hamlet* and *The Dead* proves that the more a person is affected by moral cataclysm the greater is his chance to become a personality. We should point out the impossibility of such a person to be a psychologically whole individual and of his ability to harmonically integrate into society. At the same time Shakespeare's and Mammadguluzadeh's protagonists are men of the best moral qualities.

The process of individuation in Hamlet begins when he eventually decides to go move words to deeds. He cannot demand the inner transformation of the surrounding people, since they are not ready for it. Thus he understands his mission to be an example and to cleanse the space: he clearly realises that unless the community will be "cleansed" of such a sycophant as Polonius and criminals as his uncle, the transformation of the person into the personality will be a really complicated matter.

Unlike Hamlet, Iskandar is portrayed as the individuated, the wholly matured personality. The complications of his period of becoming are given in a non-explicit way and very little is shown. We should mention that Mammadkuluzade'h masterfully uses the technique of silent poetics: the reader observes only the result of a process that happened outside of the narrative – the transformation of a naive, optimistic youth into a still young but tired of living, weary and wise Iskandar.

Jung mentioned more than once that previously relatively harmonious relations of consciousness and unconscious develop into irresolvable conflicts in modern times, conflicts which characterises the mode of life as of a society as well of individuals. In his opinion "the energetic potential of the tension" created by the conflict results in the constant renewal of society and individuals. The collective unconscious and the system of archetypes being in time cannot restore the stability; the collective unconscious, confronted with the constantly arising problems created by upheavals, resembles the two-faced Janus: it forced to unite two diametrically opposite qualities: conservatism, something required by its nature, and dynamism, demanded by the character of the XXth century.

During relatively peaceful periods of time the collective unconscious is characterised by dynamic stability and is able to restore the order. The tragedies of Shakespeare, such as *Othello*, *Macbeth*, *Hamlet*, *The King Lire* thematically and in artistic description portray the broken order of the things, which is eventually restored at the finale. Prince Fortinbras in *Hamlet* at the end of the tragedy declares the restoration of the previous state. The poet of the Renaissance period was confident that in spite of all changes and perturbations life will go back to normal in the end.

However in the circumstances of the XX-th century, when individuals and societies are subjected to permanent moral and social turbulence, the restoration of the normal functioning of the collective unconscious and the system of archetypes and their usual control over society is impossible. Mammadguluzadeh in *The Dead* and *The Madmen Gathering* described different variations of a situation characteristic for the XX-th century. After the visit of Sheikh Nasrullah to Irevan, its population is unable to live as before. The problem is not only that the fraudster's use of religious terminology and discourse broke the fanatic faith. The brutal changes in the XX-th century have a latent influence on the collective unconscious: Iskandar's attempts to change the community bring results a posteriori. The time being temporarily "out of joint" in Shakespearian times, is in the times of Mammadgulugzadeh completely "broken." The Azerbaijani intellectual, sensing at times the turbulence present in things, and at times predicting them, had a pessimistic view on the process of history: he was unconfident of the return to a normal functioning of the collective unconscious and the system of archetypes. It was impossible to define the algorithm of the cataclysms of the XX-th century, such as cyclic revolutions, world wars, the formation of the communism and fascism, and presuppose the return of the collective unconscious to normal. The works of J. Mammadguluzadeh, and later Samuel Becket and Eugene Ionesco, merely reflected the spirit of the turbulent times.

References

Dictionnaire Petit Robert, Paris, 1967.
Məmmədquluzadə C. *Əsərləri* 4 cilddə, 1 c. B.: 2004.
Шекспир У. Полное собрание сочинений в 8 томах, 1 т. М.: 1960.
Shekspir U. Polnoe sobranie sochinenij v 8 tomah, 1 t. M.: 1960.
Юнг К.Г. AION. Исследование феноменологии самости. М.: 1997.
Jung K.G. AION. Issledovanie fenomenologii samosti. M.: 1997.
Юнг К.Г. Человек и его символы. М.: 1997.
Jung K.G. Chelovek i ego simvoly. M.: 1997.
Лейбин В. *Постклассический психоанализ.* Энциклопедия. М.: 2008
Lejbin V. *Postklassicheskij psihoanaliz.* Jenciklopedija. M.: 2008

Faustus as archetype

Gonul Bakay
(Turkey)

This paper argues that the figure of Faustus as the archeteype of human endeavor and desire for unlimited knowledge and power has not lost its appeal over the ages and is still prevalent today. In the words of Beicken: "Archetypal Faust has all the elements of Western hubris and thus something of modern Everyman" (Beicken 1999: 3). This is probably the main reason why the tale of Dr. Faustus has been emulated and adapted by several western writers including Benet and Washington Irwing. In order to show how the figure of Faustus inspired and spoke to these writers on the other side of the Atlantic, I will first offer a short analyis of Marlow's play and then move on to show how the cautionary tale of Dr. Faustus is rearticulated in the American context through the examples of *the Devil and Daniel Webster* and *the Devil and Tom Walker*.

To begin with, Faustus represents the heroic aspirations of the Renaissance man. Many have seen behind the tale "the Renaissance aspirations, the discontent, the wearing unsatisfied striving after knowledge that marked the age. Many have witnessed in it a tension between one one hand: "the moral and theological imperatives of a severe Christian orthodoxy and on another hand, an affirmation of Faustus as the epitome of Renaissance aspirations."(As Jonathan Dollimore observes: "In Dr. Faustus, however sin is not the error of fallen judgement, but a conscious deliberate transgression of the limit." (Oz 1971:156)

Stephan Greenblatt finds in Marlowe's work a subversive identification with the alien, with one which flaunts society's cherished orthodoxies, embraces what the culture finds loathsome and frightening" (Greenblatt 1983: 203, 220). In Marlow's play, Faustus pursues unlawful practices, which indicates the narrowness of Faustus's universe.

One of the most important contradictions in Christian theology is: "how is evil possible in a world created by an omnipotent God?" (Oz 1971:159). Vice is in conflict with Christian teaching. When Faustus seeks empirical knowledge, he arrives at his limits. He is the malcontent. The practices of hell forbid him to know how the world was made. (Oz1971:170). As Catherine Belsey observes, "The play is poised between two problematics, a discursive knowledge which does not lead to power and an empirical knowledge which is not yet certain of its own projecy or its own authority." (Oz1971:170).

Faustus's dilemma can be examined from the twentieth century standpoint of Jung's psychology of archteypes. In Jungian Psychology, an archetype is an "unconscious idea, pattern of thought, or image inherited from the ancestors of the race and universally present in individual psyches. Jung linked the archetypes to heredity and considered them as instinctual. Whenever he looked across cultures, he found the same archetypes and thus came to conceptualize them as fundamental forces that somehow exist beyond us. They have existed in ancient myths as elemental spirits and Jung sought to link with this deep and old experience" (Golden 1985: 202). "According to Jung, the death of meaning in the mythic symbols of Christianity began during the Renaissance.- Reformation period the age of Dr. Faustus."(Golden 1985: 202)

First, Faustus, cannot comprehend the full meaning of hell. He thinks. "I think hell's a fable."(I, ıı, 125). Later, he thinks hell is a pleasant place. "I'll willingly be damned, what? sleeping, eating, walking and disputing?" (I, ıı, 136-137). There are conflicts within his psyche. "Mephistopheles is a symbol of what Jung calls the shadow, archetype of the dark, not integrated complementary portion of the physic. Looked at in terms of modern psychology, the good and Evil angels represent the opposing sides: the ego and the shadow of Christian complex, the collection of religious ideas Faustus has internalized in his personal unconscious" (Golden 1985: 206).

The perennial question that haunts readers of this famous play is why Faustus went into a pact with the devil. Some critics suggest it was because he was damned. The problem, in this sense, is one that relates to theology. Only God chooses the ones who will be damned. God does not allow Satan to have dominion over the soul of believers, but only gives over to his sway the unpious and unbelieving whom he deigns not to number among his flock. (Calvin: 1.14.). Although the good angel tells Faustus what he should do, the latter fails to follow this advice. Therefore he will be unable to claim ignorance when God taxes him with his wickedness" (Calvin,1.75). If this is so, then Faustus' fate is decided very early.

To have faith is important. "The reward of sin is death? That's hard. .... If we say that we have no sin,we deceive ourselves .... Why then belike we must sin and and so consequently die?" (Wilson 1999:249) Faith in Christ leads the way to salvation. Hilary Gratti expresses the main theme of Dr. Faustus with the words: "Marlow is here expressing one of the fundemental issues of his times. Man's new faith in his own intellectual resources against a deeply rooted Christian concept of vanity of human endeavour alone." (Wilson 1999: 250).

Faustus's desire for power has found resonance in the hearts of humans at all times, it is what makes him an important archetype. Faustus's drama can be viewed as an intellectual, rather than a moral dilemma. On the other hand, Marlow must be surely aware of the Copernican theory of the universe at the time he was writing this play. Mephistophelis answers all Faustus's questions with the accepted – though still disputed premises of the Ptolemic- Aristotelian hypothesis.

Faustus stresses his link with Wittenberg. Marlowe's strongest lines are when he writes about the tension

My God! My God, Look not so fierce on me
Adders and serpents, let me breathe awhile.
Ugly Hell gape not
I'll burn my books; ah Mephistopheles (V, ıı, 197-200)

The two scholars discover Faustus'dead body. They can also undrestand and sympathise with Faustus's desire for more knowedge.

Yet for he was a scholar, once admired
For wondrous knowledge in our Germaine schools. (V, ııı, 16-17)

The play ends with a pessimistic tone. The chorus sings of Faustus's pact with Mephistopheles as an act of negativity. All in all, the play suggests that because of strict religious controversies, there is little hope for the positive sciences to develop.

As Ingrid Schafer observes: "Among Christians, those who denounce Faust see him brasenly continuing to eat off the forbidden tree thus re-aracting the primal fall. Those who admire Faust, see him bravely continuing to strive toward ever higher levels of understanding, thus realizing his human potential. "One formed in the image of God" (Schafer 2005) As Schafer further suggests: "The difference, I believe is a sign which can at least partially traced to the radically different world – views found in Catholic thinkers of Italy and Protestant reformation Germany. Renaissance artists and thinkers tended to focus on the incarnation as a sign of God's presence in the world, while some Protestants tended to focus on original sin as sign of Satanic power in the world (Schafer 2005).

Faustus aspires to be more than man. He is a man of humble origins who has acquired great knowledge. From the start, he rejects such subjects as law, divinity and philosophy; he is more attracted to medicine and witchcraft. In his words: "a sound magician is a demi-God" (I,ı, 61). Mephistopheles doesn't tell him anything that he doesn't already know. What he wants to know is how the world was made. He wants to solve the riddle of life but does not advance in this field.

On another level, one could suggest that Faustus's problem is with his identity. To be precise, Faustus is an example of the divided self. He is not sure whether he is a spirit or a man. He wants to be more than man. He aspires to reach above human possibility and thus enters a new world of magic and illusion. Thinking that he has tried all that man is capable of, he isolates himself completely and leads a solitary existence.

On the other hand, the play stresses the importance of true repentance. The good and bad angels symbolize Faustus' struggle with his conscience. It is clear that his initial signing of the bond is not final in his damnation. It is his rejection of his humanity that finally destroys him. It is when Faustus rejects his humanity by showing no mercy to the old man that he is finally damned. Moreover, it is Faustus' resistance to relinguish his power that destroys him. Good and bad angels try to play with his mind and influence his decisions. If there was no possibility of saving his soul, they wouldn't have tried to influence him. Faustus desires supreme power. He muses:

> "Of power, of honour, of omnipotence is promised to the studious artisan. All things that move between the quiet poles Shall be at at my command." Good angel urges Faustus . "to lay that damned book aside"(I,ı,69-70) Bad angel says. " Go forward Faustus in that famous art."(I, ı,73)

From the first paragraph, the chorus sets the scene. Faustus is associated with the image of Icarus who soars too high and his waxen wings melt with the heat of the sun. He is described with the following words.

> That shortly, he was graced with doctor's name.
> Excelling in all those sweet disputes.
> In heavenly matters of theology.
> Till swollen with cunning of a self conciet
> His waxen wings did mount above his reach.
> And melting heavens conspired his overthrow
> For falling to a devilish exercise. (chorus, foreward, 17-23)

Faustus shares his desire for supreme power with his friends Cornelius and Valdes and says "it is magic that nourished me" (I, ı, 109). Cornelius urges him and says after the miracles that magic provides, you will want to study nothing else.

> To men? should sign this bill." (1,5, 65)

There are contradictions in the tale. Both Harry Levin and Anthony Burgess ask the following question "Why the terrors of Hell? Why does Marlowe try to justify the ways of God to men?"(Kostic 2009: 212) Marlowe has doubts about Hell. Lucifer had lost Heaven because of his pride. Faustus asks Mephistopheles: "How comes it that thou art out of Hell?". Mephistopheles answers: "Why this is Hell, nor am I out of it. Thinks thou that I who saw the face of God And tasted the ever eternal joys of Heaven Am not tormented with ten thousand Hells. In being deprived of everlasting bliss. ?"(I, ııı, 76-80)

Faustus is tricked by the Devil. He doesn't achieve what he is seeking, he is not satisfied. He observes: "these are but shadows, not substantial." (Marlowe, IV, ıı, 54, 55). He remains unfulfilled and disillusioned. In this context, Faustus's tale predicts the dilemma of modern man- who is never satisfied with his condition, with what he has, reaches for more until sometimes he loses all in this strife. The tale stresses the moral premise that there is a limit to man's power. Being above animals and having enough intelligence to undrestand many riddles in life, man audaciously aims for ultimate knowledge, which is dangerous. He may loose everything in this struggle. As Manley observes: "having risen to the zenith of academic accomplishments in several disciplines, he asks the perennial questian that Jung testifies to hearing from men in midst of mid- life crisis:" What now?" Jung calls this ego inflation, the chief danger encountered by Renaissance man (as well as a modern man) .With one sided intellect which values knowledge for the technical manipulative power it gives power it gives to things and people"(Manley, 203).

All in all, the Faustus motif provides an oppurtunity to explore the spectrum of attitudes in Christians towards more knowledge, more power and desire for innovation in science and technogy. In America, the Faustus motif has been extensively employed to give a moral lesson against greed and for knowledge beyond what God allowed. In what follows, I examine two well-known American tales in which the figure of Faustus is

The Devil and Daniel Webster

Benet's story is an Americanized version of the Faustian motif. Jabez Stone is an unlucky man who sells his soul to the devil. Although he has good land, he is always unlucky. One day when his wife is ill and he breaks his plow, he says: "I vow it is enough to want to sell his soul to the devil" (Benet 2004: 17). The devil arrives and makes a pact with him. Scratch is a polite, friendly man who chews tobacco and takes a drink. He is out to get Jabez's soul. As soon as Jabez Stone makes a pact with the devil his life starts to improve in every possible way, so that people start to envy him. One day the devil arrives and tells Jabez that the time has come for them to talk about the mortgage. He observes: "This being the U.S.A and me always being a religious man I began to have serious doubts about that mortgage had in courts." The stranger says. "There is courts and courts" (Benet 2004: 23). Finally Jabez Stone goes to an eminent man – Daniel Webster – to get his advice. Jabez's wife is a brave person who is not afraid of the smoke and fire. It is she who suggests to her husband to contact Daniel Webster.

The devil says his name is Scratch and he is pressed for time. Daniel Webster says "Pressed or not you shall not have this man" (Benet 2004: 38). The devil claims to be an honest American like Daniel Webster. The devil says: "T'is true the North claims me for a Southerner, and The South for a Northerner, but I am neither. I am merely an honest American like yourself (Benet 2004: 39). The devil adds, "though I don't like to boast of it, my name is older in this country then yours" (Benet 2004: 47). The devil is out to get Webster's souls also. (Benet 2004: 48)

Daniel Webster is a man devoted to a cause. He is devoted to the union. It is his vocation, something above himself. When he talks, he talks with such enthusiasm that glitter goes out from the eyes of the Judges. Similar to Faustus, Daniel has strong desires; he wants to be president, but the devil says: "a lesser man will be made president and you will be passed over" (Benet 2004: 58). Daniel Webster is a man loved and respected by all. But the devil says all men will turn against you. He even observes: "Even in New England some will say you have turned your coat and sold your country, and their voices will be loud against you till you die" (Benet 2004: 59). The last question Webster asks is whether the fight for the union he had always fought for will have a positive result? Whether the fight will be won against those that aim to tear it apart? The devil answers: "not while you live. But it will be won. And after you are dead, there are thousands who will fight for your cause because of words that you spoke" (Benet 2004: 60). Daniel Webster is delighted. He observes: "For by the thirteen original colonies, I'll go to the Pit itself to serve the union". These words aptly convey Webster's deep emotional attachment to the union which he places even above God.

In fact, Daniel Webster is an actual historical figure who lived between the years 1782- 1852. In addition to Jabez in the tale, Daniel Webster also resembles Faust in many respects. He is arrogant, proud and very ambitious. He is also very proud to be a New Hampshire man. His pride is obvious in the lines: "If 2 New Hampshire men are not a match for the devil, we might as well give the country back to the İndians"(Benet 2004: 33). The devil agrees to have a formal trial on the condition that he will appoint the members: he calls thirteen villains from American history as the jury.

As this story is an Americanized version of the Faustus tale, it hardly comes as a surprise to see that Webster's whole argument rests on the basic principles of the American constititution. First, Webster doubts Scratch's credentials as an American citizen. Webster says; "İf you can claim citizenship, then I can claim a formal trial for my client" (Benet 2004: 251). According to the Yale Journal: "Although it would not be accurate to call Webster a mercenary man, – he was much more addicted to power and glory than to Money" (Benet 2004: 453). In the end, Webster wins the case by appealing to the patriotic feelings of the jury. He speaks of how wonderful it is to be a man, to be an American. He says that many wrongs have been done in America but "something new and good had grown from it" and everybody played a part in it, even the traitors.

Webster is an ambitious man like Faustus. Moreover, he sees ambition as a virtue, not a vice. He observes: "Ambition is what? The Grand nerve of human exertion; the producer of everything excellent in virtue and in vice. Ambition in Ceasar and in Washington is the same; in each it is the wish of exceling. Thus, various are the effects of ambition. It can enslave a nation or it can burst the monacles of despotism to make the opressed rejoice" (Golden 1985).

As the writer observes: "the fascination of Webster for his contemporaries was that he seemed to lead a life of allegory in which the forces of virtue and corruption battled for his soul" (Benet 2004: 455). America considered him the greatest man of his age: "The model of ambition subdued to virtue".

The Devil and Tom Walker

Tom Walker is a meager miserly fellow who lives in a thicky wooded swamp around the year 1727. His wife is also miserly and she hides away whatever she can lay her hands on. She, moreover, has a bad temper and a loud voice. She could often be heard quarreling with her husband in the woods. The couple lives in a forlorn, faraway house. One day Tom Walker tries to take a short cut home and arrives at a kind of fort made by the İndians. He rests there for some time and gives a kick to a black mound. As he pierces the ground with his stick he encounters a shell and gives it another kick. Then he hears a voice: "let that shell alone". "What are you doing on my ground?" says Deacon Peabody. When Tom Walker asks: "what right do you have to cut down Deacon Peabody's timber,?" The devil answers: "This wood belonged to me long before one of your white–faced race put foot upon the soil. "I am a great patron and prompter of slave dealer; and a great master of Salem withches" (İrving 1983:4). Scratch tells him that there is a great deal of money buried under an oak tree by Kidd, the pirate, and he can disclose the place for him, under certain conditions.

Tom discloses this secret to his wife, but she is more greedy than he is and wants the money no matter what the conequence may be. Tom himself wants the money badly but he refuses to sell his soul. His wife goes to the woods and never returns. Tom grows anxious about his wife but is rather more anxious about the silver. Tied to a checked apron tied to a cypress tree. There is a liver tied to it. Tom says, "Old Scratch must have had a tough time of it" (İrving1983). He even thinks the the devil has done a favor to him. He decides this time to contact the devil himself. The devil insists that the money Tom Walker would gain should be used in his service. First, he asks Tom Walker to be a slave dealer, which Tom refuses. Then, they agree that Tom will become a userer. Tom starts doing good business in Boston. He increases his terms in proportion to the needs of his costomers. As he grows older he starts to think of death. One day a needy land jabber asks him for money. Tom gives the money but refuses the man's plea for a few months of delay. When the man tells him that he has made a lot of money out of him, he answers saying "the devil take me if I have made a farthing". (Benet, 2004: 49) The Devil promptly appears after these words and takes him on his saddle and rides out to the forest.

The tale is commonly referred to as "comic new England Faust". Irving endows the tale with moral ideals common in New England, a place predominantly populated by Puritans and Quakers, for whom religious devotion is very important. Ultimately, the tale aims to show people what would happen to them if they became sinners like Tom Walker.

Like Benet, Irving americanizes the Faustus tale by using various themes and symbols. The issue of slavery is one of the themes used by Irving. Although Tom accepts to become a usurer, he still doesn't agree to become a slave dealer, which he views as a graver sin. The short-cut through the swamp may symbolize the short cut to wealth. Pride is symbolized in the tale with tall trees. The moral of the tale may be viewed as the loss of the right religious way may result in moral decay. Finally, the tale of Doctor Faustus stresses the unchanging qualities in man such as pride, desire for more knowledge and more power. It also illustrates the lengths he is prepared to go to in order to satiate his thirst to become invincible. As one of the most well-known cautionary tales of all times, it also shows the dire consequences that await mankind when such unlawful desires and ambitions possess the individual. The tales of Daniel Webster and Tom Walker attest to the fact that the qualities that make Dr. Faustus who he is are the very same qualities that cause his downfall. Looking at the world today, one could unfortunately observe that these urges, desires and ambitions seem to exist in men, at all times and all places, and probably will continue to do so in future times.

References

Benet, Stephan. V.*The Devil and Daniel Webster* USA: Dramatists Play service inc. 2004.

Golden Kenneth, L. "*Myth, Psychology and Marlowe's Doctor Faustus",* College Literaure, vol 12, no:3 Fall 1985.

Greenblatt, Stephan. Renaissance Selffashioning New York: University of Chicago press, 1983.

İrving, Washington. *The Devil and Tom Walker* USA: Aerie publishers ,1983.

Jump, John. D. edt. *Dr. Faustus – Christopher Marlowe* London: Methuen and Co. Ltd, 1962.

Kostİc, M. "The Faustian Motif in Christopher Marlowe's Dr. Faustus". Facto, Series Universitatus. Linguistic and Literature, Vol. 7, No 2, 2009, (209-222).

Oz, Avraham. *Marlowe* New York: Palgrave Macmllan. Penguin books ltd. 1971.

Schafer, İngrid. "Faust reflected in the metaphysic Mirrors of the Christian Spectrum: Science as Diabolic or Divine?" Zygon, Dec. 2005, vol 40, issue 4 (891-916).

Steane, J.B. edt. *Christopher Marlowe Complete Plays* Harmondsworth, England.

Werre, Campbell and Beicken. *Doctor Faustus: Archetypal Subtext at the. Millenium*, USA: West Virginia University Press, 1999.

Wilson, Richard, edt. *Christopher Marlowe,* London and New York: Longman, 1999.

Archetype of the Russian Man in Dostoyevsky's Work

Mamed Godjaev
(Azerbaijan)

According to Carl Gustav Jung, the creator of the theory of archetypes, an archetype belongs to the collective unconscious, It is not something that has been expelled from the area of consciousness, as Sigmund Freud supposed (См. Фрейд З. 1991), but is inherited and constantly present in the unconscious psyche of a modern man.

As Jung described the term in his numerous works, an archetype is a primordial psychological phenomenon, the ancestral' perception of the world and of human beings, which does not disappear with each generation, but lives in the depths of the soul of the modern individual, who holds the very origins of the human family, the prototypes or to be more precise the potential of the primordial types in his subconscious. "Unlike the relatively thin layer of the personal unconscious, situated at the fringe of consciousness, the content of the collective unconscious cannot be "remembered" with an aid of analytic technique since it not suppressed or forgotten" (Юнг К.Г. 1999). However, archetypes can sometimes emerge into consciousness as visual images, conscious forms, as if they had been transmitted to the language of consciousness and presented to the person in dreams, in artistic inspirations, or in religious revelations. Thus, archetypal images do not correspond to their manifest content and should be perceived as the symbols of another content. Therefore it is difficult for a dreamer or a poet to recognise the image and accept it as his own creation. Like a person who does not create his dream, the genuine poet does not create his work. They both are born in dreamer's and poet's soul beyond the owners' will and consciousness.

For artistic genius the archetypes are a source of energy and imagery. They represent not only what can be directly observed, i.e. everything external and visible, but also everything impossible to perceive, all the internal, hidden, and substantial parts of the soul. One such genius who revealed the mysteries of the human's soul was Dostoyevsky.

Dostoyevsky did not consider his study of the soul to be psychology, and moreover, he distinguished it from modern day psychology. Depth psychology was a newly emerging science, not known in Russia during his time. The XIXth century science of psychology, that is, Pavlov's study of conditioned reflexes and brain activity, was a psychology of the conscious. Dostoyevsky distinguished his psychologism from the contemporary conception of psychology. "I am called a psychologist, but it is not true. I am a realist in the best sense of this word, that is to say, I portray the depths of the human soul (Достоевский Ф.М. 1972-88:65)." The depths of the human soul" he opposed to the psychology of his time. Later Dostoevsky's psychologism took the name of depth psychology, which includes Freudian psychoanalysis and the analytical psychology of Jung.

According to the theory of Jung all people resemble each other in the depths of the soul, but differ in the area of consciousness. He differentiates these two as the Self and the Ego. The person is the generic phenomenon at the unconscious level, and the phenomenon of the species at the level of consciousness. The ego is visible. It is what the person knows of himself and creates in himself. The self is archetypical, a general phenomenon, something that person does not know about himself and is unable to control. On the contrary, the hidden, archetypical source has a strong impact on his perception of the world. The ego is like the person's face, his fingerprints, different and unique. The self and the archetype are the kinds of biological essences of the organism common for everybody.

Dostoyevsky intuitively was aware of it when he said via the protagonist of *The Teenager* Makar Dolgorukov that, in the depths of the soul all people believe in God, but many of them behave like atheists. Atheism is a phenomenon of consciousness, however, faith is a phenomenon of the unconscious. Otherwise stated, an atheist is a person who does not know that he believes in God. Thus Tolstoy's Levin (*Anna Karenina*) could not understand why he, a non-believer, started to pray during Kitty's childbirth.

Western Medieval theologians also argued that the human soul is Christian in its essence. Translating it into the common humanistic concepts of faith, it would sound like this: the human soul is essentially spiritual.

The characteristic feature of Dostoyevsky's works is to represent man in two images: in a real, visible, social expression as a figure, a type, and in a deep, invisible, spiritual expression as a character, an archetype. It is generally accepted that the national Russian character, the Russian soul, found its most adequate expression in Dostoyevsky's works. Dostoyevsky managed to overcome the visible, external world and delve into the invisible, inner content of the Russian character and the Russian soul, which can be identified as an archetype of the Russian. Dostoyevsky believed that all manifestations of the Russian type compose only the form, rather distorted, of the Russian national character, the archetype, the genuine soul of the Russian hidden underneath.

The images created by Dostoyevsky are manifold, completely different from each other. For instance, the Karamazovs, the father and his three sons, are different as personalities, as types, but identical as to the archetype, the self, the Russian soul, the bearer of generic origins. They are all similar on the generic level and all the peripeties of their life lead to the same ultimate outcome – the discovery of the true self, the revelation of their real essence, which is hidden even from themselves. Their life paths are completely different in nature and their life principles tend towards the same ultimate goal, to the core of their character, to the archetype of the Russian man.

Karamazovschina – is a visible, social type, which manifests itself in various ways, while the Russian orthodox soul is an essence, the spiritual type, or rather the archetype, which manifests in the same way in all situations. The surname Karamazov[1] ("Chernomazov" is an accidental slip of the tongue of one of the characters) consist of a Turkic element which Dostoyevsky considered alien, as a historical, but not mythological factor, lacking archetypical foundation. *Karamazovshina* as a form is opposed to orthodox Christianity as a content, generic, spiritual, archetypical foundation which is superior to history as well as to milieu.

Karamazovshina as an outward appearance is most vividly and clearly represented in the image of the head of the family, Fedor Pavlovich Karamazov, in whom the form has completely suppressed the content and does not allow it to exist outside. The archetype of the Russian, a believer and a sufferer, which Fedor Pavlovich undoubtedly had, has suffocated under the thick coating of foreign layers. The head of the family is unable to discover his archetypal basis and dies tragically murdered by his own sons. In fact, it is the suicide of the type, the assassination of generic origins, which exerted a tragic influence upon all the Karamazovs.

Thus the elder Karamazov – is the typical image of the Russian man, while the youngest Karamazov Alesha – is the pure archetype of the Russian, the naked Russian soul hidden in the deranged depths of the unconscious of the other Karamazovs. Each of them is the same as Alesha Karamazov's Russian archetype, the same Russian soul lies in the depths of their hearts. However all the Karamazovs share qualities similar to that of their father, who is the typical form of the Russian character. Each of them could resemble their father, but temporarily, not forever, because *Karamazovshina* as a form is not eternal. At the same time each of them is doomed to come to the condition of the Alesha Karamazov's soul. Therefore all Karamazovs, with all their power and the Karamazov's persistence of defending their life principles, equally love Alesha, their own, generic origin, and love him like the hidden essence of their soul, like the unrealised and concealed themselves. Alesha is an expression of that archetype of the Russian, that orthodox Christian soul which for some reasons either was unrecognisably distorted (Mitya, Ivan) or died (Smerdakov) in the souls of the other brothers.

Mitya is a brawler, a martinet, a "Bourbon" as he calls himself. However, this is his mask not hisessence, his guise not his face. This is "reality", not a soul.

---

1 Kara-Turkish, meaning black.

There is another person inside him, and the character knows nothing about the other Mitya.

Ivan – is a philosopher and his philosophic ideas, his ethical principles and finally his militant humanism exibit the same form, the same "realism" as Mitya Karamazov's violent orgies.

Mitya and Ivan are different in their factual, existential manifestations, but they are similar in their spiritual, archetypal content. And the similar, typical, unchangeable i.e. soul, is embodied in Alesha, who was also touched by *karamazovschina,* but not on such a deep level as his brothers. The Karamazov's power sublimated into spiritual love, the love of God, and the love of truth. The image of a righteous man and a real humanist, a humble lover of God, is common for all Karamazovs, and this is the archetype of a Russian which constitutes the basis and the heart of every Russian. Fedor Pavlovich, Mitya and Ivan Karamazovs live in masks, in distorted and alien forms which hide their soul, their essence, and which are accepted by them i.e. the carriers of these forms, as their genuine content.

Alesha Karamazov lives without a mask, he is free from the false form, he lives with a naked soul, and the spiritual content, the archetype of a Russian is revealed almost in everything from his facial expression to his feelings and deeds. His father and brothers deeply love him and that is not a coincidence, since everyone loves in him their innermost, their dream, their mysterious wish, the hidden essence – the archetype.

The archetypal origin is expressed in each of them in the vague feeling of a furtive approval of Alesha's ethics and behaviour, in the secret understanding that Alesha Karamazov is a true human, a true Russian soul. Each Karamazov is endowed with a string in the soul that is responsive to Alesha's kindness. Almost all Dostoyevsky's characters, including that of *The Brothers Karamazov*, cross the fire of tragedy and catastrophe, which destroys all that is accidental and illusory in order to reveal the true essence, the archetype of the Russian. Fedor Pavlovich and Smerdyakov perished in the fire, unable to find their mysterious soul because they crossed the forbidden borders separating a personality and the self, form and content, an image and an archetype, a villain and a human.

Resurrection occurs only in the two brothers – Mitya and Ivan – who represent at their best two different forms of distortion and cover the archetype with a modern image, the coating of "realism". Mitya Karamazov, if one can put it this way, suffers from a purely Russian form of mental illness. It is the Karamazov's uncontrolled recklessness, the strength which was wasted by a deceptive perception of life. Ivan Karamazov is contaminated with the subtler poison of civilization, western philosophic ideas, which put the Man above God and create as a result the ethics of so called "Man-God", justifying crimes and preaching the theory of "everything is allowed".

Mitya's character is distorted in the Russian way. Thus bloody fights, rudeness and ribaldry occur. Ivan's mind is distorted in the European way by exquisite intellectual, philosophical, ideological thinking. Mitya's soul is the soul of the Russian covered by Russian trash, easier to clean up. Ivan's soul is covered with more refined and outwardly pretty junk, thus to clear it without touching the soul is impossible. Ivan is ill at the end and has to expiate his rebirth by the severe mental suffering. Father Zosima's predictions were correct: the idea troubling Ivan is resolved in a positive way. The crude feelings and passions that covered Mitya's soul are well visible from aside. He also clearly sees them but does not want to get rid of them yet. In this case he is like his father. The difference is only that Fedor Pavlovich raised the dirt to the level of his life principles, while Mitya has been a knight in the disguise of a boor, a nobleman under the mask of a thief and scamp. Ivan's soul (as primordial and great as Mitya's) is also covered with seemingly beautiful civilised ideas and theories in the form of new veritoes about human being, verities as certain as a parallel postulate about lines which supposedly never meet.

In this context, this system of measurement of Ivan's ethics is very convincing: God's paradise at the end of the world is not worth a tear of a tortured child. This is a human truth, the humanism of this world. However in the other geometrical system, parallel lines can meet; eternal harmony at the end of the world is worth human suffering, including that of children, not here, in the real world, but there, in a transcendental world, in the world of archetypes where there is no guilty and innocent, where, as father Zosima said, "every human is at fault for everything and everybody (Достоевский Ф.М. 1972-88:290). In the world of archetypes there is no "you" and "I", but only a whole living unity, a whole living organism, one particle of which cannot be accused and opposed to the rest.

Religion and belief in God, a belief in the immortality of a soul – belongs to the sphere of archetypes. God can be understood in the system of archetypes while in the system of types and images of the actual world he cannot be perceived and accepted. Ivan could not accept Him because he was thinking in worldly images and human categories. All mankind, the whole universe is a unified living organism. People are the parts of this organism. Worldly sins and faults belong not to the separate parts of the organism or separate individuals but to the whole organism consisting of everybody including children. Consequently redemption belongs to everybody and everyone should equally share it.

The archetype of a Russian is differently revealed in Ivan and Mitya. Mitya's soul is cleansed through love, not through the love-hatred towards Katerina Ivanovna, but through the love-humility toward Grushenka. His love for Katerina has boiled his blood, arousing feelings of pride, rivalry and revenge. He loves and hates her simultaneously, trying to win and conquer her by superior nobility. The love of Katerina and Mitya looks like a duel of two prides. Katerina Ivanovna's beauty suppresses Mitya, and he wants to win the arrogant beauty with his love. This is a beauty where "God fights with the devil and the battle field is people's hearts (Достоевский Ф.М. 1972-88:100). There is no touch of souls, or archetypes here. There is only the contact and the struggle of two "I", two egos.

Mitya and Grushenka's love is a love of another kind, a love beyond egoism, love expelling egoism, and as result there is a touch and amalgamation of two selves, two souls. The beauty of Grushenka affects Mitya as something dear, maternal, Russian, calm and peaceful. Since Mitya fell in love with her, he became humble, gentle and even tearful like a child, turned pure and meek as a baby. Everything artificial has disappeared and the original soul has emerged. Thus the path to his soul has been found, the archetype, as well as everything Russian, national. The native soil opens his way to belief, to God, to love for God and the human in general. The way to faith goes through love for the native soil, through the native soul. Mitya was wild as a lion with Katerina, but became humble as a kitten with Grushenka. Mitya who hit people in the face, now thinks about the crying child, cannot forget him and asks, "Why is the baby crying?" The crying child becomes the symbol of suffering mankind, and everyone is to blame for their miseries. The compassion to the crying baby comes from the depths of the protagonist's soul, from the heart of the Russian man.

Thus, Mitya makes a distinctive spiritual transcendence from the world of types and images to the world of archetypes, from the world of "realism" to the world of soul, from the human world to the world of God, the world of transcendent truth. In other words he leaves his false form and bonds with his real content.

None of Dostoyevsky's characters gain anything new, something that did not exist in them before. The same is true with Mitya. He does not develop new character features, but returns to the old, archetypal origin of the Russian character.

As Carl Jung wrote, "rebirth can be a renewal without essential changes in a man, so that the transformed personality does not change essentially, but only functionally ..." The same process i.e. transformation from the image to the archetype, from "realism" to soul, from philosophy to belief, but in another form, occurs or rather should occur in Ivan Karamazov's character. In any case Ivan's philosophy has completely failed in the narrated part of his life. Seemingly logical and humanistic, Ivan's philosophy led to crimes, to his father's murder. Smerdyakov guided by the theory that "everything is allowed" killed Fedor Pavlovich and before his suicide confessed his guilt and noted that the real murderer is Ivan. From that moment the concrete logic of Ivan and his image of being a firm humanist fractured and opened the way to the archetype, hidden in his subconscious. The hard and long process resulted in Ivan's mental illness. The outcome is unknown as it is not given in the narrative. However it is apparent that Ivan has finally known what is hidden in his soul and rediscovered himself, or to be more exact, lost his former self confronted with either his rebirth or death. Nevertheless the hope of Ivan's rebirth is much stronger than the anticipation of his death. Since he is guilty of his father's death, he killed his image in his soul even before Smerdyakov had killed him, but the question remains whether Ivan could destroy himself in his soul, could he murder God? There is no affirmative answer to this question. It means that Ivan, just as his predecessor Raskolnikov, "did not cross the border, stayed at this side". And that means that there is hope for his revival. Dostoyevsky believed in the archetype of the Russian which sooner or later will overcome obstacles, break out through all foreign coverings and appear in its pure form. What a beautiful image will emerge in this case – great, humble and heroic as Ilya Muromets, a legendary hero of Russian epic narratives. Dostoyevsky assumed an alien and false layering on the Russian national spirit, the socialistic and revolutionary theories which supposed to build a fair and heavenly life on earth without God. For him the Russian soul archetypally was the carrier of the orthodox faith and religious ethics on the foundation of which could arise a new edifice of Russian social and state life, a new social order, incarnating Christianity as well. According to Dostoyevsky in this case Christianity and the state neither will be separated nor united (as union also presupposes essentially different parts joining together) but would be the same. That was Dostoyevsky's utopia.

References

Достоевский Ф.М. *ПСС в 30-и тт.* – Л., Наука, 1972-1988. – Т. 27.
Dostoevskij F.M. *PSS v 30-i tt.* – L., Nauka, 1972-1988. – T. 27.
Фрейд З. *Достоевский и отцеубийство* // Фрейд З. «Я» и «Оно». Труды разных лет. Кн. 2.: Тбилиси, «Мерани", 1991.
Frejd Z. *Dostoevskij i otceubijstvo* // Frejd Z. «Ja" i «Ono". Trudy raznyh let. Kn. 2.: Tbilisi, «Merani", 1991.
Юнг К.Г. *Об отношении аналитической психологии к поэзии* //Юнг К.Г. Избранное, – Мн.: ООО «Попурри", 1999..
Jung K.G. *Ob otnoshenii analiticheskoj psihologii k pojezii* //Jung K.G. Izbrannoe, – Mn.: OOO «Popurri", 1999..
Юнг К.Г. *О перерождении* // Юнг К.Г. Синхрония: акаузальный объединяющий принцип. – М.: АСТ Москва. – 2010. –
Jung K.G. *O pererozhdenii* // Jung K.G. Sinhronija: akauzal'nyj ob#edinjajuwij princip. – M.: AST Moskva. – 2010.

Gods Don't Talk, Poets Talk instead of Them (Archetype of Poet)

Khuraman Mursalieva
(Azerbaijan)

The creative force in a human probably develops from his first day of existence. As consciousness develops and a desire to talk about existence takes shape there arises the era of petroglyphs, parchments etc. The advance of discourse has given rise to the creation of the desire to express everything in words, aiming for further qualitative improvement of the communicated material. It has brought about the times of myths, legends, dastans and fables ... and their authors.

If the ancient artist re-creating the hunting scene in words felt the necessity to share information, he did not necessarily think about the social resonance of his creation, and perhaps was not concerned with its figurative representation. Later, Homer and other Ancient Greek poets, for instance, had a clearly manifested artistic purpose.

The comparison between modern and ancient poets is difficult to make. What is important about both of them is not how they wrote, the subject of their songs, but that they understood their "chosenness", their calling.

Interestingly enough, not only the understanding of the poet's role, his mission and his place in society has changed according to the epoch, but the attitude towards poets and their works has also changed greatly.

In the course of time poets began to contemplate their mission, and in different epochs and cultures, different nations did things in their own way. The relations between a poet and a power, a reader and a society, formed in accordance with the understanding of the poet's role.

In oriental literature the artist is not dissolved in the crowd, he sees himself in a higher position than a simple reader and powerful ruler. He teaches both, gives them lessons of justice, mercy and goodness ...

The perception of a poet as a prophet is widespread and traditional in European and Oriental poetry. The image becomes not only the reflection of a lyrical hero but the object of research and study.

Thus, for Mirza Shafi Vazeh[1] (Цветаева 1997[Tsvetaeva, 1997]) a poet is a judge sent from heaven into the word of folly. He does not only have a talent, but

---

1 Mirza-Shafi Vazeh (Azerbaijani: Mirzə Şəfi Vazeh, 1794-1852), also known as the "sage from Ganja", was an Azerbaijani poet, who continued the classical traditions of Azerbaijani poetry.

he is a bearer of light and wisdom ("Sometimes god send the poet as a judge to the word ruled by folly").

The notion of a "poet" is an archetype well-known in literature. From the very first "pages" of folklore we are able to discern the man behind the created text. In later centuries poetry has changed, became complex and extensive, while the man creating it has always comprehended his role. In the past he glorified his own pain and suffering, and gradually the common pain and common joy, dissolving in the created. In the course of time the poet perceived his mission and chosenness. He talks about painfully important things, about the soul which aims high and is revolted by injustice ...

Depending on time and space the attitude to poets is also has changed. In the East, the poet was most respected and considered to be a wise man, equal to the great ones who are in the earth. Sometimes he was a dervish, a saint, marked by god.

At first the poet's chosenness was emphasised by admirers, and when the poet became persecuted and suppressed, he began to oppose the people, who could not understand and value him, distinguish him from the crowd.

In the XXth century the poet has become more obsessed with the own profession. It is a difficult and contradictory time. The poet began to loudly express his hidden and cherished thoughts.

The image of the poet is encountered most frequently in Russian poetry of XXth century. The poetry of the Silver Age, comparable to the European Belle Époque, did not negate the sublime in the human, and at the same time, it emphasised the merely human and worldly in him. Although it is not the broken-hearted "prophet" of Pushkin, or the "citizen" of Nekrasov or the "vast bird" of Baudelaire, s/he, the poet, is the chosen still.

Thus, Blok, for instance, shows the poet as a man who does not lack mundane qualities. Despite his chosenness and out-of-the-wordliness, at times he is too earthly. In the *Poets* Block describes (sometimes excessively) the details of the poet's worldly affairs. They are the same as the people surrounding them, they drink, fancy women, quarrel, and "Когда напивались, то в дружбе клялись, / Болтали цинично и прямо …" ("When they drank, they swore on the eternal friendship, Chattered cynically and bluntly ...").

They have the certain "set" of sins. At the same time the author opposes the true poet to a philistine, an average man, to whom he addresses the following words:

Ты будешь доволен собой и женой,
You will be content with yourself and your wife,
Своей конституцией куцей,
And your curtailed constitution,

А вот у поэта – всемирный запой,
But a poet is having a worldwide binge,
И мало ему конституций!
And constitutions are not enough for him!

The philistine cannot obtain anything that the poet has; addressing a peevish reader, for example, he says, that poet has "...spits and rain clouds, and the golden age, But they inaccessible to you..." ("…И косы, и тучки, и век золотой / Тебе ж недоступно все это!..") The poet has the great gift to see the invisible and unattainable. Recognising his mission as the chosen one, "I am snowed under by god" ("Бог меня снегом занес"), at the same time he lives among and with people. Almost like Baudelaire's poem *Albatross*, where the poet is compared with the freedom-loving bird, flying above the skies:

The poet resembles this prince of cloud and sky
Who frequents the tempest and laughs at the bowman;
When exiled on the earth, the butt of hoots and jeers,
His giant wings prevent him from walking.
(Translated by William Aggeler)

Balmont says about poets: "We are more ancient than people. We are the arcs of other planets. We are the passages of a Spirit." However the discrepency obliges the poet to remember many things, and first of all to remember that "You are the deputy of god on earth, thus God should be in your words".

A poet for Marina Tsvetaeva is a chosen one, the life of whom is "a maned curve that a calendar couldn't foretell!" The poet is a naked soul accepting the pain of other's as its own. Later the same will be said by Constantin Simonov: "There is no other's sorrow, Who is afraid to confirm this, he either kills, perhaps, or is prepared to kill" (Чужого горя не бывает, / Кто это подтвердить боится, / Наверно, или убивает, / Или готовится в убийцы).

The personality of poet is of no less importance. The concept of the poet's personality by Tsvetaeva is as follows: birth, evolution and formation, death, or rather, the stepping into immortality, the highest category of eternity.

For Tsvetaeva, this theme concerns not only creativity but life as well. For her a poet is a phenomenon creating a past, and a present, but most of all a future. He is always connected to time, he is inside time; however not in the frame of his historical period. The picture is bigger. Being a contemporary, he "creates his time, not reflects it". For a poet cooperation with his time is irrelevant to his will. The concept of time for him is always higher and larger than its usual meaning. It is an aid in the travel between past, present and future, without stumbling into their borders.

Tsvetaeva differentiates between "poets with history" and "poets without history." Here the maximalism characteristic of Tsvetaeva's thinking clearly shows itself. She does not (does not want to) consider other occasions when poets would not fit into the given scheme. Nevertheless, how one should understand her classification? Who are the "poets with history?" They are those who otherwise can be called poets with a development; those who can become novel, unpredictable, and even unrecognisable. The poets with history discover themselves all the time through all phenomena and events they meet on their way. Their main goal is a self-discovery of the soul via constant journey forward. They don't glance back to see what they were yesterday. Their journey is quick and impetuous. Tsvetaeva compares them with flying comets, as rapid as flashes, bright and distinctive. They are the true creators of art as it should be, rushing to a certain goa, and having a theme relevant to the aim. In other words, they do not have external themes. Everything concerning the world is an area of their concern. For them indifference is an unacceptable state of mind. Thus the poets with history are the conscious creators of life, their "I" equals to the world: from a human to the universal.

Tsvetaeva compares "poets with history" with arrows, aiming high, but never knowing where they will land. The best example of such poets with history for Tsvetaeva is Pushkin – the matchless and unique figure. She deeply believes that Pushkin embodies all components of the true Poet. For her the Poet can be only a singular number. Stated otherwise, all poets of the past, present and future, are manifold components of one single unity. They all eventually serve the creation of the powerful image of the Poet.

Why did Tsvetaeva name Pushkin a poet with history? She did so because one can follow the formation and development of his artistic destiny. He always aims forward, for the unknown. Unlike Lermontov, who (according to Tsvetaeva) was born purely himself, Pushkin is a pioneer, going ahead and knowing nothing of his future calling. According to Tsvetaeva, poetry discovers a mystery hidden from the eyes, and it cannot be perceived all the time. She compares the process of the creation of poetry with dreams. It is "almost identical with dreaming", almost ... If a human being could control his dreams, then the analogy would be complete. In other words the process of the formation of poetry is a phenomenon not always dependant on the personal will. The thing which does not stop working in the human brain during sleep, that which stays vigilant, (sometimes bringing beautiful fairy-tale dreams, and nightmares at other times) is similar to poetry, which does not allow a soul to sleep, and which controls the thoughts and feelings of a poet. "The self of a poet is the devotion of his soul to some dreams, the visit of some dreams, the mysterious source that is not his will, but his whole nature" (Цветаева M. [Tsvetaeva M.] 1997:76). Tsvetaeva deduces the original "Law of peculiarity" of poets, their similarity and difference. "They are similar, since all without exception see dreams. They differ in what kind of dreams they see. Similar with their ability to dream, they differ by dreams ..." (Цветаева M. [Tsvetaeva M.] 1997:76).

Poets without history ... Who are they? They are stylites, sleeping and knowing all from birth. They are already born "with their own vocabulary and a maximum of originality". If Pushkin is a poet with development, Lermontov, according to Tsvetaeva, is a poet without history. In the early poem *Sail* we already see Lermontov. Pushkin is no less talented than Lermontov; however, it would be difficult to foresee the true greatness of Pushkin in his early verses. Lermontov, though, has already shown everything he will be. He, like all poets without history, came to the world not to learn, but with a sole purpose – to say. Tsvetaeva distinguishes poets without history among her contemporaries as well; the brightest among them are Akhmatova, Pasternak, and Mandelstam. As poets without history they all are purely lyric poets. In their turn, they do not let anything alien enter their world. (That was the opinion of Tsvetaeva in 1933. She could not have known then the poem of Akmatova *Requiem,* where pure lyric is barely present.) However, Tsvetaeva very describes poets without history very strangely. They are the poets of feeling. Theirs are purely lyric poetry, and it has always existed in feelings. Feeling is a closed circle, where the beginning and the end are on the same line, where everything is in itself.

Unlike the "poets with history" who never know what will happen to them, the "poets without history" always know that nothing happens to them, that they cannot and will not have anything else except for themselves.

The poet is a chosen one, however, he is not chosen for a replete, quiet life. He is chosen to take the pain of others as his own and bring it to other's attention as their own, his, hers, ours.

Contemplating the essence of poet, Tsvetaeva notices, that he "is an answer ... The poets' thing hit itself by itself, inquired of itself – by itself".

For Tsvetaeva the poet not only becomes a person who creates poetry, he becomes the object of research, of the problem of creativity. She studies him in dynamic terms, in development and in time, like a scientist. According to Tsvetaeva, "poetry is the language of gods! The gods don't talk, poets talk instead of them".

Tsvetaeva's concept of a poet goes for the period of Homer to modern days. The poet is a creator of not only of his own life, art, and destiny, but of contemporary life, in a sense. He is a witness, a chronicler, a critic, an observer, a philosopher, a law-maker, and most importantly, he is a person who cannot lie, nor to conceal the truth, nor tell something else. As our contemporary poet Olzhas Suleymenov said:

Не всем, кто ждал, помог,	I didn't help all, who was expecting it,
ведь я не бог,	I'm not a God
что в силах одинокого поэта?	what can a lone poet do?
На все вопросы не нашел	I couldn't find answers

ответа	for all questions
но людям я не лгал,	but I didn't lie
хотя и мог …	although I could ...

The poet is the one who creates, but he can create only being free (as writes Suleymenov: "Стих может быть и не верлибром, / Поэзия была б свободной" – " The verse may be not a free verse/ Would only poetry be free"). He would not sacrifice the truth for the rhyme, quite the opposite. He is a rebel inside, rushing to give back the gift sent to him from the heavens by the Creator, to return it and not keep it silent, since he is always against all and for all.

For Tsvetaeva the poet is an entity constant and universal for all times and places, one whose main goal is to be a conductor of knowledge, to nurture the given and "return it a hundredfold".

Pasternak, for example, considers a poet to be a vigorous contributor of primordial nature. He demands from the poet only two things: to have clarity of creative conscience and responsibility for eternity.

Tsvetaeva, talking about poet's soul, emphasises a quality most dear to her, which is the "soul – our ability for pain"; the process of poetry making, beginning from the inspiration to the realisation of it on paper, is pain. For that reason while a poet is a rebel (he sees and hears all), sometimes he wants to be deaf.

The greatness of a poet is measured by his immortality, since only the immortal ones are great.

"The death of a poet is unlawful. Violent death – is horrible. Pushkin (taken as collective noun) will die as many times, as he will be loved. All over again – in the loving one. And in every loving one – eternally" (Tsvetaeva M.1997: 302.), – was saying Tsvetaeva as if anticipating verses of Evtushenko about her destiny:

Есть лишь убийства на свете запомните,
Remember, there is only murders in the world,
Самоубийств не бывает вообще.
There is no suicide at all.

According to Tsvetaeva, the poet is not tender-hearted, but generous and royal by nature. He has a mark on him, "he is marked so much that his first and vital wish is to pass unnoticed". As usual, in categorical terms, Tsvetaeva gives the formula of the poet's mission:

Поэт не может служить власти –
потому что он сам – власть.
Поэт не может служить силе –
потому что он сам – сила.
Поэт не может служит народу –
потому что он сам – народ …

A poet cannot serve the power –
since he is the power himself.
A poet cannot serve the force since he the force himself.
A poet cannot serve a nation since he is a nation ...

The only thing a poet can serve is another, greater poet." (Цветаева М. [Tsvetaeva M.] 2000:165) The poet is one, who while was gifted with a great talent, was deprived of everything else: "Since, if you, a poet, has been given the voice, the rest has been taken,"

References

Цветаева М. Поэты с историей и поэты без истории. – Произведении в 7 томах. М.: 1997. том 2.

Tsvetaeva M., Poety s istoriey i poety bez istorii

Цветаева М. Произведении в 7 томах. М.: 1997. том 1.

Tsvetaeva M. v 7 tomax M:, 1997, tom 1

Цветаева М. *О поэте.* В кн.: Благословляю Вас. М., 2000.

Tsvetaeva M., O poete. *V kn: Blaqoslovlyayu Vas*. M., 2000.

Archetype and Symbol of a Wise Old Man

Sevinj Bakish
(United Kingdom)

The present essay discusses the notions of archetype and symbol from a *Jungian point of view*, applying Jungian ideas to literature, myths, religion and culture. We will try to define different symbols of the wise old man, giving particular attention to the figure of the Muslim saint and divine helper, Khidr,[1] whose image one can find in oriental folklore as well as in classic literature and thought.

The Jungian understanding of an archetype differs from the literary concept widely accepted in academic and general circles, although both use the same term as a base – *a primordial image*. If the latter notion reveals the very broad meaning of "first original model or prototype", the former relates to archetypes lacking a certain content and form within the collective unconscious. In his account Jung equates *the primordial image* with the Schopenhaueran *idea* (C.C. Jung 1989: 446). According to Jung "the archetype is essentially an unconscious content that is altered by becoming conscious and by being perceived, and it takes its colour from the individual consciousness in which it happens to appear" (C.C. Jung 1980: 5). The term *archetype* appears for the first time in the works of Philo Judaeus of Alexandria (13 BC-45 AD) and with reference to the *Imago-Dei*, Irenaeus (130-200), and *Corpus Hermeticum*.[2]

Although Plato did not mention the term, his notion of *eidos* as the immutable genuine nature of a thing, one of the eternal, transcendent forms apprehended by human reason, resembles the Jungian term. Jung finds the equivalent of archetypes also in Lévy-Bruhl's "représentation collective", which denotes symbolic figures in tribal worldviews that are no longer a content of the unconscious but are altered by tradition and transmitted with a collective content.[3]

According to Anthony Stevens, "Jung contemplating the apparently infinitive multiformity of symbolisms created by mankind so richly complicated, so ingeniously diverse, came to realise that they were in fact variations on a number of universally recurrent themes. The theory of archetypes attributed the universal occurrence of homologous symbols and myths to the existence of universal

---

1 The name of Khidr is spelled differently in English, German and Arabic, Persian and Turkish sources: al-Khadir, (al)-Khidr, Khezr, Khizr, Khidr, Hızır etc.

2 A collection of works by unknown authors dated before the end of the third century AD and attributed to Hermes Trismegistus, that greatly contributed to Gnosticism and alchemy.

3 See: C.C. Jung, The Archetypes and the Collective Unconscious, p. 5.

structures within the human mind" (Anthony Stevens 2002: 25). As such, Jung differentiated several of the most common archetypes: anima, animus, mother, trickster, child, hero, and wise old man. As this essay will further analyse the topic, it will become noticeable that the two latter archetypes are very close to each other, the latter being the cause of the hero's psychological transformation.

Another important characteristic of archetypes, deriving from their residence in the unconscious, is that they are not determined as to content but are determined only in form or function. As Jung puts it "... this term [archetype] is not meant to denote an inherited idea but rather an inherited mode of psychic functioning... In other words, it is a 'pattern of behaviour'" (C.G. Jung 1971: 518).

We should distinguish between the archetype as such and the images, ideas, feelings it gives rise to. What we are going to discuss is the *projection* made by the archetype into our consciousness, but not the archetype itself, which is hidden and invisible as such. Thus we shall discuss the expression of an archetype in everything which can be manifested in consciousness: myths, fairytales, folklore, religion, and literature among others. Rawer, less elaborated products of the archetype are found in dreams and visions. They also present a more individual, personal content.

One significant and popular expression of archetypes is in myths and a fairytales (V.V. Propp 1986:27-30), with their personages as representatives of different archetypes. Archetypes of the hero, the (divine) child, the chtonic (or great) mother, the trickster, the wise old man, and the virgin in various forms can be found in fairytales of all times and nations. Actually what fairytales and myths do is to concretise the archetypes, shape them into known universal forms, whereas the archetypes attribute them with certain recognisable qualities. For example, the wise old man can be portrayed as a dwarf, a little man, or an old one with a grey or white beard, he can have very youthful skin or be all crinkled; he can reside in the woods, underground, or nowhere. Very often he is closely connected with nature, greenery, or the woods. He can have a green dress, beard, or skin. However his knowledge, insight, wisdom, cleverness and intuition on the one hand, and moral qualities such as goodwill, and readiness to help on the other, makes his "spiritual" character recognisable in all the manifestation of the archetype. In Sufi literature the wise old man usually has the same external and internal features: he is usually portrayed as an old man with a long white beard in white robes and headdress. In the Sufi tradition Khidr is a divine helper sent to those on a spiritual quest by god. He is sometimes called the Verdant One, an allusion to his immortality, and/or his connection with nature.[4]

---

4 In Arabic Al-Khidr literally means "The Green". See: C.G. Jung, *The Archetypes and the Collective Unconscious*, p. 240; http://khidr.org/khidr-turkey.htm.

On the other hand, we should not forget the symbolic character of mythological or "story" figures, because according to Jung, the archetype itself, residing in the unconscious, cannot be revealed unaltered. The archetype represented in consciousness is modified by the individual (in the case of dreams and visions) and collective perception (in myths, fairytales and esoteric teachings). Thus in dreams and visions we encounter mostly personal symbols, whereas fairytales, myths and legends etc. represent the universal, what common to all of humanity, a nation, or a tribe. Later in *Memories* Jung gives the definition of archetype as "an irrepresentable, unconscious pre-existent form that seems to be the part of an inherited structure of the psyche and can therefore manifest itself spontaneously anywhere, at any time" (C.G. Jung, 1963: 380).

The concept of a symbol as an important part of Jungian theory is closely related to his notion of archetype. The Jungian understanding of a symbol, although framed by psychological perceptions, stays in a close relation with philosophical concepts.

The Russian philosopher and linguist, A. F. Losev, defines the concept of the symbol in philosophical and mathematical terms, not as the actuality of the thing, but rather as its sense and abstraction.[5] In his view a symbol is not the thing or actuality itself, but a creative *principle*, not a proposition but *supposition* about it. Mathematically speaking, a symbol is not just the function or reflection of a thing but the function expanded in an infinite series. The symbol has quite a substantial character, although it consists of irrational and transcendental data. In the structure of the symbol, images of the subject and denotation are presented like two opposing poles that are inconceivable without each other. Simultaneously they stand apart and thus create a field of tension, making a symbol meaningful and alive. A Jungian understanding of the symbol resembles the Losevian because of the explicit use of dialectic which both thinkers adapted individually: Losev through Hegel's works and Jung through Kant.[6]

5 See: A. F. Losev, *Problema Simvola I Realisticheskoe Iskusstvo* [*The Problem of the Symbol and Realistic Art*] (Moscow: Iskusstvo, 1976), and *Znak, Simvol, Mif,* [*Sign, Symbol, Myth*] (Moscow: Izdatel'stvo Moskovskogo Universiteta, 1982). Unfortunately there is no English translation of these works.

6 Hester McFarland Solomon showed the resemblance of the Hegelian dialectic and Jungian transcendent function in her essay 'Hegel's Dialectical Vision and The Transcendent Function', in Mary Ann Mattoon, *The Transcendent Function: Individual and Collective Aspects: Proceedings of The Twelfth International Congress for Analytical Psychology* (Einsiedeln: Daimon Verlag, 1993), pp. 123-142. On the other hand, the so-called terminology of Hegelian dialectic was ascribed by Hegel himself to Kant. See Hegel's preface to *The Phenomenology of Spirit*, trans. A.V. Miller (Oxford: Clarendon Press, 1977), §§50 and 51, pp. 29 and 30.

According to Jung a symbol is another form of mediator; in other words, it is the union of opposites, a synthesis of thesis and antithesis. The symbol represents a constant process without an end. Consequently, Jung always calls the symbol a living thing – living because of its perpetual fluidity and ability to transform: 'So long as a symbol is a living thing, it is an expression for something that cannot be characterised in any other or better way. **The symbol is alive as long as it is pregnant with meaning** [my emphasis]' (C.G. Jung 1971: 474.). As soon as the meaning is delivered, concretised, and defined for the perceptive mind, the symbol is dead. The following notion of living and dead symbols correlates with the Losevian understanding of the symbol as a mapping of an interminable series; consequently the symbol is living when new possible meanings are created, when these meanings are fluid and at the same time adapted to the particular mapping principle. The other important distinction derived from the uncertainty of the symbol is that it depends mostly on the individual's perception, on the attitude of the observing consciousness; that is, it lives up to the expectations and framework of the mind.

Therefore the symbol, according to Jung, has a twofold nature born out of conscious and unconscious materials. The unconscious relates it with the world of archetypes, which are not clearly defined, but nevertheless give it a mythological shaping. Therefore the symbol represents an archetype reconstructed on the conscious level. Symbols of the same archetype can vary depending on individual and collective cultural perceptions bearing at the same time the essential characteristics common to humanity as a whole. Archetypes can manifest themselves appealing to the conscious through symbols. The archetype of a spirit could be manifested as an wise old man, or a trickster, sometimes combining both opposing sides within one wo/man (for example in the image of crazy and wise Bahlul in the oriental narrative, or the old hag Baba-Yaga of the Russian folktale, and her equivalent, "kupegiren gary", in the Azerbaijani folktale, who is sometimes helpful, and sometimes evil to a fairytale hero etc.). Actually here we can observe the interplay between fairytale personages which also act as symbols because of their repeated materialisation and representation in human consciousness.

In the long list of symbols signifying the archetype of the wise old man, the figure of the Muslim saint and prophet Khidr (Khidr, Al-Khidr) stands out as the ultimate source of God's wisdom and compassion. Usually Khidr corresponds to the Christian prophet Elijah.[7] The cult of Khidr (The Verdant) is rooted in pre-Islamic lore, spread throughout the whole Muslim world from Turkey to India

7 See for references on Khidr: Haim Schwarzbaum, *Biblical and Extra-Biblical Legends in Islamic Folk-Literature* (Waldorf-Hessen: Verlag fur Orientkunde, 1982), pp. 17-18.

and to Sri-Lanka.[8] The great Azerbaijani poet and thinker, Nizami, wrote about Khidr's quest with Alexander the Great, which resulted in the immortality of the saint. The figure of Khidr probably goes as far back as the first known immortal Ziusudra of Sumerian literature. Apart from the fact that both figures are the products of the same Middle-Eastern area and Semitic culture (Non-Semitic Sumerian Ziusudra was later represented in Akkadian literature as Uta-napishti), some of the similar features in the stories and personages which will be analyse later add plausibility to the assumption.

The 18th Surah from the Qur'an was selected by Jung as an example of the archetypal narrative of a psychological process of transformation being so intense that it can be considered a sort of rebirth. Entitled 'The Cave', the Surah can be divided into three sections. It opens with the Judaeo-Christian legend of the seven sleepers in a cave and their prolonged state of sleep over many hundreds of years. This story is followed by an account of Moses and his companion (as Qur'anic commentators agree, Joshua ben Nun) and their encounter with an unnamed person. Moses wants to "learn" from this man, who reluctantly takes him on as a pupil. A series of events occurs which are handled by the teacher in a most unusual fashion, perplexing Moses. The third section of the Surah deals with the character of Dhul-Quarnayn (supposedly Alexander the Great) and his fight with the mythical monsters, Gog and Magog.

Jung's reading of the Surah claims that it is an "almost perfect" description of the process of a transformation of consciousness:

> The legend has the following meaning: Anyone who gets into that cave, that is to say [...] into the darkness that lies behind consciousness, will find himself involved in an – at first – unconscious process of transformation. By penetrating into the unconscious he makes a connection with his unconscious contents. This may result in a momentous change of personality in the positive or negative sense. The transformation is often interpreted as a prolongation of the natural span of life or as an earnest of immortality (C.G. Jung 1989: 135-136).

Khidr is the most famous and respected figure among people of the vast region from Africa to Sri-Lanka and the protagonist or helper in many folk tales and legends. The only reference to him in the Qur'an is in the 18th Surah, although he is not mentioned by name: he is described by Allah as "one of Our servants, whom We had endowed with Our grace and Our wisdom" (*The Koran Interpreted* 1955: 18:54-82). Below I give the summary of the story, which was completely quoted by Jung.

Moses with an unspecified servant in the Qur'an goes in search of a place where two seas meet. When they reach this place the servant sees that he has

8 There is a holy place for all Muslims of Sri-Lanka called Kataragama, where it is believed Khidr can appear to the blessed and most devoted pilgrims. See: http://kataragama.org/islamic.htm.

forgotted their fish, which have leapt back into the sea. Unaware of their destination they journeyed past the place. At their next stop, Moses asks his servant to bring the fish, and the servant realised, that he had forgotten it on the rock at the previous stopping, where the fish "took its way into the sea". Moses realises that they were seeking a rock. Back at the rock Moses meets a mysterious man, standing on the rock where they had lost the fish, and whom he asked to teach hin Allah's grace and wisdom. However the man answered that Moses lacked the patience to experience things he did not understand. After Moses' denial Khidr allowed Moses to come with him on a journey on one condition: he should not question Khidr's actions. During the journey Khidr did three things forbidden by Law: damaged a boat, killed a youth and raised up a nearly falling wall without asking permission or demanding payment for his labour. All three times Moses questioned Khidr, and the third last time, prior to parting with Moses, Khidr explains to him the wisdom of his so called "crimes" (C.G. Jung 1989: 137-138)

The Qur'anic narrative is seen by Jung as a symbolic description of the process of individuation, the rebirth of personality which sometimes takes place during an encounter with the archetype of an wise old man. For Nietzsche the corresponding figure is Zarathustra, for St. Paul is Christ, for Moses it is Khidr (*Ibid*, pp. 120, 121,122). The same encounter, perceived as an inner development, Jung states as a real form of individuation. In this case the wise old man can be seen as an inner voice which guides the person, or as an internal friend, or helper, or guru. Khidr usually fulfils the function of guru with Sufis, according to their accounts.[9] Hence on the one hand, the story of Moses and Khidr can be considered "real", where Moses, after meeting with Khidr, becomes wiser, since he comprehends a different type of wisdom – gnosis – and the psychological process can be called a transformation. On the other hand, the encounter can also be called imaginary, and that account explains many cases of meeting Khidr by Sufis or others in search of truth. This version is described by Jung in psychological terms as an inner development, that is, *individuation*.

One important aspect of the story of Moses and Khidr is the apparent crimes of Khidr. As Jung describes his actions "Khidr symbolises not only the higher wisdom, but also a way of acting which is in accord with this wisdom and **transcends reason** (C.G. Jung, *1989:*141)**"** [highlighted by me – S.B.]. The Jungian explanation of moral observations and adherence to the law shows the dual aspect of knowledge conceived by *pneumaticos* (spiritual man) and *sarkikos* (car-

9 Usually the guru of a Sufi disciple is the existing Sheikh of the order; however sometimes Khidr was a guru for a powerful Sufi like Ibn Arabi. See in: Shaykh Hazrat Azad Rasool, *Turning Toward the Heart: Awakening to the Sufi Way*, Fons Vitae, 2002; Patrick Franke, Begegnung mit Khidr: Quellenstudien zum Imaginaren im traditionellen Islam.

nal man). In Sufi literature these types are described as higher self and lower self. While the lower self, a "carnal soul" is awake in everybody, "potentially the situation can be changed, for ultimately man is not identical with his lower self. [...] Man's authentic existence is in the Divine; he has a higher Self, which is true ... The call comes: to flight, migration, a journey beyond the limitations of world and self," as one of the Western Sufis describes his path. Khidr guides Sufis and all travellers (who can be on a spatial or spiritual journey) giving them the knowledge and the help they require: in some cases, especially in folktales, he can show the right pathway, or give a lift to the place travellers want. For example in the Azerbaijani folktale *Ashik Garib* retold by the 19th century Russian poet, Lermontov, the protagonist of the story, hurrying to the wedding of his lover, is teleported by Khidr from Baghdad to Tiflis. Nevertheless, for Sufis help consist in gnosis, a mystical and deep knowledge of the Truth. Again the difference proves the Jungian assumptions of Khidr's function as guide for *sarkikos* and *pneumaticos* men.

Jung describes Moses as *pneumaticos* and his servant (Joshua ben Nun) as *sarkikos* man (C.G. Jung 1989: 138). The deeds and the mind of Moses are rational, thus Khidr's outwardly irrational actions are incomprehensible for him. As Jung puts it: "... the animal-ancestor and creator of life ["Nun, which is a name for fish" is "the father of the shadow, of the carnal man, who comes from the dark world of the Creator"] separates himself from the conscious man, an event which amounts to loss of the instinctive psyche" (*Ibid*, pp. 138, 139). Khidr comes to reunite the missing or lost part, thus again, he fulfils the role of the wise old man.

The connection between the fish and Khidr is obvious, but not only because he appears in the place where Moses and his companion lost the fish. Jung particularly pays attention to the transformation of the forgotten fish by Khidr and reminds the reader of the nourishing character of the transformative substance or deity in Christian and other mythologies: Christ as the bread, Osiris as the wheat etc.[10] In Sufi tradition Khidr is portrayed sitting on a small island, or staying on a fish. According to Indian Muslim and Buddhist beliefs "Khidr is at home in both worlds, the dark and the light, but above all he is master of the flowing River of Life in the Land of Darkness: he is at once the guardian and genius of vegetation and of the Water of Life."[11] This aspect of Khidr (along with others) – dwelling in darkness near water, relates him to Uta-napishti (or Ziusudra) from *The Epic of Gilgamesh* (or Bilgames in the Sumerian), which was mentioned by Jung,

---

10 (Beiruter Texte und Studien), Stuttgart: Franz Steiner Verlag, 2000, particularly the 3rd part. etc.

11 As one of the forms of transformation Jung describes the Mass as a rite of transformation, where the initiate should eat the body of Christ and drink the blood in order to be reborn as a Christian: the motif of transformation of personality.

quoting Vellers' *Chider* (1909) in his work (C.G. Jung 1989: 140). Other aspect connecting Khidr with Uta-napishti are their immortality and dwelling near the sea.

Uta-napishti is the sage who earned immortality for saving people and the ancient knowledge of arts and crafts during the deluge. Gilgamesh goes in search of Uta-napishti, so he could receive eternal life from the gods. Uta-napishti's place of dwelling is supposedly Dilmun, the Elysian fields of Sumerian literature, a place "far away, where the rivers flow forth" (*The Epic of Gilgamesh* 2000: 95, XI:204-205). This place, identified by scholars as "a remote island, where the rivers of Euphrates and Tigris welled up again from the deep" (*The Epic of Gilgamesh* 2000: p. xxxii) is seemingly the place of the quest of Moses, the *Ma'jma 'al-Bahrain*, as it is stated in the Qur'an.[12]

The allusions of the story of Moses and Khidr to *The Epic of Gilgamesh* are plentiful, not only in the characters but in story line as well, although most Islamic scholars deny such connections. The similarities between Khidr and Uta-napishti as wise old men archetypes are as follows. They are both given immortality by the god(s) for their wisdom. According to one legend Khidr became immortal after a conversation with the archangel Rafail.[13] Another more common tradition narrates a story in which he earned eternal life after drinking from the Water of Life (in the next paragraph I will show the parallels to this motif). They both are renowned for their wisdom. Uta-napishti brought to Gilgamesh knowledge lost before the deluge, and Khidr also brings hidden or lost divine wisdom to Moses. Another parallel is the archetypal situation of the encounter of the hero with the wise old man. Jung mentions Moses as "the man on a 'quest'" (C.G. Jung 1989:138), which is the perfect description of a hero. Gilgamesh, like Moses, is a hero on a quest. "In the epic Uta-napishti fills the role of the *quintessential wise man* [emphasis is mine- S.B] who knows the secrets of cosmos – as it were, the meaning of life. He and his knowledge, ancient and unique among men, are the end of Gilgamesh's long and arduous quest" (*The Epic of Gilgamesh* 2000: p. xlii).

The figure of Gilgamesh in turn is reminiscent of the image of Alexander from the Alexander Romances, the collection of legends concerning the mythical exploit of Alexander the Great. In one of them, retold by Azerbaijani poet and scholar Nizami (Nizami Ganjevi 2002.) in the 12th century, Alexander makes the prophet Khidr his guide in his search for the water of life, and it is Khidr who discovers a fountain, from which he drinks, becoming immortal. He keeps his

---

12 Through it may be a Mughal tradition, a Muslim Turkic dynasty, which blended with existing Buddhism.

13 See: Encyclopaedia of Islam, ed. Bosworth, Clifford Edmund, vol. 5 entry Idris, al-Khadir and Khwadja Khidr.

eye on the spring, while waiting for Alexander to meet him, but the well disappears from sight, and Khidr himself vanishes, realising that Alexander will not succeed in his quest. Nizami continues to relate another version according to the classical tradition of Ancient Greece. Here the quest is undertaken by Ilyas (biblical Elijah) and Khidr, who sit down by a fountain to eat their meal, consisting of dried fish. The fish falling into the water comes to life, and thus the seekers are made aware that they have found the Fountain of Life, from which both drink.

Nizami then proceeds to the Qur'anic version, and interprets the Fountain as one of Grace, the true Water of Life being the Knowledge of God. Nizami attributes Iskandar's failure to his eagerness, opposed to Khidr the wise man, who finds the Water of Life without seeking it.

The figure of Alexander the Great appears in the 18th Surah as well, where he is mentioned by the name of Dhul-Qarnayn (many Western and Islamic scholars agree in this matter). Jung, after reading K. Vollers *Chider,* where there is emphasis on the relationship of Alexander and Khidr, compares Moses and Alexander. Traditionally they were both "horned". Afterwards he notes: "Vollers does not hesitate to extend the comparison to that other pair of friends, Gilgamesh and Enkidu"(C. G. Jung 1989: 145). The comparison would be exact if Vollers (and Jung as well) had used the names Gilgamesh and Uta-napishti. The similarity between Khidr and Uta-napishti was mentioned before.

The image of Alexander the Great as it was portrayed in the *Alexander Romances* and in oriental tradition bears many similar to Gilgamesh's features. Gilgamesh is a son of a goddess and a mortal. Alexander considered Heracles his ancestor and wanted to become a god, as Heracles did through his *arête.*[14] Lowell Edmunds writes: the hero "is a mortal, subject to his mortality but through a divine *arête* within him, he surpasses the ordinary limits... *Arête* is "equal to immortality." The mortal who already has within him the capacity for arête attains to an immortal, divine quality". Below, quoting Aristotle, Edmunds continues ... "an excess of virtue can change a man into a god" (L. Edmunds 1995: 183-184), especially when man is a son of a god. As antique sources suggest, after conquering Egypt, Alexander was convinced that he was the son of the god, Zeus Ammon (E. Badian: 121-122).

The above mentioned poem of Nizami consists of two parts; the first part of it *Sharafname* (*The Book of Honour*) narrates the triumphant battles of Alexander, the second *Ikbalname* (*The Book of Wisdom*) describes his wisdom, which he acquired after meeting Khidr, all real achievements which people will remember

---

14 "According to the Isaba, 882, he was given immortality after a conversation with his friend the archangel Rafail in order to establish the true worship of God on earth and to maintain it". See: http://kataragama.org/islamic.htm.

forever. In the following statement Plutarch describes Alexander as an ideal wise ruler: "But as he believed that he came as a heaven-sent governor to all and mediator to the whole world, those whom he could not persuade to unite with him, he conquered by force of arms and he brought together into one body all men everywhere, uniting and mixing them in one great loving-cup …" (Plutarch: 210)

In the beginning of the standard version of *The Epic of Gilgamesh* Gilgamesh is also portrayed as a wise king and a brave warrior who achieved his glory through the mediation of the wise old man:

> He saw what was secret, discovered what was hidden…
> Who [knew]…was wise in all matters…
> Surpassing all other kings, heroic in stature…
> A mighty bank, protecting his warriors…
> A wild bull of Lugalbanda, Gilgamesh, perfect in strength…
> (The Epic of Gilgamesh 2000: 1-2)

In the last line we encounter a constant epithet of Gilgamesh, "wild bull", which we find in the more ancient Sumer version of *The Epic of Bilgames* in variations as "the great bull", "the wild ox", almost certainly because of his relation to the Wild Cow-goddess Ninsun. This is quite an apparent allusion to the "horned" Alexander, who considered himself to be the son of the Bull-Ammon. Another interesting point is, that the purpose of the heroic battle of Bilgames with Huwawa (Akkadian Humbaba) described in the Sumerian epic is to make his name live forever, "since no man can escape life's end" (*Ibid*, p.151, lines 4, 5), which is the equivalent of the Alexandrian arête.

Alexander and Gilgamesh both were in search for immortality; both reached the end of the land in their quest. Both "saw the deep": one of Alexander romances narrates the episode of his descent to the sea-floor enclosed in a glass vessel. There is the parallel motif in the *Epic of Gilgamesh*, where Gilgamesh in order to obtain the sea-plant, the source of youth, dives to the bottom of the sea. At the end of their days, after encountering the sage (Khidr in the case of Alexander, and Uta-napishti with Gilgamesh) they both achieved not immortality, but wisdom, and both become a kind of deity.

The numerous parallels between the two images are derived possibly from the oriental conception of the ideal sovereign, which was already known in the Sumerian period. In the hymn of Shulgi of Ur "he [the king Shulgi] portrays himself as the ideal ruler: a rare combination of sage, soldier, sportsman, diviner, diplomat, patron of learning, and happy provider of all good things for his land and people" (S.N. Kramer, *Shulgi of Ur: A Royal Hymn and a Divine Blessing* in http://links.jstor.org/sici?sici=0021-6682%281967%292%3A57%3C369%3ASOUARH%3E2.0.CO%3B2-S). The ancient Greek culture (specifically Plato's and

Aristotle's ideas) in which Alexander was raised had a similar tradition[15] which most probably came from eastern customs.[16] This tradition continues in oriental folklore (The image of king Bahram),[17] in classic literature and later Persian literature (*Shah-name* Firdowsi); in rgw oeuvres of Nizami such as *Seven beauties*, *Xosrov and Shirin* and especially *Iskandarname* it reaches its apogee. *Iskandarname* consists of two books, *Sharafname* and *Iqbalname*. The poem narrates the three stages in Alexander's life; in the first part *Sharafname* (literally the *Poem of Glory*) Alexander is in the search of fame and glory and thus conquers the known world; the second part Iqbalname (literally the *Poem of Blessedness*) narrates Alexander's quest for truth and knowledge, which results in Alexander's acquiring divine philosophy, that is, monotheistic religion. The difference between the mythological Alexander (as he is portrayed in Alexander Romances and Nizami's poems) and the previous kings, in that Alexander completes his quest with the help of the wise old man and accordingly excels other kings in fame and wisdom. Thus Khidr, performing the role of the wise old man helps Alexander to gain hidden knowledge, to fulfil his real potential and his destiny, in other words to become not immortal, but wise.

Showing parallels among Moses, Alexander, and Gilgamesh we established the pattern of an archetypal heroic quest in search of wisdom. All heroes on their quest (the parallels can be broadened to the romances and epics of the European Middle Ages) meet the wise man, who gives them a clue, shows them the right path, or in case of defeat explains to them the highest wisdom gained from their defeat, which at the end becomes the hero's highest achievement, such as in the stories of Gilgamesh and Alexander.

The wise old man, the name given by Jung to the archetype of the mediator between god and people, is a complex figure. First of all, as Jung states "if the name "Lucifer" were not prejudicial it would be very suitable for this archetype" (C.G. Jung, *1989:* vol. 9, part 1: 37). On the one hand, the name of Lucifer indicate his connection with light (in a Latin means "light-bearer"), but on the other hand he is the personification of evil, and "... the devil in Christian mythology

---

15 Arête (Greek: ἀρετή) – meaning excellence of any kind, usually translated as "virtue". Different époques of Greek culture had different perception of arête.

16 Plato's *Republic* stated an ideal paradigm for a just ruler, and Aristotle's *Politics* for the rule of reason.

17 Xenophon, the Greek soldier and historian, wrote the biography of the Persian Emperor, Cyrus the Great, potrarying him as a just ruler for the edification of the Greeks. According to Richard Frye "he [Cyrus] became the epitome of the *great qualities expected of a ruler in antiquity*, and he assumed heroic features as a conqueror who was tolerant and magnanimous as well as brave and daring. *His personality as seen by the Greeks influenced them and Alexander the Great ...*" (Encyclopaedia Britannica Article).

represents the shadow" (C.G. Jung, *1989:* vol. 9, part 1: 322). The name of Lucifer indicates how the image could convert into its contrast, therefore, the relativity of good and evil.

In *The Phenomenology of the Spirit in Fairytales*, Jung further explains his position. He says that first of all, the archetype of the wise old man is a personification of spirit, or god. Consequently Jung explains the expression of the Khidr's representation in Islamic tradition as "The Angel of Face" being "the symbolisation or "incarnation" of Allah"(C. G. Jung, *1989:* 145). Next, Jung reiterates in almost all his works "the uncertainty of all moral valuation, the bewildering interplay of good and evil" (C. G. Jung, *1989:217)* and that the realm of god is "beyond good and evil" of human values.[18] Thus he explains the appearance of this archetype in different fairytales as good or evil spirits. Just like the deeds of Khidr travelling with Moses could be considered evil by the standards of a common man, the actions of malevolent spirits or creatures have a beneficial effect at the end of stories.

The core of the problem in reality is the comprehension of knowledge and/or truth by a carnal and a spiritual man. The collection of Arabian fairy tales "Thousand and One Nights" being mere entertainment narrative for a carnal man, for a Sufi was a manual for achieving gnosis, knowledge.[19] This tradition that the same text could be considered as sacred or profane depending on interpretation had deep roots in Oriental literature. Myths were once sacred texts, but losing the clue to their symbolical interpretation, they began to be considered as fiction, which is also the modern understanding of this word. The Russian scholar, Vladimir Propp convincingly showed the mythological roots of fairytales; consequently through time they lost some links in the plot and become fairytales (See: V.Propp 1969). The fairytale images in the "disguise" of dragons, dwarfs, and giants, different good and bad old men, mermaids and witches etc. hide very old archetypal features. In fairytales bad personages actually can bring good outcomes and vice versa.

The archetype of the old man, which lost its sacred meaning of hidden mystical knowledge transformed later into a dual figure. Jung gives an example of Merlin, who "seeming, in certain of his forms, to be the incarnate of good and in others an aspect of evil." (*Ibid*, p. 227)

---

18 Chapter vi in: http://www.iranica.com/articles/bahram-the-name-of-six-sasanian-kings.

19 "Good and evil are feeling-values of human provenance, and we cannot extend them beyond the human realm. What happens beyond this is beyond our judgment: God is not to be caught with human attributes. Besides, where would the fear of God be if only good- i.e., what seems good to us – were to be expected from him?" in C.G. Jung, 'A Psychological Approach to the Dogma of the Trinity' (1942), CW 11, *Psychology and Religion: West and East,* pp. 107-200.

In my view, the reason why the figure of Khidr did not transform into the rigid fairytale personage with explicit and controversial opposites is that this image is still alive for believers in modern Islamic tradition as the guardian and mediator of sacred gnosis, thus keeping his dialectical nature.

Strictly speaking the Jungian archetype is an ahistorical and acultural concept, since it dwells in unconscious and is irrelevant to the social context. It becomes historical when it is filled with historical content and becomes cultural when it is loaded with cultural tradition. For example, Alexander characterises the archetype of the ancient Greek hero of the 4th century BC. But his image also bears ahistorical and acultural, universal features which can identify him with any hero of any time. Moreover, it can be identified with any person as well (a modern time hero), as James Joyce showed in "Ulysses", correlating Blum with Odyssey.

The archetype is a living concept, living because its attributes, and its content always shift, always change. In fairytales and myths the wise old man can appear as a green man, a dwarf, a youthful god, cabiri in the ancient Mediterranean beliefs, Hermes Trismegistos in alchemy, or as Zarathustra for Nietzsche. Of course, this changeability is related to the ambivalent character of this archetype. At the same time, the archetype has some rigid forms, which help to recognise and differentiate them. As Jung elucidates, archetypes "require dialectical procedure" (C.G. Jung, *1980:* 40).

In "Nietzsche's Zarathustra" there is an extensive report, given by Professor T.Reichstein, about the functions and different representations of the archetype of the wise old man in different cultures. On the one hand the wise old man possesses an extraverted side: as judges, lawgivers, or teachers and introverted side. On the other side: as sorcerers, priests, initiators; furthermore "he can become the embodiment of the supernatural or the deputy of God or Demon." (C.G. Jung 1988: 301)

In those stages of civilizations where the inner and outer world are not separated (perhaps not yet distinguished by the primeval human mind), the extraverted and introverted aspects of the wise man appear in single individual." (*Ibid*, p.301) I suggest that more importantly the division of the wise old man into two aspects is connected with logical and intuitive thinking. The former comes from man's logic, his understanding of life, rooted in practice and experience. The latter is derived from the connection with the divine, with the collective unconscious, one would say with a god. It is something that cannot be explained and understood by logic.

Khidr has exactly that function in Islamic culture. "In the most civilised as in the primitive form, the outer and inner aspects of the wise old man appear together in one individual. The most highly developed form is that of the inspired teacher, called the "Guru" in the East." (*Ibid*, p.302)

Now returning to the analysis of the 18th Sura from Jungian perspective, we can make the following assumptions. The Prophet Moses can be explained as an extraverted and mostly logical aspect of the wise old man, the teacher, the giver of the new order of things, the rational thought of God. His commands are usually explainable. Khidr is an introverted and intuitive aspect, the soul of God possessing gnosis; something unexplainable, but nevertheless, his advice and actions one must follow in order to reach the goal. Logically thinking and therefore submitted to the law, Moses cannot see the reason of Khidr's actions. Moses is a prophet and has brought the word and the law of God to people. He symbolises the logical and visual sides of knowledge that is, thinking and sensation. Khidr's deed is born from gnosis, the intuitive side. Khidr appears where there was a fish. He is a personification of the fish, which symbolises the collective unconscious, the inner, intuitive connection with god. This aspect of Khidr also explains why in oriental fairy and folktales (*dastans*), he is a protector of lovers. In oriental literature, love being the strongest feeling, is given by God to chosen ones. In the Sufi tradition love also symbolises the human desire of God.

It is not surprising, therefore, that the archetype of the wise old man in the East took the form of the most reverent and friendly figure of Khidr, who according to some Quran commentators (Al-Tabari, Al-Bukhari, Al-Suri) was the saint – awliya, and/or a prophet – nabi.[20] Khidr accumulates all that is necessary for the archetype qualities: elusiveness, on the one hand, with many accounts of his existence witnessed by Sufis, and even ordinary people.[21] The figure is also connected with the collective unconscious, a notorious representation in human consciousness. But most importantly, as can be derived from the previous statements, it is purely psychological in nature, which explains Khidr's above mentioned qualities. The cult of Khidr combining the practical with gnosis makes him a perfect example of the archetype (and symbol in this case) as the living process, as Jung said in *Psychological Types*: "It gives a co-ordinating and coherent meaning both to *sensuous* [emphasis is mine – S.B] and to *inner* [– S.B] perceptions …" (C.G. Jung, 1989 vol. 6: 445).[22]

The present essay, inspired by Jung's scrupulous psychological research of the 18th Sura, analysedthe archetype and symbol of the wise old man and his effect on the hero through the study of the image of Khidr. Closer examination of the connections to another important archetype, the hero on a quest, will be the material of a future paper.

---

20 See, for example: http://ishk.net/sufis/lessing_ commandingself.html.

21 See: http://khidr.org/khidr.htm and http://sunnah.org/ msaec/articles/khidr.htm.

22 See: Warren S. Walker and Ahmet E. Uysal, *An Ancient God in Modern Turkey: Some Aspects of the Cult of Hizir*, in Journal of American Folklore 86 (1973), Lubbock: Texas Tech University, taken from http://khidr.org/hizir.htm; also Asiff Hussein, *Kataragama – The Land of Khidr*, in Sunday Observer, 31/08/2003 taken from http://www. sundayobserver. lk/2003/08/31/fea17.html.

References

Anthony Stevens, *Archetype Revisited: an updated natural history of the self*, 2nd ed-n London: Brunner/Routledge, 2002.

Jung, C.C., *Definitions,* in *Psychological Types,* in Collected Works vol.6, London: Routledge & Kegan Paul, 1989 (In all future references CW stands for Collected Works)

Jung, C.C., *The Archetypes and the Collective Unconscious*, in CW vol. 9, part 1, 2-nd ed-n, London: Routledge & Kegan Paul, 1980

Jung, C.G., *Nietzsche's "Zarathustra": notes of the seminar given in 1934-1939 by C.G. Jung,* edited by James L. Jarrett in 2 volumes, Princeton, N.J: Princeton University Press, 1988

Jung, C.G., *Foreword to Harding: "Woman's Mysteries",* in CW v.18, London: Routledge & Kegan Paul, 1971

Jung, C.G., *Memories, Dreams, Reflections*, Recorded and ed. Aniela Jaffé. trans. Richard and Clara Winston, New York: Pantheon,1963

Badian, E., 'The deification of Alexander the Great' in *Alexander the Great: Antique and Modern Perspectives* edited by Joseph Roisman Lexington, Massachusetts: D.C. Heath and Company, 1995

Edmunds, L., 'The Religiosity of Alexander' in *Alexander the Great: Ancient and Modern Perspectives*, edited by Joseph Roisman Lexington, Massachusetts: D.C. Heath and Company, 1995

Ganjevi, Nizami, *Iskandarname*. Azernesr: Baki 2002. (Unfortunately there is no English translation of this book, except for first part of it *Sharafname* translated and published in 1889.

Lamborn Wilson, Peter, *Introduction to the Sufi Path* in http://www.hermetic.com/bey/intro-sufi.html.

http://khidr.org/khwaja-khadir.htm.

Plutarch, 'The Mixing of Greeks and Barbarians', in Alexander the Great: Antique and Modern Perspectives.

Kramer, S.N., *Shulgi of Ur: A Royal Hymn and a Divine Blessing* in http://links.jstor.org/sici?sici=0021-6682%281967%292%3A57%3C369%3ASOUARH%3E2.0.CO%3B2-S.

The Koran Interpreted, trans. A.J. Arberry London: George Allen & Unwin, 1955

The Epic of Gilgamesh, trans. by A. George, Penguin books: London, 2000.

Propp, V.V., Istoricheskie Korni Volshebnoj Skazki, (The Historical Roots of a Fairy-tale), Iz-vo Leningradskogo universiteta, 1986.

Propp, V., *Morfologiya skazki*, Moskva: Nauka, 1969 (in Russian).

Part 4
Archetypes in Language and Translation

The Role of Translation in the Integration of Western/Christian Archetypes in Contemporary Arabic – Islamic Literature

Saddik M. Gohar
(UAE)

Due to the efforts of literary translators and missionaries, major Western / Christian archetypes have been integrated into Arabic literature written by Muslim writers and disseminated in traditional Islamic communities in the post WWII era. Such a process of adaptation, which includes the recollection, citation, rephrasing, and re-writing of Western / Christian legacies to fulfill indigenous purposes, is part of the issue of hybridity and interculturation which characterizes the contemporary experience of political and cultural globalization. By assimilating Christian archetypes (like Christ) and religious narratives (like the crucifixion and resurrection) as well as related literary traditions into Arabic-Islamic literature, post-war Arab writers ironically rediscover their religious and nationalist myths and ancient Islamic legends, particularly the historic narrative of al-Hussein, the martyr of Karbalaa, which shaped the cultural history of the Middle East and the Arab world.

Preface: Translation in Ancient Arab-Islamic History

Translation in the Arab-Islamic world is not a modern phenomenon, but one that is deeply rooted in Islamic culture and history. The Abbasid dynasty which lasted for two centuries (750-935) witnessed a wide interest in translation, particularly during the reign of the caliph al-Ma'mun in the beginning of the ninth century. Before he claimed the throne, al-Ma'mun, whose mother was of Persian descent, ruled as the governor of Khurasan (Eastern Iran) in the city of Merv from 809 to 818. There he became acquainted with the Banu Musa family members, who were interested in science and medicine. When al-Ma'mun became caliph, the Banu Musa were given paramount positions in the new government.

As part of the rising elite who enjoyed political and financial privileges in the court, they affirmed their social prestige by providing unlimited support to translation. Due to the great efforts of the Abbasid court and the personal enthusiasm of the Banu Musa family, the chief patrons of science and knowledge, translation became fashionable in ruling circles. According to the thirteenth – century biographer Ibn

Khallikan, the Abbasid emperors encouraged the translation of literary, scientific, medical, and engineering books because" their noble ambition was to master the ancient sciences and the books of the classical scholars and they devoted themselves to this project". They sent agents to the Byzantine Empire to bring the latest publications on science and art to be translated into Arabic (Kennedy: 2004; 255).

Combining their political role with a keen interest in the cultural heritage of other nations, the Abbasid caliphs attracted translators from distant lands and far off places by offering generous rewards.

The Abbasid court in Baghdad encouraged the production of reliable and elegant translations which required considerable expertise. As the leading and discerning patrons of the translations of scientific texts, the Banu Musa paid a monthly salary of five hundred dinars for top-quality translators, providing them with accommodations and other amenities. This sum was equivalent to the salary of a senior member of the bureaucracy or the high-rank officers in the army. As a result, qualified translators flocked to Baghdad, such as Hunayn ibn Ishaq (d.873), a Christian from the Ancient Arab city of Hira in southern Iraq, to offer their services. Ibn Ishaq was a master of Greek, Syriac, and Arabic; therefore, he was assigned the mission of visiting the Byzantine Empire in search for manuscripts and medical texts, notably texts by Galen and Hippocrates.

Qusta ibn Luqa (Constantine, son of Luke – d.922) was a native Greek speaker and a famous translator living in the city of Baalabak (ancient Heliopolis) in Lebanon who came to Baghdad with Greek manuscripts as potential texts for translation. Like Ishaq ibn Hunayn, who wrote a book entitled **History of Physicians** in addition to his work as a translator. Ibn Luqa produced original works on medicine, nutrition, sexual pracitces, astronomy, and Euclid's geometry. In addition to Hunayn ibn Ishaq and Qusta ibn Luqa, a third translator came from the dusty deserted town of Harran located in southern Turkey on the Syrian border. The third of the great translators appointed by the house of Banu Musa was Thabit ibn Qurra, the Sabian (b. 826). As a Sabian, ibn Qurra preserved Hellenic literary culture and was a master of Greek, Syriac, and Arabic. He was presented to the court of the caliph al-Mu'tadid (892-902) who was himself a speaker of Greek and had a keen interest in natural sciences. Ibn Qurra gained a reputation and much respect as the translator of key books on mathematical and astronomical sciences. Due to his expertise in the field of mathematics, he was a distinguished translator and author of several treatises on topics as conics, which were admired by foreign scholars and scientists (Kennedy: 2004; 256).

Translation, Inter-Cultural Dialogue and The Attitude toward the West

During the first confrontations between the Arab world and western imperialism (during the era of the Crusades), Arab scholars dealt with Europeans as colonizers who came to annihilate their countries. Nevertheless, they reveal an admiration for the science and culture the western invaders brought to the East (Gohar: 2008; 376). Such an ambivalent attitude provided the first spark that gave an impetus toward the translation of western works into Arabic. Historically, beginning with the eighteenth century, scholars and writers from different Arab-Islamic countries have encouraged the translation of western arts and sciences which were supposed to lead to the establishment of an intercultural dialogue with western civilization. Even during the early colonial period and due to an awareness of western culture through the translated texts of western arts and sciences (besides the translation of the Bible by western missionaries), prominent Muslim thinkers, such as Mohamed Abdo and Refaa al-Tahtawi, worked toward the dismantling of the barriers separating the Arab world and the West.

In the first half of the 20th century, Taha Hussein and Tawfik Al-Hakim argue that in case the Arabs "are not able to establish an Oriental civilization, at present, they should follow the example of Turkey and simply become part of the European nations." (Hussein: 1938; 2). They point out that "since Arabic-Islamic civilization has been influenced for a long time by the Mediterranean Sea and its culture, an attempt should be made to build bridges with Europe" (Hussein: 1938; 3). Apparently, the prominent Arab-Muslim scholars mentioned above defended western culture and scientific achievements, calling for the Arabs to be assimilated into a global civilization. For example, Taha Hussein points out that Arab culture is not only Islamic, but also has its deep roots in the Mediterranean civilizations of the Greeks and the Phoenicians. Hussein argues:

> Is Egypt East or West? Is the Egyptian mind Eastern or Western in its imagination, perception, comprehension, and judgment? More succinctly put: which is easier for the Egyptian mind to understand, a Chinese or a Japanese or an English or a Frenchman? The Egyptian mind has had no serious contact with the Persian mind. The Egyptian mind has had regular, peaceful and mutually beneficial relations only with Greece and the Near East. In short it has been influenced from the earliest times by the Mediterranean Sea and the peoples living around it. (Hussein: 1938; 4).

Through mutual interaction and cultural entanglements with western civilization, the Arab world, according to Hussein, would rediscover itself by restoring what the Arabs had given to the West during the golden era of Islamic civilization. Furthermore, the ambivalent attitude toward western civilization which could be traced back to the era of the European Crusades, manifests itself in the Arabic literary tradition since the late 19th century until the 1940's. In these works the West is depicted as the hegemonic power against which the Arab poet/writer attempts to express himself and emphasize his own culture and identity. Ironically, the impact of the West on the Arab world, due the translation movement and other factors, reached a culmination during the era of decolonization and Arab nationalism. Consequently, the ambivalence toward Western civilization characterizing the literary works of the pre-WWII era is replaced by a tendency to be fully involved in the western cultural project.

Due to a variety of reasons, among them the state of stagnation that dominated Arab culture for decades, young poets in the era of decolonization initiated a local poetic tradition aiming to break the state of complacency integral to Arab culture. Moreover, in the aftermath of WWII, the barren cultural situation and the miserable political conditions in the Arab world, encouraged a young generation of Arab poets to turn westward for cultural nourishment and inspiration.

Though literature written in indigenous languages is often concerned with the construction of national and cultural identities, the situation in the Arab world in the post WWII era pushed modernist Arab poets toward the West in an attempt to develop a poetics of hybridity able to confront the new challenges emerging in the region. Discovering that the Arabic literary heritage had nothing to offer the Arab world in an era of national turmoil and international transformations, Muslim Arab poets, such as Badr Shaker Al-Sayyab, Abdul-Wahhab Al-Bayati, and others turned toward the West for cultural nourishment. Adapting **Christian narratives** to fulfill indigenous purposes, they were attracted to Western literature, particularly T.S. Eliot's critical and literary heritage.

M.M. Badawi argues that "the interest of Arab poets and critics in Eliot after the Second World War, made Eliot appear in Arabic literary canon as a synonym for modern English poetry" (Badawi: 1975; 2). Eliot's impact on the Arabic literary scene in the post WWII era coincided with the emergence of political movements and military coups whose aim was to undermine the foundations of an old system and establish a new order. Thus, Arab poets from different countries were mostly interested in Eliot's narratives of death, rebirth, and salvation because they found in them reflections of the socio-political situation in the Arab world in the aftermath of the Palestinian tragedy in 1948, and the rise of tyrannical regimes in the region. (Gouhar: 2011; 48).

Therefore, by the end of WW II, Eliot's literary heritage constituted the major source of influence of western literature on contemporary Arab poets. Being interested in Eliot's poetry, modernist Arab poets responded passionately to Eliot's masterpiece, **The Waste Land**, establishing an analogy between the stagnant situation in the Arab world in the aftermath of WW II and the wasteland myth in Eliot's poem. As representative of the post-war revolutionary spirit, the modernist Arab poet seeks salvation for the Arab people in western traditions, incorporating Eliot's Christian narratives and cultural myths:

The wasteland that is his society is thirsty for rain. The barrenness that is his nation is longing for fertility. But Tammuz has to be killed by the wild boar and suffer the darkness of the underworld before he returns to the wasteland in spring, filling it with abundance and fertility. The Phoenix has to be burnt down completely before it can rise again from its own ashes. Prometheus has to suffer the sharp beak of the vulture as a price for the divine fire he has given mankind. Sinbad, like Ulysses, has to suffer loss in alien lands before he comes into his own. Only through the cross is Resurrection possible (Boullata: 1976; XII).

Like Eliot, who passed through the experience of the First World War, the Arab poet witnessed the catastrophic ramifications of the Palestinian tragedy and the emergence of post-colonial regimes and puppet governments responsible for the curses and defeats which affflicted the Arab world. Explicitly, Eliot's wasteland narratives fit the situation in the Arab countries during the post WWII era, where an entire order of things had crumbled. The theme of the barren land waiting for the rain of fertility restored through blood, death, and resurrection attracted the new generation of Muslim Arab poets led by Al-Sayyab and Al-Bayati. The political upheavals in the Arab world in the aftermath of WWII which threatened to dismantle the roots of Arab culture, find an echo in Eliot's wasteland narratives. Therefore, in post WWII Arabic poetry, Eliot's discourses about a fallen civilization are appropriated and recycled to fit into local political contexts to serve indigenous interests. Arab poets incorporate Eliot's modernism and literary heritage, utilizing symbols, myths and motifs inherent to Western thought and alien to the core of Islamic traditions. In other words, western modernism opened wide horizons for the WWII generation of Arab poets to appropriate Eliot's poetic strategies in order to fit the drastic transformations in the region (Gouhar, 2012; 69).

The Use of Western/Christian Narratives in Arabic-Islamic Poetry

The translation of T.S. Eliot's literary and critical works, particularly his great poem, **The Waste Land,** into Arabic, immediately after WWII, was considered as a turning point in modern Arabic literature and culture. For a variety of reasons, Eliot's theory of tradition and his modernist techniques dominated the poetic scene in the Arab world after the Second World War. In **Studies in Arabic Literature**, Shmuel Moreh argues:

> Shakespeare, Shelley and the Romantic poets of the West did not exert so deep an influence on Arabic poetry as did T.S. Eliot who almost cut it entirely from its roots. Eliot's work changed the form and technique of Arabic poetry as well as its contents to an extent that has no precedent in the whole history of Arabic poetry (Moreh: 1976; 216).

Attracted to Eliot's criticism of a dying civilization, Arab poets found a reflection of their own predicament in Eliot's modernist poetry. Salma Khadra Jayyusi argues that Arab poets were attracted to Eliot basically because they found in his "implicit use of the fertility myth [in "The Waste Land"] an expression of ultimate love and an emphasis on potential of self-sacrifice." She points out:

> It was the idea of the cycle of sacrificial death that leads to rebirth which attracted them most. From the mid-fifties to the early sixties, Arab poets repeatedly drew an analogy between the aridity of Arab life after the 1948 disaster in Palestine and the aridity of the land in the fertility myth, saved from complete waste only by death and the spilling of blood, analogous to the falling of rain over a parched land (Jayyusi: 197; 724).

After the Palestinian tragedy in 1948 and the rise of dictatorial regimes in the Arab world in the 1950's, the image of the wasteland waiting for resurrection became a reflection of the state of collapse and desolation in which the Arab world was plunged. Due to Eliot's impact, Arab poets employed myths and symbols obtained from Eastern and Western sources, modern and ancient history, in order to express the pains and hopes of a nation shattered by recurrent defeats and dominated by political corruption. The poetic techniques used by the Arab poets who came under Eliot's influence differ from one poet to another and from one period to another. For example, Eliot's method of deploying speech-like language or allusions, used by Arab poets in the 1950's gave way to the use of personae and masks in the 1960's, which paved the way for engagements in textual structures that gave way in turn to further experimentation, which resulted in poems of profound complexity.

Inspired by Eliot's myths and archetypal images, poets like Al-Sayyab, Abdul-Sabur, and Al-Bayati struggled to liberate Arabic culture and literature from fossilized traditions and a stagnant heritage. Therefore, modernist Arabic poetry, in the post WWII era, was characterized by an increasing use of Christian and western legends, reshaped to integrate narratives of contemporary significance in the Arab world. Further, modernist Arab poets were fascinated by Eliot's view of tradition, his conservative religious thinking, his resourceful poetic techniques, and his use of myth. Exploiting Eliot's rich traditions of poetic symbolism, Arab poets utilized western legends, Christian symbols and western archetypal figures like Prometheus and Sisyphus to articulate native issues integral to the Arab world in an era of great transformations.

As a result of integrating Eliot's theory of tradition, modernist Arab poets were able to discover their own indigenous figures in Arab history, like Sinbad,

Antara, the pre-Islamic Bedouin warrior, and Al-Hallaj, the Persian Sufi who was slaughtered by the Abassid rulers in Baghdad in the tenth century, due to his religious beliefs. Nevertheless, unprecedented attention has been given in modernist Arabic poetry to the hardships, sacrifices, and martyrdom of Jesus Christ. For example, the Iraqi poet, Al-Sayyab, attempts to draw explicit parallels between his own suffering under tyrannical Arab regimes and the torture of Christ on the cross. Discussing the use of Christian motifs in Arabic poetry, S. Moreh argues:

> The favorite symbol is Christ to symbolize the poet who sacrifices himself for his country and people. Other symbols connected with the crucifixion are used, such as Christ bearing the cross which stands for the burden of the sacrifice on the way to Golgotha – the long path of suffering along which the poet has to pass. (Moreh: 1976; 247).

In Palestinian poetry, for example, Christ is associated with the Palestinian refugees, and in Iraqi poetry he is associated with the Iraqi Marxists, brutalized by Abdul Karim Qasim's regime (Gouhar: 2011; 97). Furthermore, the Algerian revolutionaries, persecuted by the French occupation forces, are also associated with Christ on the cross (Gouhar: 2011; 99). In this context, Mohamed Said Al-Ashmawi emphasizes the existence of a cultural dialogue between modernist Arab poets and their western predecessors in which the Arab poets take from the West what they found appropriate for their culture and literary tastes (Al-Ashmawi: 1981; 149).

As a whole, modernist Arab poets have succeeded in assimilating western and Christian cultural traditions, adapting them to serve the needs of their societies in the post WWII era. For example, the frequent references and allusions, in modernist Arabic poetry to figures such as Christ, Lazarus, Judas, Delilah, Cain, Saint Augustine and Mary Magdalene in addition to narratives of crucifixion, incarnation and redemption, indicate the tendency of Muslim Arab poets to integrate western culture into the core of their poetry. Further, the excessive appropriation of western traditions involving mythic figures such as Oedipus, Ulysses, Aphrodite, Adonis, Odysseus as well as motifs dealing with fertility, resurrection and ritualistic sacrifices is an indication of a tendency on the part of Muslim Arab poets to incorporate western civilization, with its Christian and pagan aspects, to articulate indigenous purposes and local narratives (Alasgmawi: 1981; 150). Therefore, prominent Arab critics praised Arab poets, who extensively used symbols associated with Christian teachings and theology as well as western traditions in their attempt to explore the socio-political conditions of the Arab world in the aftermath of WWII (Al-Hawi: 1980, 81).

For example, in the poetry of Al-Sayyab, Christian and western narratives are appropriated and recycled in order to express the poet's attitude toward the political situation in Iraq and the Arab world in the era of de-colonization. Utilizing Eliot's literary heritage as inter-text, Al-Sayyab explores political issues of great significance (Al-Hawi: 1980; 82).

However, some Arab critics argue against Al-Sayyab's modernist poetry because it is characterized by an excessive use of Biblical motifs and symbols derived from western culture and religions. The poet's use of Christian narratives and his treatment of themes such as sin, suffering, crucifixion and salvation, led cynical conservative critics to point out that the reader of Al-Sayyab's poetry "would undoubtedly come to the conclusion that the Muslim poet was converted to Christianity" (Al-Sadani: 1988; 106). In other words, Al-Sayyab's attempt to work within western Christian traditions is sometimes considered as a rejection of the poet's Islamic heritage and Arab culture. Nevertheless, the poet sees his poetic initiative as an investment of his rightful inheritance as a human being. Therefore, whether he draws his symbolism from western sources or from the ancient near East, "it was with a universal connotation rather than a narrow local nationalistic one" (Loya: 1971; 198).

Being convinced that Jesus Christ belongs to all humanity and his death "symbolized the salvation of the whole human race" (Loya: 1971, 197), Al-Sayyab associates himself with Christ on the cross. The bleeding wounds of the poet, who lives in exile and poverty, are supposed to bring resurrection to his barren country. Explicitly, Al-Sayyab utilizes Christian narratives, appropriated from western literature to articulate political issues integral to the poet's local community. Using Christian traditions to convey his personal tragedy as an outcast and a political exile who was forced to stay in Diaspora after being persecuted in his own country, Al-Sayyab transforms western/Biblical narratives into a poetics of protest. As a voice of opposition to the Iraqi regime in the 1950's, Al-Sayyab was frequently traced by the agents of Abdul Karim Qasim's government who considered him to be a traitor due to his political views. In different poems, the Iraqi poet, isolated, exiled and cut off from his roots, identifies himself with Christ, while the Iraqi dictators are associated with Judas. The poet hopes that his spilt blood would lead to the redemption of his native land and the removal of the curse brought by Qasim's regime (Loya: 1971; 198).

In his famous poem, "Christ after Crucifixion", Al-Sayyab also incorporates images of suffering and salvation surrounding the crucifixion narrative, identifying Christ with Iraqi political refugees, banished from their country due to their ideological views. In spite of the apparent religious overtones of the poem, it offers a vision of political transformation at a crucial stage in the history of modern Iraq. From the beginning of the poem, the Iraqi poet is transformed into a Christ figure carrying the burden of the cross. He points out that he is lonelier than Christ, expressing his longing for someone to take him down from the cross, to chase away the birds of prey from his wounds and remove the crown of thorns. In spite of the great pains and suffering he passes through, the crucified poet is not yet dead: "after they brought me down I heard /the long wail of winds sweeping through the palms /and footsteps growing more distant / the wounds, therefore, on which they have kept me/nailed all through the evening have not killed me" (Bishai: 2001; 53).

Furthermore, the analogy between Christ, whose steaming blood brings fertility to the earth and the Iraqi poet whose sacrificial death would lead to the salvation of his country dominates the text of Al-Sayyab's poem: "when even the darkness grows green / warmth touches my heart/and my blood courses through its soil/my heart is water and the ear of corn/whose death is resurrection" (Bishai: 2001; 54). Due to his persecution under the Iraqi regime, in the 1960's, Al-Sayyab is transformed into a fertility symbol using Christian symbolism to articulate a local political narrative: "I died so that bread may be eaten in my name/with the coming of the new season/How many lives shall I live? (Bishai: 2001; 54). In addition to his appropriation of Eliot's season imagery, integral to **The Waste Land**, to fulfill domestic purposes, Al-Sayyab utilizes the condition of Christ and his crucifixion to create a narrative of political salvation and resurrection: "I have become the future in every tomb/I have become the seed/I have become a generation/and one or some drops of my blood/flow through each heart" (Bishai: 2001; 55). In **The Waste Land**, Eliot uses seasonal imagery and Christian symbolism to articulate narratives of death, fertility, salvation and resurrection integral to his aesthetic vision: "April is the cruelest month, breeding/ lilacs out of the dead land, mixing/memory and desire, stirring/ dull roots with spring rain/winter kept us warm, covering/earth in forgetful snow, feeding/a little life with dried tubers/summer surprises us" (Eliot: 1980; 37). While Eliot used the cycle of seasons and the tale of crucifixion to express his religious perspective and moral vision, Al-Sayyab appropriates them as objective correlatives to articulate an ideological/political narrative, different from Eliot's original context.

Exploiting the ritualistic potential of the crucifixion story (the New Testament is not considered a legend) as a narrative of torture, sacrifice, and martyrdom, Al-Sayyab transforms Christ into a symbol of Arab nationalism and revolution against hegemony and tyrannical policies: "the eyes of suns devour my road/In which fire dreams of my crucifixion/whether made of iron or of flames/the gaze of my people is like the light/of the heavens, of memories and love/they hear my burden and moisten my cross/How small is my death and yet how great" (Bishai: 2001; 57).

As a cry of protest against the injustice of the political and military establishments in Iraq in the 1950's, Al-Sayyab's poem identifies the leaders of the Iraqi government with evil figures like Judas: "I came back/Judas grew pale when he saw me/for I was his secret/he was a black shadow" (Bishai:2001;55). Depicting his confrontation with the forces of evil symbolized by Judas, Al-

Sayyab speaks in the voice of Christ establishing an analogy between Christ and the Arab nationalists, persecuted and brutalized by tyrannical regimes: "I froze in his [Judas] thought/He feared death should reveal itself in his eyes/(they are a rock behind which he hid/his grave from people)/Do you come from the world of the dead?/Death comes once/could it have been false? This is what he thought when he saw me" (Bishai: 2001; 55). Drawing on the story of the crucifixion, Al-Sayyab, tortured and tyrannized during Qasim's reign, identifies his suffering and sacrifices with Christ: "Did they not crucify me yesterday?/here I am in my grave/let them come – I am in my grave/ who knows who I am? Who knows?/ and Judas's friends! Who will believe their claims? (Bishai: 2001; 56). The Iraqi poet's sacrifice of self for the sake of his own people repeats what Christ did for humanity. In different parts of Eliot's **The Waste Land**, there is a recreation of this act of sacrifice and martyrdom.

The extensive use of Christian images in Al-Sayyab's poem reflects the sweeping impact of western culture on the Muslim Arab poet (and his generation), who attempt to introduce new patterns of symbols and myths into Arabic literature. Evoking crucifixion as a sacrificial ritual which brings salvation to the earth, Al-Sayyab becomes a Christ-figure offering his blood for the sake of his people: "here I am naked in the darkness of my tomb/yesterday I was wrapped/like suspicion, like a blossom/beneath my icy shroud/ moistening the blood red flower" (Bishai:2001;56). Depicted as a symbol of the struggle of the Iraqi nationalists who die for the sake of their cause, Christ, in Al-Sayyab's poem, is transformed from a spiritual religious figure into a revolutionary rebel resembling the poet himself. Therefore, the concluding lines of the poem give an impression of political salvation achieved through the symbolic death of the poet who believes that the Arab world is in dire need of a Christ figure to bring about the resurrection of a dead homeland: "After they had nailed me and I/had turned my eyes towards the city/I could hardly tell the plain from the wall from the tomb/there was something stretching as far as the eye could see/like flowering forest/and at every turn was a cross and a grief-stricken mother/praised be God/such is the city in labor" (Bishai: 2001; 57).

After great anguish and pain, the poet is able to see the Iraqi city in a state of labor which is the result of the poet's sacrificial death: "when one day I warmed the bones of children with my flesh/when I exposed my wound and dressed another/the wall between us and God will be destroyed" (Bishai: 2001; 56). In Eliot's **The Waste Land**, salvation took place only after the collapse of the sinful cities and the destruction of London Bridge, symbols of western civilization: "London Bridge is falling down, falling down, falling down" (Eliot: 1980; 50). At this point in the poem, Eliot's central persona is able to "set my lands in order" and map out the way for salvation after great suffering: "to cartage then I came/burning burning burning / O Lord thou pluckest me out / O Lord thou pluckest / burning" (Eliot: 1980; 46). Blending the pains of Christ with those of St. Augustine, Eliot expresses a splendid tale of sin, confession, and resurrection rooted in his religious doctrine. Similarly, in Al-Sayyab's poem, the redemption of Iraq and its people is only possible after the annihilation of a tyrannical government, an epitome of injustice and brutality. Thus, the political upheaval in Iraq which inevitably culminates in the assassination of Qasim is the ultimate aim of the poet who was brutalized by the agents of the regime: "And soldiers came and reached/even my wounds and heartbeats/they came, all those who were not even dead/they came to me just as the palm tree/Laden with fruit bursts into view/when a flock of hungry birds/from a poor village lights on it" (Bishai: 2001; 57). For the sake of the salvation of his cursed country, his wasteland, the Iraqi poet sacrifices his blood and the best years of his life dreaming of a better future for his homeland.

In "City of Sinbad", Al-Sayyab also utilizes major Christian figures like Christ, Judas and Lazarus in order to reflect his political views toward the dictatorial regimes emerging in Iraq and the Arab world after WWII. The poet points out that there is no possibility of redeeming the Arab world as long as it is governed by dictatorial regimes and repressive governments. Therefore, in "City of Sinbad," Christ is dead and Lazarus, who represents the Arab nation, will not be resurrected. Further, in Al-Sayyab's poem, Eliot's fertility symbols are used in a reverse context, and even when rain falls, it comes in the form of blood. Integrating Eliot's **Waste Land** narratives and Christian legends, the poem, in its symbolic structure, embodies a state of sterility and barrenness integral to the situation in the Arab world in the aftermath of the Palestinian tragedy and the emergence of the refugee problem.

Appropriating the rain motif, a symbol of fertility in Eliot's Western paradigm, Al-Sayyab uses it in a different context as an emblem of plague and disease: "there is death in the streets/and barrenness in the fields/all that we love is dying" (Khouri: 1974; 97). In his attempt to depict the political scene in the Arab region after the catastrophic events which brought about the displacement of the Palestinians in 1948, Al-Sayyab utilizes western myths assimilated from James Frazer's **Golden Bough** and Eliot's Christian traditions. Eliot's literary heritage is adapted to fit the Arab poet's ideological perspective where the Arab world is portrayed as a wasteland and moral wilderness. Emphasizing a state of barrenness and sterility, Al-Sayyab denounces the Arab homeland drawing from Greek and Babylonian mythology, where Adonis is dead and Ishtar dies of thirst: "And in the village, Ishtar is dying of thirst/there are no flowers on her forehead/and in her hands there is a basket, its fruits are stones/which she casts at every woman" (Khouri: 1974; 103).

Lamenting the miserable conditions of his own country (Iraq) and the Arab homeland, after the defeat of the Arab armies in the 1948 war with Israel, Al-Sayyab deploys narratives of corruption and decay to articulate his vision of a world on the verge of collapse. In his poetic vision, the fertility gods of the Middle East are dead and Ishtar's basket is full of stones, instead of flowers and fruits. The death of Adonis and the barrenness of Ishtar, symbols of rebirth and resurrection, signify the inevitable failure of the Arab dream of nationalism and the unity which was expected in the era of decolonization. In its symbolic overtones, the poem indicates the emergence of tyrannical regimes in the Arab world in the aftermath of WWII. The defeat of the Arab armies in the 1948 war with Israel triggered a cycle of catastrophic events culminating in the collapse of Arab aspirations and nationalist dreams. Crystallizing a state of moral bankruptcy and defeat, Al-Sayyab wonders: "Is this Adonis, this emptiness?/and this pallor, this dryness?/Adonis! Behold the defeat of heroism/death indeed has shattered every hope within you" (Khouri: 1974; 97). In addition to its explicit castigation of policies which led to the miserable situation in the Arab world in the post WWII era, particularly the useless war of 1948, Al-Sayyab's poetry aims to achieve social reform and prosperity in a region plagued by recurrent defeats and cursed with dictatorial rulers.

Explicitly, Al-Sayyab's poems, "Christ after Crucifixion" and "City of Sinbad", constitute an example of a transnational poetics which attempts to establish a dialogue between the Arab world and the West narrowing the cultural and civilizational gap that separate peoples on both sides. By transforming Christian narratives into a poetic mechanism serving domestic Arab perspectives, which are different from their original western context, Al-Sayyab provides an example of hybridity and acculturation integral to the era of globalization. In other words, the interaction between the Muslim Arab poet and Western traditions which leads to the construction of a hybrid poetics taking as its core the religious heritage of what is traditionally categorized as an alien/colonial heritage seems to be an indication of a trans-cultural dialogue rather than a clash of civilizations. The engagement of western narratives and myths in contemporary Arabic poetry will open new horizons for religious tolerance, paving the way for mutual understanding between East and West in an era of global conflicts.

References

Al-Ashmawi, M. Zaki. "Azmat al-Shir fi al-Aser al-Hadith / The Crisis of Poetry in Modern Times". Fusul 4 (1981): 149-167.

Al-Hawi, Eliya. Al-ramziya wa al-Siryaliya fi al-Shir al-gharbi wa al-Arabi / Symbolism and Surrealism in Western and Arabic Poetry. Beirut: Dar Al-Thaqafa, 1980.

Al-Sadani, Mostafa. Al-Taghrib fi al-Shir al-Arabi al-Mouser / Westernization in Contemporary Arabic Poetry. Alexandria: Manshaat Al-Maaref, 1988.

Badawi, M.M. *A Critical Introduction to Modern Arabic Poetry*. London: Cambridge University Press, 1975.

Bishai, Nadia, Tr. Ed. *Badr Sheker Al-Sayyab: Selected Poems*. Cairo: General Egyptian Book Organization Press, 2001.

Boullata, Issa, tr.& ed. Modern Arabic Poets. London: Heineman, 1976.

Eliot T.S. *The Complete Poems and Plays (1909-1950)*. New York: Harcourt Brace Jovanovich Publishers, 1980.

Jayyusi, Salma Khadra. *Trends and Movements in Modern Arabic* Poetry (2 volumes). Leiden: E.J. Brill, 1977.

Gouhar, Saddik. "The Integration of Western Modernism in Postcolonial Arabic Literature: A Study OF Abdulwahhab Al-Bayati's Third World Poetics". Third World Quarterly, V. 29. No.2 (2008): 375-390.

Gouhar, Saddik . *Singers in the Waste Land: Voices of Protest in Modern Poetry*. Verlag Press, Saarbrucken (Germany), 2011.

Gouhar, Saddik. Cities of Darkness and Fear: Integrating Western Discourses in Arabic City Literature. Lambert Academic Publishing, Saarbrucken(Germany), 2012.

Hussein, Taha. Mustaqbal althaqafa fi Misr/ The Future of Culture in Egypt. Dar Alma'aref Press, Cairo: 1938.

Kennedy, Hugh. When Baghdad Ruled the Muslim World: The Rise and Fall of Islam's Greatest Dynasty. Cambridge, MA: Da Capo Press, 2005.

Khouri, M and H. Algar, tr & ed. *An Anthology of Modern Arabic Poetry*. Berkeley: University of California Press, 1974.

Loya, Arich. "*Al-Sayyab and the Influence of T.S. Eliot*". The Muslim World LXI.3 (July 1971): 187-201.

Moreh, S. *Modern Arabic Poetry 1800-1970*. Leiden: E.J.Brill, 1976.

Symbols and Archetypes as Foundation of Phraseological Units in Languages

Khalida Isa-zada
(Azerbaijan)

Research regarding the interaction of language and culture in the conditions of international and intra-ethnical integration is most important in the development of the contemporary linguistics science. This issue, based on the principle of language's anthropocentricity, relies on the main concept of anthropological linguistics – the concept of the world view. An especially important role in the formation of the linguistic picture of the world is played by phraseological units, or idioms, with meanings that are connected to the background knowledge, practical experience, and cultural-national traditions of native speakers of the language.

Phraseological units comprise one of the most important means of preserving and communicating information about a people's history, national psychology, culture, and national mentality. According to V.N. Telia, the phraseological composition of the language is a "mirror" in which linguistic-cultural commonality identifies its national self-awareness [Telia V.N., 1999]. Phraseological units have high linguistic stability. They participate in establishing a common meaning as well as in day-to-day communications from generation to generation.

Stability and reproducibility of phraseological units usually correspond to the stability and reproducibility of the pertinent cultural practices, rituals and social strategies [Bragina N.G., 2003: 3]. Analysis of phraseological units helps to identify which part of any given language expresses the universal and which part is relevant only to the specific situation of a certain nation, preserving its experience, and reflecting its national creative work.

The subject of interrelation between language and culture has been attracting the attention of linguistic scholars for a long time now. The roots of this issue have been traced to the works of V. von Humboldt's who believed that material and spiritual cultures as well as national characters externalize themselves in a language. Language in its turn is not a direct reflection of the world but an indirect link between a human and the world around him. It was V. von Humboldt who introduced the concept of "inner configuration" into linguistics.

Humboldt considered inner configuration to be a multi-faceted phenomenon, originating from the spirit of the people or their national-spiritual force. According to him, "the inner configuration of the language contains the specifics of the world perception by the native speakers of different languages". [V. von Humboldt, 1984]

The distinguished Russian linguist, A.A. Potebnya, considered inner configuration in the context of a psychological approach to the phenomenon of language: "Inner configuration of the word is a relationship between a thought and consciousness; it shows how a person perceives his own thought" [Potebnya A.A., 1892:102]. Thus, inner configuration, connected with the "etymology and psychological insights on motivation of the meaning" is an important component of the semantics of phraseological units [Baranov A.N., 2010: 4].

According to V.V. Vinogradov, "inner configuration of the word is an image underlying the meaning and spiritual culture of that language system in which the given word or word combination originated or modified" [Vinogradov, V.V., 1974:17-18]. It's a method of expressing meaning in linguistic units as perceived by the speaker, and it is differently presented in different languages. Figurativeness, as a distinguishing feature of phraseological units, is realized in inner configuration.

Thus, inner configuration is not only houses the figurative meaning of the linguistic expression but it is also a method of pointing out the actual meaning of the expression, its reasoning and motivation.

> "Reasoning and motivation can be described as a method of picturing a given meaning in a word, ..., it's an imprint left in a word by the thought movement that took place at the time when the word first originated. Motivation unfolds the approach of a human thought to a given phenomenon is ; this is the approach that existed at the time when the word first originated, and that is why the motivation, reasoning sometimes is called "the inner configuration of the word" [Maslov Y.S., 1998: 45-46].

According to V.A. Maslova, first a certain prototypical situation emerges in the world, which then becomes a situation corresponding to the literal meaning of the phraseological unit.

The meaning remains attached to the situation, and then it gets rethought, forming an image of the phraseological unit based on the original meanings of the words in the prototypical situation. This way forms the inner configuration "which contains the main information related to the culture.

In the inner configuration of the phraseological unit the "traces" of culture are present, such as in myths, archetypes, customs and traditions, reflecting historical events and elements of material culture" [Maslova V.A., 2004: 84].

The concept of cultural codes became one of the important aspects of research on cultural meanings conveyed through phraseological units of different languages.

> "Cultural code is a system of signs of material world that became carriers of cultural meanings. In the process of reclaiming the world by humans, these codes gained significant that is recognized and decoded while the codes are apprehended by the interpreter." [Kovshova, M.L., 2008:60].

Cultural codes represent a special link in the interpretation of phraseological units in the process of their apprehension in the light of cultural perceptions.

Phraseological units are correlated with cultural codes through their components.

Perceptions and situations underlying the phraseological units of different peoples, have much in common, since they rely on words denoting the commonalities of the ways of living, natural conditions, fauna, main human occupations, etc. These keywords become symbols, archetypes.[1]

As is known, any archetype is a stable image widespread in the culture, and it appears in the consciousness of the individuals across the board.

Phraseology presents itself as a repository of archetypes that express the results of the centuries-long experience inherited from the preceding generations.

For example, in many phraseological units, the German language still retains the archetypes indicative of German-Scandinavian mythology as well as the mythological systems of other peoples: *mil Feuer und Schwert ausroltten; die Sache ist ins Wasser gefallen; die Macht des Schicksals; verschieden wie Tag und Nacht sein,* etc.

But the symbolism common to the main characteristics of the conveyed situations may differ in its specific manifestations.

It is worth noting that language itself plays a significant role in the formation of phraseological units. To be more precise, particular intralingual means help to form phraseological units in the context of each specific language.

It would be a fair observation to make that more or less similar images or symbols in different languages are tied to animals.

Thus, in many cultures a horse is a symbol of luck and success in life, but in proverbs the thought is often expressed that the success, luck and everything else denoted by those two words have to be earned by a person.

For example the Lezghi proverb *Чарадан балкIандал алайди кьарада жеда* (That he who mounts another person's horse may find himself in the mud), in our opinion, is an equivalent of the ancient myth of *Helios's Chariot*, or the Russian saying *do not sit in a sleigh that doesn't belong to you.*

The ancient myth is a symbol of something tempting but inaccessible – one has to think that it's not right for him – having climbed on the top, he will be burned. The Russian saying expresses prohibition. The Lezghi proverb expresses a shared experience, it warns a person: if you mount a horse that is not yours, then you will find yourself in mud.

---

1 As is known, archetypes are images, formed in ancient times, accumulated in the collective subconscious of subsequent generations. They collect sensuous, aesthetical and cultural perceptions and are inherited along with brain structure" (Jung: 147).

We would like to note that in many languages there is a parallel between the phraseological units based on observation: Russian "*слепой, как крот*", "as blind as a mole", Italian «*cieco come una talpa*" and French «*aveugle comme une taupe*».

There is another agreement between Russian «*нем как рыба*» *("mute as a fish"),* the Italian "*muto come un pesce*", and the French «*muet comme une carpe*».

Thus, phraseological units, perceived through the prism of cultural knowledge, that includes archetypical forms of world comprehension and animistic perceptions, reflect universal methods for the interpretation of objective reality.

References

Баранов А.Н. *Внутренняя форма в значении и толковании идиом: тавтология или часть семантики?*//Известия РАН. Серия литературы и языка, 2010, том 69, №3, с. 3-15.

Baranov A.N. *Vnutrennjaja forma v znachenii i tolkovanii idiom: tavtologija ili chast' semantiki?*//Izvestija RAN. Serija literatury i jazyka, 2010, tom 69, №3, s. 3-15.

Брагина Н.Г. *Память и прошлое: языковые образы, культурные практики.*//Известия АН. Серия литературы и языка. 2003, том 62, №5, с. 3-13.

Bragina N.G. Pamjat' i proshloe: jazykovye obrazy, kul'turnye praktiki.// Izvestija AN. Serija literatury i jazyka. 2003, tom 62, №5, s. 3-13.

Виноградов В.В. *Русский язык.* М., 1972, с. 9-45.

Vinogradov V.V. *Russkij jazyk.* M., 1972, s. 9-45.

Гумбольдт В. О. *Избранные труды по языкознанию.* М., 1984. с. 156-180.

Gumbol'dt V. O. *Izbrannye trudy po* jazykoznaniju. M., 1984. s. 156-180.

Ковшова М.Л. *Анализ фразеологизмов и коды культуры.* //Известия РАН. Серия литературы и языка, 2008, том 67, № 2, с. 60-65.

Kovshova M.L. *Analiz frazeologizmov i kody kul'tury.*//Izvestija RAN. Serija literatury i jazyka, 2008, tom 67, № 2, s. 60-65.

Маслов Ю.С. *Введение в языкознание.* Изд. 3, М., 1998.

Maslov Ju.S. *Vvedenie v jazykoznanie.* Izd. 3, M., 1998.

Маслова В.А. *Лингвокультурология: учебное пособие.* 2 издание, стереотип. М., 2004.

Maslova V.A. *Lingvokul'turologija: uchebnoe posobie.* 2 izdanie, stereotip. M., 2004.

Потебня А.А. *Мысль и язык.* Изд.2, Харьков, 1892.

Potebnja A.A. *Mysl' i jazyk.* Izd.2, Har'kov, 1892.

Телия В.Н. Первоочередные задачи и методологические проблемы исследования фразеологического состава языка в контексте культуры// Фразеология в контексте культуры. М., Языки русской культуры, 1999. с. 13-24.
Telija V.N. Pervoocherednye zadachi i metodologicheskie problemy issledovanija frazeologicheskogo sostava jazyka v kontekste kul'tury//Frazeologija v kontekste kul'tury. M., Jazyki russkoj kul'tury, 1999. s. 13-24.
Юнг К. Г. Проблемы души нашего времени. СПб., 2002.
Jung K. G. Problemy dushi nashego vremeni. SPb., 2002.

Part 5
Archetypes in New Transformation or Fan-fiction

Dostoevsky's Underground Man as a Literary Archetype in Postmodern Literature

Hatice Övgü Tüzün
(Turkey)

Although it is hard to mark a definitive moment when the anti-hero came into existence as a literary type, Dostoevsky's Underground Man is undoubtedly one of the most memorable characters in this category. "In the literary work on *Notes from the Underground,* the protagonist is always called Underground Man (pod-pol'nyj chelovek), as if he were an archetypal entity, rather than "the narrator," an accepted literary convention of the Icherzihlung" (Matlaw 1958: 101). Generally speaking, the term Underground Man" refers to a condition of being marginalized, self-effacing, and to a large extent antisocial. The defining feature of the Underground Man is his "hyperconsciousness" that results from his intelligence and sensitivity on the one hand, and his pathological dislike of action on the other. He is described as "the anti-thesis of the normal man, for example, he is a man of heightened awareness, who has, of course, emerged not from the womb of Nature but from a test-tube," (Dostoyevsky 1972: 21). He is moreover an incurable skeptic, paralyzed by his overanalysis of everything in life. A spiteful misanthrophe, the Underground Man avoids commitment to pursue individual freedom but, ironically, often finds the burdens of freedom hard to bear. All in all, he is a man of several contradictions doomed to suffer eternally from the burdens of his consciousness.

In contemporary literature, Dostoevsky's Underground Man finds a multitude of famous descendants. He is, in other words, a seminal literary figure, a precursor to a certain type of individual. There is something about Dostoevsky's character that resonates not only with the spirit of his times, but that also embodies a sensibility we recognize only too well today. The aim of this paper is to examine the character Ambrose in John Barth's "*Lost in The Funhouse*" as an heir to the legacy of the archetypal Underground Man. Despite several differences in terms of age, nationality, culture, and the historical era in which they were created, Ambrose and the Underground Man are temperamentally akin and thus, there are remarkable similarities with regard to the ways in which they think and feel. In what follows, I will point out to some of these similarities and illustrate how Ambrose may be considered a postmodern reincarnation of the Underground Man.

One of the most critically acclaimed short stories of the latter half of the twentieth century, "*Lost in the Funhouse*" depicts the story of a thirteen-year-old boy's trip to the beach with his family on the fourth of July during World War II. Having learned that the beach is covered in oil and tar from the fleet off-shore, the group decides to go through the funhouse. Ambrose gets lost soon after, and during the process of finding his way out of the dark corridors, he comes to some realizations about himself, most significantly, that he is constitutionally different from others who do not look too much into things. On another level, the story is an example of metafiction in that it constantly calls attention to its own artificiality through the interruptions of an intrusive narrator, who is often identified with Ambrose himself. The disjointed and disorienting prose parallels the inner workings of the main character's mind in which the reader gets lost. As an exceptionally introspective young man with a troubled psyche, Ambrose is very much reminiscient of the Underground Man who suffers due to similar pressures exerted on his being.

In the translator's introduction to the Penguin edition of *Notes From the Underground*, Coulson states that Dostoevsky's anti-hero is "a man turned in upon himself, a man of heightened awareness and self-consciousness whose sensitivity to slights drives him alternately to retreat into his corner, his underground, and to revenge himself for his humiliations by humiliating others" (qtd. in Dostoyevsky 1972: 9). Indeed, the Underground Man's struggle with himself, with others, and ultimately with life itself, is an important theme of the book. A similar feeling of being "out-of place" stems from hypersensitivity, and the consequent retreat into one's own world can also be seen in the case of Ambrose who is presented as an outcast:

People don't know what to make of him, he doesn't know what to make of himself, he's only thirteen, *athletically and socially inept*, not astonishingly bright, but there are antennae; he has some sort of receivers in his head; things speak to him, he understands more than he should, the world winks at him through its objects, grabs grinning at his coat. Everybody else is in on some secret he doesn't know; they've forgotten to tell him. (Barth 1988: 88, *italics original*)

Like the Underground Man who suffers from what Lethcoe calls "a paranoid persecution complex" (Lethcoe. 1966:13), Ambrose is haunted by a feeling that the whole world is conspiring against him. Torn by inner conflicts, detached from his fellow human beings, Ambrose is very much like his predecessor whose reflective mind is a curse rather than a blessing. Both the Underground Man and Ambrose are doomed paradoxically because they are endowed with the 'gift' of heightened awareness, which many around them lack. Alienated not only from their surroundings but also from themselves, they feel uncomfortable in the world and under their skin. What exacerbates their sense of ontological insecurity is the sense that they are the unfortunate victims of a nasty hoax, the victims, perhaps, of a cosmic joke.

How to cope with the myriad difficulties life presents them seems to be the main question for both characters. After all, one needs to *be* something, have a firm sense of being and feel grounded, in order to take a stance against the sea of troubles he is forced to cope with. Unfortunately, both the Underground man and Ambrose seem to suffer from an identity crisis, or rather a crisis of being, that makes it impossible for them to salvage a firm footing in themselves. The Underground Man complains that

Not only could I make myself malevolent, I couldn't make myself anything: neither good or bad, neither a scoundrel nor an honest man, neither a hero nor an insect. Now I go on living in my corner and irritating myself with the spiteful and worthless consolation that a wise man can't seriously make himself anything. Yes, a man of the nineteenth-century ought, indeed is morally bound, to be essentially without character; a man of character, a man who acts, is essentially limited. (Dostoyevsky 1972:16)

Although Dostoevsky created the Underground Man as a caricature of the 19th century Russian intellectual whose self-serving philosophising takes him to absurd conclusions with tragic consequences, the self-induced 'suffering' of the hyper-conscious individual whose intellectual gifts become self-destructive is a motif one often comes across in postmodern literature as well. As a representative postmodern writer, Barth is preoccupied with the plight of such characters who suffer in the throes of a persistent identity crisis, yet also find it impossible to give up the effort to make something of themselves. It is, then, possible to suggest that "although Barth's heroes are unable to define themselves through their narratives, they experience an almost desperate need to continue the attempt" (Worthington 2001: 115). Like the Underground Man who mourns the impossibility of making himself anything and feels like an empty signifier, Ambrose feels that he needs to somehow become someone, feel that he is "somebody" by narrating his existence to himself. However, his self-conscious self-reflexivity inhibits his efforts in this direction and leads him to acknowledge, instead, the multiplicity of self-hood: "You think you're yourself," he says, "but there are other persons in you" (Barth 1988: 85). He is, in short, too conscious to be a real person and live life spontaneously.

Ambrose's painfulful acknowledgement of his own artificiality makes one recall the Underground Man's revealing observation that the man of heightened awareness does not emerge from the womb of nature but from a test-tube. According to Bernstein: "The self-contempt of figures like the underground man is due to his "haunted sense of only acting according to "type," of lacking authenticity even in their suffering, where they most need to feel original" (Berstein. 1992:22). Ambrose, too, shares similar feelings since he is constantly chased by the ominous sentiment that he is not a *real* person. Thus, the thinking man is inevitably alienated from his very own nature and is held hostage by his own mind. A good example that illustrates how an overactive mind leads to the detachment of the person from himself can be found in a scene where Ambrose can not stop thinking even at a moment when he is supposed to be immersed in a feeling of ecstatic sexual pleasure. When a supposedly innocent game of Masters and Niggers with Magda takes on another dimension Ambrose has what is perhaps his very first sexual experience: "But though he had breathed heavily, groaned as if ecstatic, what he'd really felt throughout was an odd detachment, as though someone else were Master. Strive as he might to be transported, he heard his mind take notes upon the scene: "*This is what they call* passion. *I am experiencing it*" (Barth 1988: 84, *italics original*). Ambrose's stream of consciousness shows that instead of simply having an experience, he feels the constant need to distance himself from that experience through a veil of mental description (Worthington 2001: 125). Both Ambrose and the Underground Man can never live in the moment and thus can never seize the day precisely because their overdeveloped self-consciousness will always keep them from directly experiencing their own lives.

In the light of these observations, one could suggest that individuals like the Underground Man and Ambrose are overwhelmed by the centifugal forces in themselves that pull them in several directions. Unable to find their center, they cannot prevent the disintegration of the self even in the very attempt of anchoring it. Consequently, they experience severe inner turmoil, feel mentally paralyzed and unable to move in any direction. It is revealing that the Underground Man is aware that his condition is the result of "the normal fundamental laws of over-acute consciousness, and … the inertia that [is] the direct result of those laws" (Dostoyevsky 1972: 30). Likewise, Ambrose's main problem is a self-consciousness which prevents him from actively participating in life, and which ultimately gets him lost in the funhouse, which represents life itself. The very first sentence of the story captures the heart of the matter: "For whom is the funhouse fun? Perhaps for Lovers. For Ambrose it is a place of fear and confusion" (Barth 1988: 71). An acute feeling of fear and confusion is what life itself has in store for Ambrose, who is haunted by self-consciousness, alienated from family and society, and seeking out a valid and viable self. Under such circumstances, he cannot help but feel that "there was some simple, radical difference about him; he hoped it was genius, feared it was madness, devoted himself to amiability and inconspiciousness (89)."

The acknowledgement of oneself as rather peculiar, as someone not like the rest and thus something of an oddity, is a feeling one also finds in the Underground Man who, from an early age, is tormented by the thought that nobody else is like him and he isn't like anybody else: "I am one person, and they are everybody, I would think, falling into a b?rown study" (Dostoyevsky 1972: 49). By the age of twenty-four, he tells us, his life was already "gloomy, ill-regulated, and as solitary as that of a savage. I made friends with no one and positively avoided talking, and buried myself more and more in my hole" (60). The incurable sensation of loneliness that this frame of mind engenders leads people like Ambrose and the Underground Man to isolate themselves from others, towards whom they have ambivalent feelings. On the one hand, they admire their ignorance, which is in fact a blessing, a freedom from the burdens of the contemplating consciousness. On the other hand, they depise them for the very same reasons.

Consumed by self-alienation, Ambrose envies his brother Peter's normalcy by saying that "the truth was, his brother was a *happy-go-lucky youngster* who'd've been better off with a regular brother of his own" (Barth 1988: 91). The Underground Man, on the other hand, remains torn between his contempt for the unthoughtful men of action and his undeniable envy of their spontaneity and zest for life. He reaches the conlusion that he does not have a place in their world: "Now I'm living out my life in a corner, teasing myself with the malicious, useless consolation that an intelligent man cannot turn himself into anything, that only a fool can make something of himself" (Dostoyevsky 1972: 16). This does not, however, mean that Ambrose and the Underground Man do not have the need to connect with others. In fact, what exacerbates their suffering is that they can neither obliterate nor consummate their yearning for human warmth and intimacy.

The Underground Man hates himself because he longs desperately for love, and he realizes that he will always be cut off from it by his own nature (Paris 1973: 516). His main problem seems to be that he longs for companionship but wants it only on his own terms. Thus, it comes hardly as a surprise that he has severed all ties with almost all of his friends. He loses his only remaining schoolfriend Simenov when he irritates the hell out of everyone, making a fool of himself during Zverkov's farewell dinner. His treatment of the good-hearted prostitute Liza is no less scandalous. On the night of their first encounter at the brothel, he launches on a tirade about the unhappy lot of prostitutes who end up in the gutters and then regrets having teased her for sport when she starts crying. Feeling bad about himself, he gives her his address and tells her to visit him, but when she shows up some days later he goes into a frenzy and humiliates her. In a similar vein, Ambrose wants to be like the lovers for whom the funhouse is fun, but is left on his own when Magda leaves with Peter. Too self-absorbed like the Underground Man to respond efficiently to the immediacy of life, Ambrose misses the precious moments that he can share with others.

If there is no peace for such individuals in this world, can Ambrose and the Underground Man find some peace in alternative realities? Given their overactive imaginations, dreaming seems to offer a possible avenue of satisfaction for both characters. For instance,

> Ambrose amuses himself by inventing romantic fictions (his affair with Peggy Robbins), realistic fictions (his peaceful domesticity with Magda), even prosaic fictions ("he fell into his habit of rehearsing to himself the unadventurous story of his life, narrated from the third person point of view,"). In fact, Ambrose seems to have too much imagination, to the extent that his tendency to fictionalize existence nullifies his ability to experience existence. (Malmgren 1987: 8)

Like Ambrose who seeks solace and hope in imaginative fictions, the Underground Man repeatedly attempts to escape the misery of his life by imagining himself as a "doer." He imagines himself engaging in retaliatory actions to avenge the wrongs inflicted on his pride, but, eventually, he fails to carry out his plans. In both cases, the characters are rendered unfit for action due to the power of their imaginations. It is therefore possible to suggest that the very possibility of an "authentic" and self-fullfiling existence seems to be out of the question for the vulnerable, imaginative, and highly conscious individual, who is an excellent observer of the inner processes of his mind, but inept when it comes to the actual experience of living.

Towards the end of his account, the Underground Man declares that:

> … a novel needs a hero, but here all the features of an anti-hero have *purposely* been collected, and most of all, the whole thing produces a bad impression, because we have all got out of the habit of living, we are all in greater or less degree crippled. We are so unused to living that we often feel something like loathing for 'real life' and so cannot bear to be reminded of it. We have really gone so far as to think of 'real life' as toil, almost as servitude, and we are all agreed, for our part, that it is better in books. And what is it we sometimes scratch about for, what do we cry for, what do we beg for? We don't know ourselves. And it would be worse for us if our stupid whims were indulged. Just try giving us, for example, as much independence as possible, untie the hands of any of us, loosen our bonds, and we […] After all, we don't even know where 'real life' is lived nowadays, or what it is, what name it goes by. (Dostoyevsky 1972:122-123)

This lengthy quotation illustrates the governing ideas that go into the Underground Man's thinking and actions. It also heralds the emergence of a new kind of hero, namely the anti-hero, as the representative of modern consciousness. According to the Underground Man, the anti-hero is out of tune with life, estranged from himself and others, and imprisoned by his own mind. Oppressed by his environment, he withdraws into himself and leads a solitary existence. The Underground Man is aware that he has lost track of 'real life' which he finds terribly burdensome and irritating. Dazed and confused, he drifts about not knowing what he wants or what he is doing. Although the young Ambrose does not yet have the bitterness of the Underground Man, he has the makings of the same character. The experience he has during the visit to the funhouse functions as a rite of passage that gives him a level of maturity beyond his years.

Ambrose's new found awareness about life and himself only serves to accentuate his feeling of out-of-placeness and leads him to question his role in life: "He wishes he had never entered the funhouse. But he has. Then he wishes he were dead. But he's not. Therefore he will construct funhouses for others and be their secret operator – though he would rather be among the lovers for whom funhouses are designed" (Barth 1988: 97). Unlike the Underground Man who experiences his difference from others only as a curse, Ambrose shows a willingness to make something of his potential as an outsider who is endowed with extraordinary sensibilities. Although he would have preferred to be like ordinary people for whom the funhouse is simply fun, he knows he will never be like them. Given the fact that he cannot be ordinary and lead a simple life with its simple joys, Ambrose decides to accept himself as a gifted individual with a high creative capacity. Recognizing in his inner turmoil an impetus for artistic creation, Ambrose feels that he can put his potential to good use by becoming a constructor of funhouses. Indeed, the possibility of finding a creative outlet which can give a sense of purpose to his life is most probably the only hope for Ambrose who is otherwise on his way to join the Underground Man in his Underground.

Conclusion

According to Hall "it is Dostoyevsky's distinctive achievement in *Notes from the Underground* to have portrayed and analysed a contemporary revolution, the anguished moment when the old myths of Enlightenment's rationalism give birth within apparently continuous forms to the new myths of individualism and the radical opposition between the 'self' and the 'other'" (Hall 1981: 132). As a well-known polemic against scientific determinism and Chernyshevskian rationalism, *Notes From the Underground* shows that man doesn't always act within the laws of reason. In fact, as the Underground Man makes clear at several points in his narrative, he may find himself doing things that may be deemed irrational and contrary to his apparent advantage just to prove that he can exercise his free will. As Hall further suggests, the foregrounding of the irrational forces within the human psyche and the consequent undermining of the Cartesian definition of the ego is indeed a revolution with far reaching consequences that materialise especially during the second half of the twentieth century.

From this perspective, it is possible to read *Notes From the Underground* as a prophetic book that presents this paradigm shift through a character who is overwhelmed by the irrational and contradictory urges that pull him in several directions. The confused, introverted, and self-destructive anti-hero who gets lost in the maze of his mind is ironically an attractive figure that has enjoyed enduring appeal.

Presenting an old story in new ways, Barth revamps this particular breed of the anti-hero, giving him a postmodern twist. Like Dostoevsky who wrote a hundred years before him, Barth subscribes to the idea that "a hero could no longer speak with confidence and coherence, and so define himself, since under contemporary philosophical pressure the old cogito, ergo sum had become a farcically painful lie" (Klinkowitz 1982: 408).

All in all, no "redemption" seems to be possible for Ambrose and the Underground Man who try to lead anxiously examined lives. Feeling manipulated by forces beyond their control, they find it hard to keep focused and 'sane.' On the other hand, although they are lost and suffer from inner paralysis, they also find a kind of perverse pleasure in their torment and seem to find cause for celebration in their difference. One could perhaps suggest that Ambrose is not as doomed as his predecessor, since he comes to feel that the excruciating self-consciousness that marks him as "different" comes with the gift of a lively imagination that can help him become an artist. However, even finding this creative outlet does not seem to console him, since he would rather be like the others who enjoy life and feel at home in this world.

Ultimately, both *Notes From the Underground* and *Lost in the Funhouse* dramatize the quest of the individual for his place in the world. Nothwithstanding the differences in their age and cultural orientation, the Undergound Man and Ambrose are of the same fabric and hence, suffer due to pressures stemming from similar psychological dynamics. Both are acutely conscious beings who deeply suffer from the absence of authentic, self-realizing existence. Their stultifying self-consciousness inhibit the immediate experience of life and render them unfit for the serious business of living. In both cases, heightened consciousness leads to inertia and the characters continually withdraw from the world, forced outside the stream of life. The distorting prism of their subjective perception makes it impossible for them to find peace wherever they turn. Thus, although both characters long to overcome their self-consciousness and make contact with the world, their failure to do so characterizes their existence.

References

Barth, John. *Lost in the Funhouse*. New York: Anchor Books, 1988.

Berstein, Michael A. *Bitter Carnival: Ressentiment and the Abject Hero*. Princeton University Press, 1992.

Dostoevsky, Fyodor. *Notes From the Underground.* London: Penguin Books, 1972.

Hall, J.R. "*Dostoyevsky's 'Notes from the Underground'*" The Modern Language Review, Vol. 76, No. 1, Jan., 1981

Klinkowitz, Jerome. "*John Barth Reconsidered.*" Partisan Review, 49, 1982.

Lethcoe, James. "*Self-Deception in Dostoevskij's Notes from the Underground*" The Slavic and East European Journal, Vol. 10, No. 1, Spring, 1966.

Malmgren, Carl D. "'From Work to Text": The Modernist and Postmodernist Künstlerroman. Novel 21, No. 1, fall 1987.

Matlaw, Ralph E. "Structure and Integration in Notes from the Underground" PMLA, Vol. 73, No. 1, Mar., 1958.

Paris, Bernard J. "*Notes from Underground: A Horneyan Analysis*" PMLA, Vol. 88, No. 3, May, 1973.

Worthington, Marjorie. *"Done with Mirrors: Restoring the Authority Lost in John Barth's Funhouse"* Twentieth Century Literature, Vol. 47, No. 1, Spring, 2001.

The Mill Archetype in Literature

Elnare Garagyezova
(Azerbaijan)

The mill archetype is one of the interesting archetypes met with in the literature. A mill appears to be a symbol of abundance and provision, since it is a place for grinding the flour required for breadmaking. However the symbol of mill does not express only abundance and good things in the literature. This archetype has been transformed over time, and has begun to signify the place of evil.

The Mill in Mythology

The mill archetype has appeared since the times of ancient myths. One Altaic myth narrates the creation in a mill of the present human generation out of the grinded-up dead bodies of people who died during deluge (Соколов М.Н.1978: 132-156). Thus according to the myth, the mill was one of the tools used by God in the creation. On the other hand, since mills were built far from the places of human dwelling, they were believed to be related to evil forces. "Since mills and fields were away from settling places they were considered to be a place of the unknown, a border between nature and culture, chaos and harmony in the general landscape. It is a meeting point of the evil and good, reality and myth (like in *Dəyirman* (*The Mill*) and *Şeytan* (*Satan*) by M.Sulejmanly)" (**Asif Hacılı. 2002:67**). The figure of the Mill Mother in the mythology of Tatar Turks is believed to be a holy spirit living in the mill. An abundance of bread, flour and grain are associated with this mythological being. "The Mill Mother or The Mill Master is usually imagined as a smeared in flour short old woman or a man with covered in white flour hair, eyelashes, beard, and moustache. According to Tatars' belief, the Mill Mother would not let the evil forces to come near the mill and keep them away from bread and flour; as well as guard people coming to grind grain."(Çulpan Zaripova Çetin.2007: 1-32)

In some myths about hell, the mill is the attribute of the underworld. "A mill and fire are depicted together on the background of many Bosch's paintings. Probably, the contemporaries of Bosch considered a mill to being a symbol of the hell." (http://ergotism.info/ru /Д_Абсентис_МирБосха_Пылающиемельницы.htm)

Another interesting fact: the words As, Asia, Asiyab were widely used in the classic Turkish literature as the synonyms of the mill in its primary meanings and as metaphors and symbols. (Birici S. 2007: 97-113)

The Mill as a Drinking Place, Distillery

The association of the mill with evil in Azerbaijani literature occurs in the works of M.Sulejmanly *Dəyirman* (*The Mill*) and *Şeytan* (*Satan*). In the novel *Dəyirman* the mill is described as a drinking place, a nest of the forbidden and evil. According to one of the personages, the mill is the dwelling of Satan ("Şeytanın yığnaq yeri"): "The sinful people were talking about virtue with incomplete sentences, and broken words, repeating "they are searching for sin in me". There were sinless, with words – long live, well done – they were kissing the sinful. Only a Kebab-shop keeper was not drunk, was not sober either, he was collecting money." (Süleymanlı M. 1993:324) It would be appropriate to compare M.Sulejmanly's kebab-shop with a tavern from H. Malot *Sans Famille*. The drinkeries in both novels are places of evil, and both have the extraordinary ability to attract people. Remi, the protagonist of *Sans Famille* is interested in the place where merry voices always sound and in the events that go on there (http://lib.ru/INPROZ/MALO_G/ bez_semji.txt). In *Dəyirman* one who has once stepped into the mill becomes addicted to the place and can't give up going there. Remi meets Vitalis in the drinkery. The mill-turned-into-kebabshop is also awakened by the shepherd's visit. There is an image of an orphan child in the both works. Remi, earning a living with hard work, in the end is rewarded with happiness, but the Ayat's (*Dəyirman*) fate, passesing through more terrible sufferings, remains unknown.

The transformation of the mill into a drinkery is a known event in history. A famous example is the **Moulin Rouge** in France. The Red Mill was a cabaret built in 1889 by Joseph Oller in Montmartre. It was marked by the red windmill on its roof. The Moulin Rouge is famous as the birth place of a modern form of seductive dance, the cancan (http://en.wikipedia. org/wiki/Moulin_Rouge). Similarly a two hundred years old mill in Datça (Turkey) has been restored and begun to function as a café (news.otpusk.uz/archives/2251).

Mill and Satan

Sometimes the mill is described as a dwelling place of the Satan. In the novel *Şeytan* Satan comes out from a mill. "Satan became a handful of dust, and came out from the chimney of the mill ... Satan fell dead from the hole of the mill, and came out alive. The miller was sitting in the front of the milled grain. The sound of grinding stone was causing pain in his head; the miller was counting his earnings. Satan blended with the flour dust, and sat into the miller's heart" (Süleymanlı M. 2006:144). Thus here the mill is also considered as the attribute of hell.

However, in my opinion, the transformation of the mill into an evil place starts in folklore, which has been most clearly reflected in the Azerbaijani epos *Koroglu*. Kechel Hamza (Hamza the Bald) deceives the protagonist Koroglu in the mill where the brave hero Koroglu suffers defeat at his hands (Koroğlu. 2005: 169-170.)

It should be noted as well that in some Christian countries the motion of wings or the wheels of the mill during some religious holidays, for instance, Christmas night, was considered to be a bad sign (http://ec-dejavu.ru/m/ Melnitsa. html). According to Slavic beliefs, Satan can disguise himself as a miller (Энциклопедия символов и знаков //http://sigils.ru/). In a short story *The Wild Mill* by Alexander Grin a miller wants to kill the stranger staying in his house (lib.ru/RUSSLIT/GRIN/dikmel.txt), but hides, frightened by the sunlight falling upon him. A fear of light indicates he is an evil force. This can be compared with the Zoroastrian philosophy of the light and darkness of to some extent, as light represents good and dark evil in Zoroastrianism. Probably it is connected with the Azebaijani expression "an evil time", by which twilight is sometimes called. Actions such as sweeping the house, cutting one's nails, combing one's hair, sleeping, and washing are forbidden during this time. According to some superstitions, forbidding these actions are a safeguard against genies, evil spirits. Some say bathing or sleepsing at this time time it can make one ill, while others believe that one's sleeping at that time can cause his loss of fortune, because fortune is given at that time. According to Y.V Chemenzeminli's essay *Zoroastrian traditions in Azerbaijan* this superstition is derived from Zoroastrians beliefs: "Azerbaijanis call the twilight "the evil time": "I had told that Zoroastrians believed the Universe is the battle of darkness and light. This battle is repeated during every twilight period: the day fights with the night, ending with the victory of the night and darkness over the light. Defeat of the light is considered to be "evil". According to the folk belief to be sad, to hold hands in one's bosom, cause children to cry and not to burn the lamp during the evil time is a sin because the fundamental rule of Zoroastrian is to courageously withstand the evil and harm." (Çəmənzəminli Yusif Vəzir.2005:313.)

There are certain connections between the plots of A. Grin's story and Russian fairy tales about Baba Yaga. Baba Yaga first feeds the person coming to her home, and then she tries to devour the guest when he falls asleep. Accordingly the miller feeds the protagonist, gives him a place to sleep, and then while the guest is asleep, binds his arms and feet and tries to kill him. No less interesting is the assumption of the Baba Yaqa's hut originating from a mill (http://www.blogbuster.ru/2006/01/27/genezis-izbushki-na-kurih-nozhkah/).

Why Don Quixote of Cervantes fights with a mill? Some critics noted that the motif probably derives from the author's subconscious. The author's irrational fear of the mill is reflected here. According to D. Absentis, it is related with the belief that the mill is the abode of Satan. The fight with the mill is the symbol of human's battle with fears distorting the truth and preventing real life from being lived. **Salvador Dali,** depicting the mill in one of his drawings, once noted that these giants are the failures and the negative sides living in his self which must be destroyed. The philosopher and poet Jorge Angel Livraga wrote that Cervantes in the novel Don Quixote has symbolically given the advice: "When you have enough courage to attack the giants they always turn to a simple windmill (http://community. livejournal.com/bezgranitz/).

Modification of the function of the mill

The mill is used for the grinding wheat into flour, which is the reason of it being the symbol of the abundance and provision. However at times the function of the mill undergoes a change. In some folklore motifs the mill does not grind flour. In the *Poetic Edda* of Norse mythology the mill Grotti grinds out wealth, and the mill Sampo in Kalevala (Finnish mythology) gives salt and money. However, sometimes a mill can grind human bones as well. "K. Librekht studying the dark theme of "the red wheat" came to the conclusion that here a trace of ancient human sarcrifice in wheat grinders is reflected." (http://ec-dejavu.ru/m/Melnitsa.html)

In the story *The Dream Mill* by Liana Daskalova we meet with another modification of the function of the mill. The fairytale-style piece narrates a story about a boy Misho who wants to see his dreams in full colour in order to depict them in his drawings. With the purpose to find coloured dreams, Misho travels the world. He has heard that dreams are born in the forest, so Mishoe goes to the forest. After long searches he sees in the forest a mill by the little river. It appears that the mill grinds out dreams, and the miller regulates the colour of them. (http://www.litru.ru/?book=56424&description=1)

Mill as a basic space

The mill is a space where the story of love and self sacrifice takes place in the short story *Değirmen* (*A Mill*) of Turkish writer **Sabahattin Ali.** The narrative is about the fate of the gipsy Atmaca, who falls in love with the miller's daughter. Interestingly, she is portrayed as cripple. The head of the gipsy group dreams about the miller's daughter and Atmaca: "I saw Atmaca under the big plane tree waiting impatiently the whole night, his hands wide open, the miller's daughter running to him with the great joy at the sides of her mouth, and unseen before rosiness on her pale cheeks. But when they were to embrace each other an odd shapeless bulk went between them, whirling like a wheel growing and pulling them apart" (http://aruz.com/ hikayeantolojisi/hi_sabahattinali_degirmen.htm). Apparently, in the dream of the tribal leader, the wheel, which can be understood as a symbol of the mill, separates the two youngsters. Later the narrative reveals to the reader that in order to prove his love to his disabled lover Atmaca, the most skilful musician of the gipsy tribe damages his arm in the mill.

In the story ***The Old Mill* of the Belarusian writer Aleksei Kulakovski,** narrating the events of the Second World War, a group of children helps partisans to make the old mill their headquarters. From the mill they watch Nazi soldiers and inform the partisans about their actions. Petrik, the leader of the children dies while following a German. From that time on the old mill became like a huge monument, Petrik's grave. The green grass near the mill became the most sacred and dear place for children of the whole village (readr.ru/author/ kulakovskij-aleksej).

The image of the mill appears also in the novel **of H. Miralamov. *The Bullet Shot in the Mountains***, which narrates an event which takes place during the Garabagh war.[1] Inhabitants of the village gather together for revenge in the old water mill. They all live here as a family and fight with the enemy (Mirələmov H. 2005). "The Mill is a death any moment, the Mill is the place of rescue as well, the Mill is the fort for an attack and driving the enemy from the borders of the homeland. And everything – the whole plot and the content of the novel takes place around it." (http://kamran58.azeriblog.com/2008/12/27/huseynbala-mirelemovun-halal-haqqi)

Thus, in the research we looked into the history of the mill archetype, its appearance in folklore and beliefs, and in the literature, examining different layers of meaning and expressions in modern times. Our conclusions are as such:

- The mill archetype in literature does not express only abundance and gain. It was subjected to modification, and also signifies the place of evil.
- In fictional literature the mill sometimes is described as a drinkery, the nest of forbidden.
- Satan can be disguised as a miller in the some mythologies.
- The function of the mill undergoes a change in some cases.

1 The on and off war between Armenia and Azerbaijan since 1991, active armed conflict in 1991-1994.

References

Абсентис Д. *Христианство и спорынья. Глава 9. Мир Босха. Пылающие мельницы.*\\http://ergotism.info/ru/Д_Абсентис_МирБосха_Пылающиемельницы.htm.

Absentis D. *Hristianstvo i sporyn'ja. Glava 9. Mir Bosha. Pylajuwie mel'nicy.* \\http://ergotism.info/ru/D_Absentis_MirBosha_Pylajuwiemel'nicy.htm.

Birici S. *Klasik türk edebiyatında Âsiyâ* // Fırat üniversitesi sosyal bilimler dergisi. Cilt: 17, Sayı 1. 2007.

Çəmənzəminli Yusif Vəzir. *Əsərləri.* Üç clddə. III cild. Bakı,"Avrasiya press", 2005.

Çulpan Zaripova Çetin. Tatar Türklerinde Mitolojik Varlıklarla İlgili Mitler ve inanışlar(İyeler ve Yaratıklar) /Bilig. Güz. 2007.

Даскалова Л. *Мельница снов.* //http://www.litru.ru/?book=56424 &description=1.

Daskalova L. *Mel'nica snov.* //http://www.litru.ru/?book=56424 &description=1

Hacılı A. *Mifopoetik təfəkkür fəlsəfəsi.* Bakı: Mütərcim, 2002.

Koroğlu. Bakı, "Lider nəşriyyat", 2005.

Кривошеина А. *Мельница*/http://community. livejournal.com/ bezgranitz/.

Krivosheina A. *Mel'nica*/http://community.livejournal.com/bezgranitz/.

Кулаковский А. *Старая мельница.* //readr.ru/author/kulakovskij-aleksej.

Kulakovskij A. *Staraja mel'nica.* //readr.ru/author/kulakovskij-aleksej.

Мало Г. *Без семьи*\\http://lib.ru/INPROZ/MALO_G/bez_semji.txt.

Malo G. *Bez sem'i*\\http://lib.ru/INPROZ/MALO_G/bez_semji.txt.

Мельница_ Символы, сигилы, знаки, амулеты_ Энциклопедия символов и знаков //http://sigils.ru/.

Mel'nica_ *Simvoly, sigily, znaki, amulety_* Jenciklopedija simvolov i znakov //http://sigils.ru/ jjj.

Mirələmov H. *Dağlarda atılan güllə.* "Azərbaycan", N7-8, 2005.

Грин А.С. *Дикая мельница.*// lib.ru/RUSSLIT/GRIN/dikmel.txt.

Grin A.S. *Dikaja mel'nica.*// lib.ru/RUSSLIT/GRIN/dikmel.txt.

Соколов М.Н. *Христос у подножия мельницы-Фортуны. К интерпретации одного пейзажно-жанрового мотива Питера Брейгеля Старшего* // Искусство Западной Европы и Византии. М., 1978, с. 132-156 (в сокращении). http://ec-dejavu.ru/m/Melnitsa.html.

Sokolov M.N. *Hristos u podnozhija mel'nicy-Fortuny. K interpretacii odnogo pejzazhno-zhanrovogo motiva Pitera Brejgelja Starshego* // Iskusstvo Zapadnoj Evropy i Vizantii. M., 1978, s. 132-156 (v sokrawenii). http://ec-dejavu.ru/m/Melnitsa.html.

Süleymanlı M. *Dəyirman* // Çağdaş Azərbaycan povesti. Bakı, Yazıçı, 1993.

Süleymanlı M. *Şeytan* // Seçilmiş əsərləri. Bakı, Şərq-Qərb, 2006.
http://aruz.com/hikayeantolojisi/hi_sabahattinali_degirmen.htm.
http://en.wikipedia.org/wiki/Moulin_Rouge.
http://kamran58.azeriblog.com/2008/12/27/huseynbala-mirelemovun-halal-haqqi.
http://news.otpusk.uz/archives/2251.
http://www.blogbuster.ru/2006/01/27/genezis-izbushki-na-kurih-nozhka.

Symbolization of Celestial Bodies as an Archetype in the Azerbaijani New Period Poetry

Gunay Garayeva
(Azerbaijan)

Poetry evokes out of words the resonance of the primordial world
Gerhart Hauptmann (13)

The notion of "primordial image" – or archetype appeared in the scholarly world as a claim *about the union of the personal and collective unconscious in an individual's behaviour*, was put forward by Swiss scholar Carl Gustav Jung, founder of analytical psychology. *Archetype* is a Greek word formed by combination of two words (*arche* – primordial, first; *tipos* – image), and means a primordial image or primordial form.

Guided by the notion that apart from human consciousness and cognition, the creative process is connected with "the unconscious and impulses arising from it", Jung writes: "The creative mind, its unconscious, is able to return to life those primordial feelings, experienced by a nation throughout its history and relive them again. Therefore, a real work of art is the expression of not only the artist's personal thoughts and impressions, but also, first of all, of feelings and excitements, experienced by a nation throughout its history. Therefore, creative enthusiasm disconnects the artist from personal thinking, personal impressions, contemporary demands, conjunctures, and merges him with primordial feelings, images, as well as makes him live with primordial feelings, talks to the nation its ancestors' language, thinks with its symbols, and for a moment, the artist turns into a beating heart and speaking tongue of history and the nation." (Qocayev M. 1998: 38).

An archetype symbolically passes on information about the national ethnos' cultural and historical existence, its manner of thinking, and lifestyle to future generations, and protects the ethnos' existence in a mythic model. On the one hand the appearance of the primordial image's informative transmission, crystallized in memory, ties the nation to its traditions, and on the other, it gives a real opportunity to the generalization of features, individualizing it.

As a primordial image, an archetype is a presentation of the nation's mythic model. While the main idea is to express the feeling and mindset of an ethnos or a nation as a general and collective creative product in the broad sense, in a symbol, the inclination away from an individual creative fantasy towards common memory is stronger. The symbol is a mythic archetype which is based on national and moral values, standing on a certain ethnic and political space. Regardless of time, the same peculiarity turns the created image-symbol into an archetype, and creates its own image chain on a national baseplane.

The ethnos' mythological inventory is a rich source for study in which, based on the mythic model, creative literary works in different stages are transformed. "Archetypical images have always accompanied human beings as a source of mythology, religion, and art. In these cultural forms occurs gradual planing of mixed images, and they turn into a comprehensive symbol according to their forms and contents. Mythology is a primordial means of usaging archetypical images". (http://dic.academic.ru /dic.nsf/enc_myphology/1657) As for us, a rich and interesting image presentation from the view point of a solution of the problem takes its initial source from mythology, the myth model, too.

The order and movement of the *Moon*, *Star*, *Sun* and other celestial bodies and the relations between them were symbolically embodied and presented in the images of heroes, for example in the Turkic epic – "Oghuz Kagan" – the khan's three sons are named *Sun*, *Moon* and *Star*. Other creation myths form the basis of the mythological making appearances as objects and anmes with deep mythological layers. Such names also appear in ceremonial songs, legends, such as in Mullah Nasreddin anecdotes, and in eposes widely-known in the Eastern literature, such as "Tahir and Zohra", "Mehr-Mah", "Mahmehri and Khurshud", "Princess Sanubar". Other examples are in such astral literary works as "Gutadgu bilik" by Yusuf Balasagunlu, and "Mehr and Mushtari" by Assar Tabrizi. These images of celestial bodies were leading symbols of the literary and philosophical thoughts and took up a place in national symbolism.

In the early 20th century in Azerbaijan romantics such as Huseyn Javid, Muhammed Hadi, Abbas Sahhat, Abdoullah Shaig and Jafar Jabbarly used symbols as a method of analyszing public and social problems, as well as a way to surreptitiously express their hopes and aspirations about the future. In the new period poetry the poet's used these images to express feeling and emotions in response to complicated socio-historical condition, aesthetic principles of the romantic Turkic literature, and artistic and philosophical concepts bound up with national traditions. One of the most commonly used images was the *morning star* (Venus). In poetry this image is a poetic symbol, fulfilling the romantic hero's thoughts and goals, characterizing his wishes and intentions and bright hopes about the future. "The Morning Star", a poem written by Ahmad Javad in 1914, is one interesting example. At the initial stage of the poet's creative activity, relations between the social environment and the individual, between the adventure and hero, and between the poet's feeling and emotions, provoked by hard and complicated socio-historical conditions were, for the first time, defined in this image's symbolic and associative shades:

So long lasted this dark night,
Come to my help, o Morning star!
I can not sleep; at least you come to me,
To my scream, o Morning star![1]
(Əhməd Cavad 1992: 119-120)

The *Morning star* shines in the sky as a herald of daybreak and morning light. The poet takes the harmony promised by the star in the nature as an artistic symbol of bright, clear wishes for the nation's morrow, which has been hiding invisible among and lost in dark, tangled clouds:

Turbulent whirlwind, tangled roads,
There are gloom and abysses on my way.
Come to me, as the string of my life cries,
Ah, come to my help, o Morning star![2]
(Əhməd Cavad 1992: 119-120)

The image of the *Morning star* is in the centre of this poem. The image-symbol created by the poet's artistic thought has two poles. One of them is a visible image, while the other is an invisible one, the side, standing behind its content. The visible image is the side of a word, object or item, existing in nature, or reality It does not necessarily create a symbol. Being symbolized, the image requires an invisible side apart from the visible one, and they are bound up with each other by logical association. This is one of the specific, distinguishable sides of symbolism. The poet preserves the natural harmony in the *Morning star* image, while, on the other hand, hinting at its invisible side, he inculcates a symbolic feature into it. Association, especially logical association, is one of the principal things that go into the creation of a symbol. Apart from Ahmad Javad, a number of poets of the same time used the *Morning star* symbol and different shades of this image in their creative works.

In the new period poetry the symbol of the *Morning star* was one of the artistic images, showing and defining the poets' emotional concussions, his confused thoughts and concrete ideals and goals within certain time frame.

1 Translated from Azerbaijani by G.G.:
"Bu qaranlıq gecə nə qədər sürdü,
Yetiş imdadıma, ey dan ulduzu!
Barı sən gəl, mənə yuxu gəlmədi,
Yetiş fəryadıma, ey dan ulduzu!"

2 Translated from Azerbaijani by G.G.:
"Qudurğan qasırğa, çarpaşıq yollar,
Yolumda zülmət var, uçurumlar var.
Yetiş ki, ömrümün karvanı ağlar,
Aman, gəl dadıma, ey dan ulduzu!"

Tradition lives in an artistic word. It doesn't die, but changes its form, improves its content and becomes substantial through development. In the new period poetry, the *Moon* and *Star* symbols, which have a specific content of meaning and are personified mostly together, are bound up, first of all, with century old national traditions, with the ethnos mentality and ancestors' memories, passed along like an artistic baton. Like the *Star* image, the *Moon* is also a symbol, taking up an important place in the Turk's sacred and artistic memory.

From this point of view the *Moon* has attained the features of a poly-semantic symbol in most of the world mythologies, as well as in the Turkic mentality. "In the Siberian shaman mythology the *Moon* is related to the world's night and dark part, while the *Sun* – with its day and light part. (In the description of the *Earth* on shaman and tambourines, the *Moon* is placed to the left of the tree of life, on the dark background). In the Chukchi myths, Celes, a creature, bringing disaster upon people is related to the *Moon*". (Abbasova M. 2004: 5)

The *Moon* cult was represented in various periods and cultures, e.g. the *Crescent* was a holy symbol of Astarte for the Babylonians and Chaldeans, Isida for the Egyptians, and Diana for the Greeks. Or in the Christian mysticism, Crescent Maria praises the feminine principle, bringing light to dark night. Being symbolized for various purposes, the *Moon* attained particular importance in Turkic culture, ethnos mentality, creation epic, as well as in legends, eposes and other genres with its rich content and interesting symbolic shades. "In Islam the *Crescent* together with the *Five-Pointed Star*, which is a sign of sacred authority and resurrection, symbolizes the Paradise."[3] (Semboller ve işaretler 2010: 23) From just this point of view, it is hard to understand the symbol of *Moon* in the Muslim and Turkic cultures as something borrowed from other cultures. "The *Moon* cult, which is typical for different epochs and cultures, gave rise to a rich mythology and symbolism related to it ... The symbol was adopted by the Turks after their victory over the Christians. The Turkish sultan began to use it as a symbol of his power. The *Crescent* became the symbol of Islam, and is opposed to the *Cross*."[4]

The existence of images of the *moon* and *star* on bas-reliefs of the Kouti tribes can be found in these areas from the 3rd century BC, drawing attention to the antiquity of these cultures. In the new period Azerbaijani poetry, these symbols are reanimated, first of all, by being bound up with traditions.

---

3 Translated from Turkish by G. G.: "İslamda hilal kutsal otorite ilə dirilişin simgesi beş köşeli yıldız ile birlikteyse cennet sembolüdür."

4 Translated from Russian by G. G.: "Культ луны, характерный для различных эпох и культур, породил богатую мифологию и связанную с нею символику… Символ был перенят турками после победы мусульман над христианами. Турецкий султан стал использовать его как знак своего могущества. Полумесяц стал символом ислама и противопоставляется кресту".

As can be seen in following pieces from the poems: "I asked the *Stars*, They said, "It is the *Moon*!", I went to the *Moon*, but he is mournful without you" ("Where are you from?"),[5] "Asking the *Star*, the *Moon*",[6] "My eyes are looking for you" ("The lover's grief"),[7] "The *Star of Life* no longer rises, we didn't see the *Moon* and counted stars at night" ("My sorrow"),[8] "The *Star of God*, that beautiful houri, my flag, found shelter in the *Moon* in her arms" ("To the flag of Azerbaijan"),[9] "In your arms you gave a place to the *Star* and *Moon*" (Goy Gol),[10] "That charmed and wan look of yours reminds me of a beautiful houri" ("To the *Moon*"),[11] written by Ahmad Javad, as well as "What to do? Alas, I have not got an intellectual dad",[12] "I have not got a *Moon* to announce my wistfulness",[13] written by Muhammed Hadi, the *Moon* and the *Star* were symbolized as free, sovereign and independent attributes of the Azerbaijan Republic.

The *Moon*, *Star* and *Sun* are unitifed primordially. The meaning, as well as the idea and content attained by this trio in the ethnos mentality transformed into various forms in different periods and literary epochs, returning to its initial form again. In examples of folklore, especially in our epics ("Tahir and Zohra" can be a real example to this – G.G.), the togetherness and union of the *Moon* and *Star* is based on the presentation of the unity of the person of the lover-beloved. This conception, existing in astral works appears in new period poetry by returning to memory the tradition in an artistic symbol.

The *Moon* and *Star*, symbolizing the Republic and its major attribute – the national flag were poetical elements frequently addressed in poetry, both during the national independence period and after the failure of independence. Because of artistic examples, symbolizing the flag and independence with these poetic figures, poets underwent unjust attacks, pressures, and were condemned for expressing "their deepest sorrow and action with mystical and symbolical images, and non-political aestheticism" (Mammad Arif) in the media (reference). Apart from the poetry of Ahmad Javad, in other poems such as "I shall cry" ("Mən ağlaram") by B. Seyid-Zadeh via the hemistich "When I see the *Moon*, I cannot look at it, as my eyes are blinded, When I see a *Star*, I grieve, When I see the

5 "Yıldızlardan sordum: – "Aydır!" dedilər, Aya getdim, o da sənsiz mükəddər ("Haralısan?").
6 "Soraraq yıldıza, aya".
7 "Araraq gözlərim səni" ("Aşiqin dərdi").
8 "Doğmaz oldu artıq sağlıq yıldızı, ay görmədik, gecə saydıq yıldızı" ("Dərdim").
9 "Allahın yıldızı, o gözəl pəri, sığınmış qoynunda Aya, bayrağım" ("Azərbaycan bayrağına").
10 "Qoynunda yer verdin yıldıza, aya" ("Göy göl").
11 . "Sənin o sevdalı, solğun baxışın, xatırladır mənə bir pərizadı" ("Aya").
12 "Mən neyləyim, eyvah, ziyalı pədərim yox".
13 "Əfkarımı parlatdıracaq bir qəmərim yox".

Moon, I remember your face, When I see a *Star*, I am lost in sorrow",[14] as well as "The *Moon*", a poem by H. K. Sanyly, the images of the *Moon* and *Star* mournfully and effectively express national and spiritually dramatic nature, as well as lyrical thoughts.

Black burns on your breast,
Tells you have grief in your heart.
Will you have a new spring?
Will you meet your lover, Moon?![15]
(XX əsr Azərbaycan poeziyası antologiyası 2003: 50)

Although regret, parting, separation, sadness and a pessimistic mood related to the *Moon* and *Star* are leading lyrical thoughts, this mood is of transient character, as feelings and experiences formed in relation with a notion are related to optimism, too, generalizing the image's content.

Don't descend to the rascal that rises gradually,
Don't fold up your figure, turning into a bow,
Don't believe every word; don't rely on every power,
Kiss five-pointed star, Moon.[16]
(XX əsr Azərbaycan poeziyası antologiyası 2003: 51)

Another interesting point in the new period poetry is connected with the deconstruction of the *Moon* image. The image of *Moon – Half-moon* (Crescent), which arises in classical Oriental literature, in Sufi and tasavvuf poetry, as well as in ashug poetry, is often compared with a beauty's eyebrow, or describes slimness and grace of her body, while the fourteen-night *Moon* is likened to the roundness of her face. For example, Imadaddin Nasimi writes:

My heart is burning from your love; tears are running
from my eyes,
My heart is cloaked in grief over separation.
The pretender blames me, reproaching me for her love,
It is not necessary to throw so many stones at a break,

14 Translated from Azerbaijani by G.G.: "Ay görəndə baxmam, gözüm qamaşır, Ulduz görcək dərdim başımdan aşır, Ay görəndə üzün düşür xəyala, Ulduz görcək qərq oluram məlala."

15 Translated from Azerbaijani by G.G.:
"Köksündəki qara-qara yanıqlar,
Söyləyir könlündə dərdü qəmin var.
Olurmu səninçün heç yeni bahar?
Edərsənmi öz yarınla görüş, Ay?!"

16 Translated from Azerbaijani by G.G.:
"Getdikcə ucalan alçağa enmə,
Bькьb qamətini kamana dџnmə,
Hər dilə inanma, gьcə gьvənmə
Beşguşəli ulduz ilə öpüş, Ay."

My body has grown thinner and become like a new
moon from grief
since I met *half-moon* like eyebrows.[17]
(Nəsimi İ. 1985: 74)

Unlike a classical hero, who compares his beloved's eyebrows and her body to the *Moon* or *half-moon*, while praising her beauty as a lover, the romantic hero of the new period substitutes the abstract beauty with the new lover-beloved image by giving the *Moon* a new image, at the same time keeping its existing the traditional figurative quality.

Now dreams about her is not mine,
I will never liken any eyebrow to the *half-moon*,
I have gone mad, since I was charmed by you,
"I know", you said, though you didn't come.[18]
(Əhməd Cavad 1992: 130)

Here the beauty praised by the lover is not an imaginary beloved. Her eyebrow and body are not compared to the *half-moon*. The symbol of the *half-moon* expresses the new lover's national codes and features.

It would not be right to consider the *Moon*, *Star*, *Sun* and other celestial bodies, as exponents of lyrical *Self*, his desires and wishes. Touching upon this problem in his "Poetics of the Azerbaijani romanticism", K. Aliyev, an Azerbaijani literary critic and scholar, writes: "... the problem of using symbols in the Azerbaijani romanticism, or inclination towards symbols was not a new occurrence in our literature, but now it had a new character. This arose directly from the new life itself and this life's reflection within the romantic method."[19] (Əliyev Kamran 2002: 143)

Such natural attributes as the *moon*, *sun* and *star* were also among the leading symbols of the naturalist literary and philosophical thought in the Middle Ages. Undergoing transformation during transition from folklore to written literature, the unity of *moon and star* was substituted by the *Moon and Sun* unity in the Middle Ages. In the poem called "Gutadgu-bilik" by Yusuf Balasagunlu, the main charac-

17 Translated from Azerbaijani by G.G.:
"Yanıram eşqindən, axır gözlərimdən yaşlar,
Firqətin dərdi çıxardı ürəyimdən başlər.
Müddəi tən edübən başıma qaxar eşqini,
Sınığa lazım deyildir bunca atmaq daºlər,
Qəmdən incəldi vücudum, oldu yengi ay kimi,
Gözlərimə tuş olalı şol hilali qaşlər."

18 Translated from Azerbaijani by G.G.: "Artıq bənim yarım deyil xəyalı/Heç bir qaşa bənzətmərəm hilalı/Bir dəliyəm sənə məftun olalı/Bildim" deyib durdum, niyə gəlmədin?"

19 Translated from Azerbaijani by G.G.

ters Gun Toghdu[20] and Ay Toldu[21] are taken as symbols of law and happiness. In Oriental naturalal philosophy, the images of *Moon* and *Sun* symbolised as a new lover and beloved, attain a deep philosophical content. In mythologies around the world, the *Sun* is the male element, while the *moon* the female. The *sun* and *moon* perceived as husband and wife belongs to a number of cultures.

The Moon turned into a half-moon, seeing your
half-moon eyebrows,
The rose was stained with its own blood, seeing
your ruddy cheeks.
If the Moon's half gets light from the Sun
See this Moon that lightens the Sun with just its half.[22]
(Nəsimi İ. 1973: 116)

In Irfani philosophical poems, poetical elements of the celestial bodies are used to describe the beloved's *sun-like* and *moon-like* face." Artistic symbols did not remain stable. These images' contents changed and attained new shades of meaning in poetry influenced by the historical development of literary and philosophical thought.

In most romantic literary works as well as in the new period poetry, the sun *provides constant* heat. The sun preserves its ancient symbolic pithiness. "Being a source of heat, the Sun symbolizes vitality, passion and youth. As a source of light, it represents clearness as well ... Its rise and set symbolizes birth, death and vitality."[23] (Semboller ve işaretler 2010: 6)

The *Sun*, symbolizing truth, independence and freedom in literary works by Turkish romantics (Abdulhag Hamid, Namig Kamal, Tofig. Fikrat, etc.) could not help but influence Azerbaijani romanticism with the same content feature. The *Sun* is represented as a symbol of liberty, independence and freedom in such poems as "Parlaq baxışla nurunu gör afitabının" ("Bariqeyi-inqilab"), "Ey Şərq günəşi, çıx bulut altından, əyan ol, Zülmati-mühitatımıza sübhfəsan ol! Ey yer günəşi, parla bu yer sübhə bürünsün, Yırtsın şu qaranlıqları ki, yolda görünsün ("Bahari-əfkar"), "Aliheyi-Hüriyyətə!", "Ya leyl", "Bariqeyi-zəfər parlayır, istiqbal bizimdir" by Muhammad Hadi, as well as those written by Huseyn Javid.

Azerbaijani poetry, embracing features of primordial figurativeness, is bound up, first of all, with traditions, and ethnic symbols. The mythic model in an informa-

20 *Sunrise* – English translation by G.G.

21 *Full Moon* – English translation by G.G.

22 Translated from Azerbaijani by G.G.: "Hilalə döndü qəmər qaşların hilalından/Boyandı qana qızıl gül yanağın alından/Ayın hilalı, əgərçi günəşdən aılr nur/ Bu ayı gör ki, günəş nur alır hilalından."

23 Translated from Turkish by G. G.: "Sıcaklık kaynağı olaraq Günəş canlılıq, tutku ve gencligi simgeler. İşık kaynağı olarak aydınlanmayı da temsil eder ... Doğup batışı doğum, ölüm və diriliyin sembölüdür."

tive way to presentat the national symbolic repertory, on the one hand, while the e symbol's transformation has managed to make the content more substantial, on the other hand. From this point of view, the primordial image turns into a continuation of not only the period and time when it was formed, but also on the national and moral plane, a sacred and artistic baton passed between yesterday and today, and today and tomorrow.

References

Abbasova Mətanət. Klassik Azərbaycan hekayətində bədii simvol (1900-1920). Bakı, 2004 (PhD thesis).

Ауэр А. *Символ.* Литературная учеба. 1983, № 5.

Aujer A. *Simvol.* Literaturnaja ucheba. 1983, № 5.

Azərbaycan ədəbiyyatı tarixi. Bakı, Elm, 2004.

Əhməd Cavad. *Seçilmiş əsərləri.* 2 cilddə, 1 c, Bakı, Azərnəşr, 1992.

Əliyev Kamran. Azərbaycan romantizminin poetikası. Bakı, Elm, 2002.

Hadi M. *Seçilmiş əsərləri.* Bakı, Şərq-Qərb, 2009.

Qocayev M. K.Q.Yunq. Analitik psixologiya və bədii yaradıcılıq. Mütərcim, 1998, № 2.

Nəsimi İ. *Məndə sığar iki cahan.* Bakı, Gənclik, 1973.

Nəsimi İ. *Seçilmiş əsərləri.* – Azərbaycan Klassik Ədəbiyyatı Kitabxanası. 20 cilddə. 5-ci cild. – Bakı: Elm, 1985. – 368 s.

Sasani Çingiz. Orta əsrlər Azərbaycan poeziyasında naturalist ədəbi-fəlsəfi fikir. Bakı, Elm, 2007.

Semboller ve işaretler. Alfa, 2010.

XX əsr Azərbaycan poeziyası antologiyası. I kitab. 1920-ci illərin poeziyası. Bakı, Elm, 2003.

Юнг К. Г. *Архетип и символ.* http://www.klex.ru/2x4.

Jung K. G. *Arhetip i simvol.* http://www.klex.ru/2x4.

Hauptmann, Gerhart February 2012. chttp://classiclit.about.com/cs/ profiles writers/p/aa_ghauptmann.htm.

On the relation of analytical psychology to poetry by Carl Gustav Jung http://www.studiocleo.com/librarie/jung/essay.html.

Психологический словарь. Архетипы. http://psi.webzone.ru /st/ 302000.htm.

Psihologicheskij slovar'. Arhetipy. http://psi.webzone.ru/st/302000.htm

Quotations on Sound, the Name and the Word http://www. trismegistos.com/ MagicalLetterPage/Quotations.html.

Энциклопедия знаков и символов http://www.znaki.chebnet.com/s10. php?id =560.

Jenciklopedija znakov i simvolov http://www.znaki.chebnet.com/s10.php?id =560.

Энциклопедия мифологии. Архетипы. http://dic.academic.ru/dic. nsf/enc_ myphology/1657.

Jenciklopedija mifologii. Arhetipy. http://dic.academic.ru/dic.nsf/enc_ mypholo gy/1657.

Part 6
Mythology Archetypes and Totems

Archetypes of Turkic Culture

Anuar Galiev
(Kazakhstan)

The study of the formation of the social structure of Turkic peoples of Central Asia has a long tradition. The same can be said about the traditional organization of Kazakhs into three *zhuzes* (hordes). The most popular theory by V.V. Bartold suggested that they are related to three the geographical zones of Kazakhstan (Бартольд [Bartold]1925).

However this hypothesis does not take into consideration other phenomena of Kazakh culture.

This paper offers a semiotics analisis of Kazakh society as well as of formation of the classical structure of Turkic society. I suggest that the social structure is a reflection of a more general spatial model of socio-cosmos, a kind of matrix or archetype, to which all cultural phenomena correlating (Раевский [Raevskiy]1990). The cosmic model represents the image of Space, which helps to construct the phenomena of an earthly world for human understanding.

In human representation space is traditionally divided into three parts: upper, middle, and lower. The idea of a tripartite space is manifasted as a World River, a World Mountain, and as an antropomorphic model.

Spatial zones are compared to parts of the human body, an idea that is related to the mythological notion that the universe was created from a body of the first human. In "A Hymn of Purusha" (Rigveda, X, 90) there is a narrative about gods sacrificing the giant first human Purusha.

The gods cut his body into several parts: the sky was created out of the head, the earth out of his feet, and other parts of Purusha became various social groups: from his mouth came Brahmins (priests), from his hands the warriors, and from the hips the peasants (Бонгард [Bongard] 1985: 165).

The differentiation into the groups took place as a result of the formation of social groups with three distinct functions: 1. religious, 2. military, and 3. economic (Дюмезиль [Dumesil] 1986: 25.). Harmony among these functions is necessary for a balanced social life.

People speaking Indo-European languages give us many examples of separation into three social groups. However we are only going to analyse those that are connected to the territory of Kazakhstan. These are the Iranians (East Iranian) tribes of the Sakas, Scythians, and Alans. They occupied the steppes of Kazakhstan during the ancient times.

The Nart's epic of the modern Ossetians – descendants of the East Iranian Scythians, Alans and Sarmatians-has many examples of tripartite systems (Nart Sagas 1987: 48).

As shown above, ancient Indo-European society had a threefold social model. In Indian and Iranian traditions each social group was also associated with spatial zones. Priests were connected to the upper heavenly sphere, warriors occupied the space between heaven and earth, while peasants were relegated to the earth and the sphere of fertility (Гафуров [Gafurov] 1972: 31.).

Furthermore, each function was transferred to a person by a certain gift-symbol. The Indo-Europeans knew many such symbols. The first mythological king of Iran known from the *Avesta*, Yima, divided society into three classes, and received the divine gifts of a golden arrow and a lash from Ahura-Mazda. The gifts were to help him to expand the earth which couldn't fit the groing population of human and cattle. Since then these objects became emblems of the Iranian people (Кузьмина [Kuzmina] 1977: 62).

In the tomb of the "golden man" of Issyk, archeologists found a lash wrapped up with a golden ribbon, a golden arrowhead and a bronze mirror. The Roman historian Quintus Curtius Rufus in the "History of Alexander" (VII, 8, 17 18) wrote about the magical heavenly gifts of the Sakas. Peasants received a plough and a yoke for a bull, warriors received a spear and an arrow, and the priests were given a bowl.

The Scythians of the Black Sea Coast narrated almost the same legend to Herodotus (History, IV, 5-7). The three sons Targitaj, who was the ancestor of the Scythians, found a plough and a yoke, an axe, and a bowl, which had fallen from the sky in a fiery light (Ibid. p. 93). Each of these gifts represents one of three functions: a plough and yoke – economic, a pole-axe – military, the bowl – religious (Абаев 1990: 424). According to D.S.Raevski, each object corresponds to one of the brothers. The three social groups founded by the brothers became the three social classes (Раевский [Raevski] 1985: 27). Fairy tales about three brothers are widely spread in the world. They are directly connected to one of the three functions lead by each brother.

Kazakh oral tradition also explains the origin of the three Kazakh *zhuzes* as originating from three brothers. A.I Levshin (Levshin A. 1832: 5) recorded such a Kazakh legend. When the khan (king) died, the people were divided among his three sons. These groups began to be called by the birthrank of the princes: Senior, Middle, and Youngest.

As was shown above, Indo-Europeans connected each brother with one of the functions which was symbolized by a certain object. V.I. Abaev, the outstanding Ossetian scientist wrote: "Similar legends exist outside the Indo-European world. For example, Kazakhs have the legend about three brothers who were ancestors of the Kazakh people. The gods gave Adaj an arrow, Arghun writing, and Usun a shepherd's staff. As a result, the descendants of Adaj became warriors, those of Argyn "scholars", and Usun's descendents became shepherds" (Абаев 1990 [Abaev]: 425-426).

This information shows that Kazakhs connected the origin of the *zhuzes* with three brothers. Each brother carries out a specific social function, and each function is connected to a particular symbolic object. One variant of the legend even names the carrier of the military function. His name is Alash, which is also the name of the legendary first king and ancestor of the Kazakhs.

One fairy tale connects the military function with the youngest brother. The other two brothers try to kill him The younger brother concentrates all symbols in own hands, which means the three functions merge into one. But Kazakh tradition differs from this fairy tale. As the Kazakh scientist C.C. Valihanov wrote: "The principle of differentiation conditioned by the right of elders and the strength of the tribe, which derives from the ancestral origins, has a big impact on their family law and was accepted completely in genealogical sense; since the relationship of hordes and the families of the hordes correlates with the principle of blood kinship, and the relations of families to their horde correlate to the relation of a son to a father, to the oldest family of the oldest tribe correlates to the relationship of a nephew to an uncle. Most characteristic of this tradition are the disputes of the steppe bards about the excellence of their tribe and their ancestor."(Valikhanov Ch. 1985:148) In other words, the oldest zhuzes were considered to be more respected by right of primogeniture (For comparison, Indians consider the boy-Brahmin to be above the old man-Kshatry). The names of *zhuzes* (Senior, Middle, and Youngest) also show that the system of *zhuzes* is hierarchical. The nomination of zhuzes rests on the principle of hierarchy and not on the time of the origins.

This conclusion corresponds to the information given. The analysis shows that the Kazakh's national tradition connects the origin of *zhuzes* with three brothers, whose relationship is hierarchically constructed. The national legend relates each brother,that is, a *zhuz* with one function, that is, a symbolic object:

1. The staff is a symbol of manhood; it is the source of abundance; it assists in the creation and maintenance of the herd, the main wealth of a herdsman. The staff is also a sceptre, an attribute of a shepherd-king, who resides over Society and the Cosmos. Kazakhs consider the staff to be the symbol of the Senior *zhuz*. As a symbol of the economic function it promotes the idea of abundance.
2. A feather is most probably a later alteration of an older functionally identical symbol (. Abaev V.I., ibid. p.425). It is the symbol of the Middle *zhuz* and holds an "ideological" function.

3. The spear is a symbol of the Youngest *zhuz* and has a military function. The "History of Alexander" (VII, 8, 17-18) relates the story about how the spear was a symbol of military function for the Sakas. In German mythology the military function is symbolised by a sword.

The old Turkic ethnogenetic legend also narrates a story about symbolical objects-gifts. Oguz Khagan, the ancestor of the Oguzes, married two girls. The first girl came down from the sky on a blue beam, associated with the elements of light. The second girl was found in a tree hollow, associated with the elements of water, earth, and sky. From the first wife three sons were born, who received the names Sun, Moon, and Star. The children of the second wife are called Sky, Mountain, and Sea. Oguz Khagan hides a golden bow and three golden (silver) arrows in the steppe and sends his sons to hunt for them. The three elder sons find the bow, the three younger ones find three arrows (Fazlallah Rashid al-Din 1987: 60). The elder sons receive more honour, as a bow is more important than arrows.

The story further relates that the six sons of Oguz Khagan each had four sons. The twenty four grandsons of Oguz Khagan became the ancestors of the twenty four Oguz tribes. The legend of the Turks reminds us of the legend of the Indo-Europeans, but it also has distinctive features relelated to the core of the problem. The golden objects of the bow and arrows would symbolize a military function according to Dumesil. However if the Indo-European objects establish a functional hierarchy between religious (ideological), military and economic powers, the hierarchy here is defined by master and subordinate (Dumezil J. 1990: 160-161).

Furthermore, the magic objects – bow and arrows – of the Turkic legend present symbols of male and female genders. The arrow, as connected with the bow, serves as a metaphor for the union of the masculine and feminine, the idea of harmony and order in Cosmos. The bow and an arrow are descriptions of Turkic society. In his analysis of the social structure of the Central Asian nomads J.A. Zuev has shown that the military system was projected onto their system of family relationships, with such markers as the left wing – the centre – the right wing (Zuev, Y. 1981: 65).

This construction described not only marriage customs and military organization, but also the whole structure of Turkic society. However such a threefold social organization did not belong to the Turks alone.

The Turkic social organization can be represented in the form of a bow which has two parts and a centre, expressing the idea of military function. But the tripartite organization did not have only a military function. Its basic function was the regulation of marriage customs as well as the coordination of military actions. The Turkic social organization can be defined as a "horizontal organization", but this term is conditional.

The names of sons of Oghuz Khagan from the legend of Oguz Khagan and an inscription in honour of Kul-Tegin, correlates with the names of sons of Targitaj, marking vertical zones of the Cosmos. Thus, Kazakh society has a combination of "vertical" and "horizontal" positions. Kazakhs, as well as other people of Central Asia were divided on the principle of "the left" – "the right", but thes tribes were placed into the structure of *zhuzes* which was not based on this division. In other words *zhuzes* had no "left-right" divisions. which makes the nature of Kazakh *zhuzes* different from Turkic, and similar to the Indo-European social division.

As was mentioned before, the Indo-European tripartite organization is based on the performance of functional duties, and this creates a substantial difference between the two types of tripartite societies. The legend about *zhuzes* and their functional nature provides grounds for considering this type of the organization as similar to the Indo-European type.

This conclusion is further supported by the use of colour symbolism used in Central Asian societies. The three zones of space were marked by three colours (white, black, red). Some Turkic people compared one colour of this triad with one social group (Turner V. 1983: 102-103)

Kazakhs also used a colour code. The Kazakh tribe of Argyn, was divided into three groups: white (ak), yellow (sary), and kara (black). Other tribes of Kazakhs – Kangly, shared ak (white), sary (yellow), kyzyl (red), and kara (black) (Kaydarov A.T. 1984: 41).

In Indo-European Society every functional group correlated to the certain Cosmic zone, and as we would expect, with a certain colour. For example, the Indian terms *varna* and Iranian *pishtra* means colour (Gafurov B. Op. cit. p. 31).

The color white represents the top zone of space. Kazakhs sacrificed white horses that were considered sacred because of their colour (Argynbaev H.A. 1989: 258).

Colors are connected with social groups and the latter with spatial zones. We could suggest that the social groups originated from the three age groups. W. Brandenstein considered that three sons of Targitaj are representatives of three age groups. The association of the age groups with colours can be noticed in one Kazakh custom. If a flag flutters on top of a yurta it means that a member of the family has died. If the flag is red, it means that a young man died. A black flag means that the dead person was middle aged, and a white flag means that the deceased was an old man (Valikhanov Ch. 1984: 333). Thus, there is a connection between certain colours, ages and social statuses. This connection is clearly seen in an initiation ceremony. The ceremony is represented in a number of Kazakh magic fairy tales, especially in the ethnogenetic legend about Alash Khan.

Alash-khan (the Motley Khan) is the main character of the legend. His name is also related to horses. J.A. Zuev (Zuev, Y. ibid. p. 2.) has paid attention to the name “Alat”, or “Skewbald horse”. According to him, the name does not refer to the breeding or the possession of motley horses. Rather this name symbolizes “collecting” and “mixing” with women from the four parts of the world (from the conquered or vassal countries) by the victorious king. The Central Asian people used a horse of a certain colour to symbolise each of the four principal directions. Therefore, the name Alash referred to his ability to gather wives from all conquered parts of world, that is to be a successful ruler.

The conclusion of J. A. Zuev is correct, but it should be modified. Colours of horses are not only symbols of the four horizontal principal directions. Horses are also markers of a vertical tripartite spatial model. When archaeologists excavated a barrow of Arzhan, they found that some of the horses buried there were light in colour, with the majority of horses being golden-red colour, like in imperial barrows of the Scythians. The different colours of horses suggest that the Arzhan ruler concentrated both the spiritual and secular power in his hands. For comparison, the tripartite nature of the imperial attributes of the Iranian kings was expressed in their red attire and a headdress with coloured ribbons (Kuzmina E.E., ibid, p.96).

Thus, the correlation of the *varnas* (colours) of priests, warriors, and peasants, and the colours of horses is established. Therefore the name of Alash-khan means Colourful King (or the Motley horse). His name refers the combination of the three social functions.

Indians used to have a ceremony called *radzhasuyya,* in which an applicant for an imperial rank should be of the *varna* of the *kshatriya*. He was converted to Brahmin *varna*, then again back to *Kshatriya varna*. Thus the ceremony of *radzhasuyya* symbolised the combination of both military and sacral functions in hands of the king.

M. Mori is of the opinion that the role of the first Turkic khagans was connected with shamans-smiths. We see that these social roles (the leader, the shaman-smith) were combined in late Turkic tradition. As we see, the king held in his own hands not only military but also religious functions. But there is still a third function – economic. The king should hold this function as well. We can find such a ritual among the Indians. The king on his coronation day was to eat the food of simple shepherds. This myth suggests that the legendary – ancestor-ruler was brought up in a family of simple people who were connected to the production of material goods.

The economic function became fundamental, as Ancient people held the king to be responsible for the fertility of the earth and the prosperity of the people. The combination of the three functions which are designated by three colours gives us “diversity of colour,” that is, “Alash”. But each colour marks one of the three worlds, and therefore we can assume that Alash is the embodiment of such tripartate space. This reminds us of the work of the famous Osset scientist, V.Uarziati. He wrote that the Kazakh khan, Alash, has an Osset double, called Alguz (Uarziati V. 1995: 237).

The following facts confirm our conclusion as well as show the way for understanding the nature of the three social functions The tri-functional character of Kazakh society proves true, compared to the Turkic and Indo-European (Indo-Iranian) society and spacial models.

Indo-European model

(Scythians)

Upper	Middle	Lower
Upper World	World of Manhood	Underworld
Heaven	Mountain	Water

Turkic model (Traditional World of Turks of Southern Siberia 1990: 101).

Upper World	**Middle World**	**Underworld**
Heaven	Joining Heaven to Earth	Bottom
Top of World Mountain	Foot of World Mountain	Cave of World Mountain
Crown of World Tree	Trunk of World Tree	Roots of World Tree
Source of World River	Middle of World River	Mouth of World River

As we see, there is no big difference between the Turkic and the Indo-European models;. They are based on a universal human model.

However, a difference is revealed in comparing Turkic and Indo-European societies, which is illustrated in the charts below.

Indo-European model

Scythians:			
Name of three Brothers	Koloxai	Lipoxai	Arpoxai
Symbols	Bow and arrows	Bowl	Plough and yoke
Social Groups	Warriors	Priests	Peasants
Indians:	Kshatriya	Brahmins	Vaisyas
Functions:	Military	Religious	Economical

Turkic model

Existence	Male	connection between male and female	Female
Symbols	Arrows	Connecting arrows and bow	Bow
Side	Left	Center	Right
Brothers	Youngest		Eldest

Comparison of these models shows:

1. The Turkic model is a military-patrimonial model
2. The Indo-Europeans model is a functional one. The set of elements of the Turkic model is characteristic for horizontal model of space (left and right). The Indo-Europeans model is a vertical model (upper, the middle, a lower). The Kazakh model looks as follow:

Kazakh Model

Brother	Eldest *zhuz*	Middle *zhuz*	Younger *zhuz*
Symbols	Staff	Book (Feather)	Spear
Functions	Economic	Religious	Military

Functions which were marked by symbolical things correspond with the spacial zones. The scheme shows that the Kazakh social model is close to the Indo-European model. The tripartite space and tri-functional societies were modelled in various rituals. The purpose of these sacral actions is evident in the creation of social space. The idea of divisding society into three functional groups also appears in the ritual practices of the Kazakhs. For example, it shows up in the arrangement of a dwelling. Many researchers consider the house to be a model of the world.

Kazakhs consider the house (*yurta*) to be an anthropomorphic spatial model. The frame of the *yurta* is called *Uiidyn suegic*, that is "skeleton", and the back of the house is *arkasy* (back) аркасы (Kunanbaev A. Shakhanova N. 1990: 20-22)

Thus, the *yurta* corresponds to a body of a person in whom all elements of space are incorporated. The *yurta* has a number of features of a vertical model. The place of honour is intended for the most esteemed visitor and the master of the house. It corresponds to the top zone of the universe. When Kazakhs welcome a visitor they say *Zhogary shygynys, that is* "Passing upward" (Traditional world of Turks of Southern Siberia 1988: 65).

The space near the door is connected with the opposite idea. This part of the house is associated with children. This shows the social status of a person is connected with a certain space in a house. The Turks coordinated this status with the concepts of "top and bottom", and also with the concepts of "left and right". We can read in an inscription in honour of Kul Tegin that on the right there are chiefs ("Shad"), and at the left stand "Tarkhans" and mandatives (Malov S.E. 1951: 33, 35, 38, 41-43).

Observing the custom of the order of special occupation was an integral part of Kazakh ritual. During the ritual of the election of the *khan* (crowning of a king) a certain order was observed. Representatives of tribes occupied certain places near the carpet on which the new ruler was lifted (Velyaminov-Zernov V.V. 1864: 2,434). This order was observed also near the throne. In various ceremonies and rituals, including the order of occupation of places, the least senior tribe of the senior *zhuz* was placed before the most senior tribe of the middle *zhuz* (Sultanov, T.I. 1982: 98).

This ritual was observed at all levels. We see it both at the family level and at the level of relations between *zhuzes*. During rituals, *zhuzes* did not associate with members of a family, but with brothers, ancestors of *zhuzes*.

Hence, the ritual order for the occupation of places in the social model takes place both in the vertical and the horizontal levels. These levels consist of three sections. The horizontal level has such markers as a left-hand side, the centre and the right hand side. The left-hand side is female, the most honourable part. The right side is the male part. This horizontal model is wide-spread among the Turkic and Mongolian people. But its traces can be seen in the practices of the people of Europe. For instance, in a Catholic church, the left is the women's place, and the right the men's place. As seen above, Turkic people assigned a hierarchy for these areas: the centre, the left side, and the right side.

Among the Kazakhs the vertical tri-partite arrangement is connected to the vertical tripartite model of space. The place of honour corresponds to the top zone of the universe and the senior *zhuz* and the eldest brother. The intermediary zone of space is connected to the centre of the house and the middle brother. The bottom zone of space corresponds to the youngest brother and the space near the door. In rituals each zone is connected with one of the *zhuz*. This correlation is also observed at meals. The ritual meal is necessary for establishment of social relations. It is a display of the act of society's creation and spatial assignments. Its purpose is the maintainance and reaffirming of space.

M.M.Bakhtin has shown that the ritual meal is a universal celebration of life over death. To each member of a ritual meal corresponds a certain place as well as a certain part of meat from a sacrificial animal. The correlation of a share of meat with the participant of a meal is the display of an archetype. It is the creation of different parts of a society and space from a certain part of a body of the first sacrificial, human victim.

The Turkic tradition considers that Igat-Irgyl-Hodzha, the vizier of Oguz Khan, initiated the custom of distribution sacrificial meat. Irgyl distributed meat as follows: The right wing tribes, *bozok,* received the right scapula and a pelvis, while the left wing tribes, *uchok,* were given the left side of the animal (Fazlallah Rashid al-Din, ibid, p. 64-67). Spacial arrangement and society are presented in the Turkic tradition as the interaction of male (right) and female (left) elements. Other examples of the existence of this principle are shown in the chart below:

MALE	FEMALE
Arrow	Bow
Right wing	Left wing
Right side of home	Left side of home
Right side of animal's body	Left side of animal's body

We find this principle also in thetraditions described in "Oguz-name and in the social structure of the Siberian Turks and Kirghiz.

The Hun model is similar to the Turkic model. Huns were divided into two parts, each consisting of 12 tribes. The 24 tribes of Oguzes, Huns, Turkman, and the 12 tribes of Kimaks originated from the 24 ribs of the first human as a result of a primal act of sacrifice. This tradition is found among the Altay Turks who call a tribe a *seok*, meaning "bone". The Indo-Europeans and the Semitic people also have the tradition of division into 12 parts (12 tribes of Israel).

The sacrificial animal is divided into three parts in Indo-Europeans tradition. The Ossetians have a proverb: "The first honour is the honour of the head, the second honour is the honour of the neck, and the third honour it is for the scapula". Hosts distribute these three parts to guests during meal time. Each part corresponds to the age of the guest. Kazakhs give a head to the most senior and dearest visitor. The second person receives the pelvis. Ribs are distributed among other visitors. This material testifies to the Kazakh tradition which differs from the Turkic, but is close to Indo-Iranian (Indo-European).

Each *zhuz* corresponds to a certain brother, a place in the house, and a section of meat. Each place in the house corresponds to a part of a body of an animal. The sacrificial animal corresponds to the body of the first legendary victim. The Kazakh model of the world reconstructed the Indo-European myth about Purusha. The basic idea of the myth and ritual is the reconstruction of harmony, that is, the repetition of an archetype. M. Eliade wrote that a ritual is the repetition of an action of the gods who created space and a society. Ancient people thought that the world was created from a body of the first human. In order to repair the broken world, they repeated the act of a human sacrifice. Thus the action of sacrifice symbolised the rebirth of the world and the victory of a life over death.

The substitution of an animal victim for a human victim was a grand event in the life of mankind. This action is reflected in the biblical story about Abraham and his son and in the Islamic tradition of ritualistic animal sacrifice. But the idea about the creation of the world from a body of a victim has not died out. People repeat this archetype in rituals and traditions whenever they wish to restore harmony.

We have made attempts to restore the model of Kazakh space and society. This model is tripartite. The tripartite model reflects social relations. The social model of Indo-Europeans included three elements and three functions. Therefore in Indo-European society there were three social classes. One group was connected with a military function, another with the economic, and a third connected with religious functions. Symbolic objects reflect the characteristic of these groups.

The society of the Turkic people was based on a system of intermarriage practices and military organization. This society was divided into the left wing, the centre and the right wing. This system was also infused with symbolical objects (bow and arrows). The bow was a feminine existence, the arrows were symbol of the masculine one.

Thus there are two different types of societies. Their rituals and ceremonies recreate the social systems of both Turks and Indo-European peoples. The *Zhuz* structure of Kazakh society was based on mytho-cosmological beliefs, where the three parts of Kazakh land represented Cosmic zones and served to establish Kazakh society

References

Abaev V.I., *A Trojan horse*, / Abaev V.I. Selected Works. Vladikavkaz. 1990.

Abaev V.I., *Notes on the Trifunctionality*. in Abaev V.I., Selected Works. Vladikavkaz, 1990.

Argynbaev H.A., Traditional Forms of Marriage among Kazakhs, in Ethnic History and Culture of Central Asian and Kazakhstan nations, Nukus.1989.

Bartold V.V., The History of Research in Eastern Europe and Russia.

Bongard-Levin G.M., Ilyin G.F., *India in Ancient Times.* M., 1985.

Dumezil J., *Scythians and Narts.* M., 1990.

Dumezil J., Supreme Gods of the Indo-Europeans, M. 1986.

Eliade M., *Cosmos and History.* M., 1987.

Fazlallah Rashid al-Din, *Oguz-Name.* Baku.1987.

Gafurov B. *Tajiks.* M., 1972.

Kaydarov A.T., On the Historical and Linguistic Characteristics of the ethnonym “kingly”, in Turkic Onomastics, 1984.

Kunanbaev A. Shakhanova N., Yurt in the Traditional World views ¬ nomadic Central Asian-Kazakhstan region.A., 1990.
Kuzmina, E. In the Country of Kawat and Afrosiab. M., 1977.L., 1925.
Levshin A., Description of the Kirghiz Cossacks or Kirghiz-Kaysak hordes and steppes, S-Pb., 1832, Part 3.
Malov S.E., Monuments of the Ancient Literature, M.-L. 1951.
Nart sagas, , M, 1987.
Potanin G.N., Oriental Motifs in Medieval Europian Epic, M., 1969.
Rajewski D.S, The World Model of the Scythian Culture. M., 1985
Rajewski D.S., Scythian Society and the G. Dumezil's Three-Functional Concept, Iranian and Alanian Studies, Vladikavkaz, 1990.
Sultanov, T.I., The Nomadic tribes of the Aral Sea Region, XV-XVII centuries, M., 1982.
Traditional World of Turks of Southern Siberia, Inst-Birsk. 1990.
Traditional world of Turks of Southern Siberia. Novosibirsk. 1988.
Turner V., *Symbol and Ritual.* M., 1983.
Uarziati V., On the History of Ethno-Symbolism Alan-Ossetians, Nomadic Culture at the Turn of Centuries, A. 1995.
Uarziati V.S., On the "fyng" table and the ritual food of Ossetians, in Literary Osetiya,1990, N4.
Valikhanov Ch., *Diary of the Trip to Issyk-Kul,* in Collected Works in five volumes. A., 1984.
Valikhanov Ch., *Kyrgyz Genealogy* / Valikhanov Ch... Collected Works. in five volumes. Volume 2, A., 1985.
Valikhanov Ch., *Kyrgyz Lineage.* In Collected Works.
Velyaminov-Zernov V.V., Investigation of Kasimov kings and princes. S-Pb., 1864.
Yudin V.P., *Hordes: White, Blue, Grey, Gold ...*// Kazakhstan, Middle and Central Asia in the XVI-XVIII centuries. A.,1983.
Zuev, Y. The Historical projection ofKazakh genealogical legends, in Kazakhstan in the Era of Feudalism. A. 1981.

Artistic Personification of Opposites: Analyses of "Medea" by Sandro Shanshiashvili

Irina Modebadze, Tamar Tsitsishvili
(Georgia)

The contrast between East and West,[1] also topical of the present time, was very important during the whole history of those people whose culture developed at the borders of Asia and Europe. The reason behind focusing on the similarities and differences of Eastern and European cultures is closely related to the search for national identity, which found wide reflection in the literatures of these peoples, including Georgian literature. Often the *East-West* opposition is artistically resolved in a literary piece by treating it in terms of what is "*mine and what is the other's*" in conflicts between characters who have different mentalities, national characters, and behavioral models.

This problem becomes especially acute in the beginning of the 20th century when in the *East-West* dichotomy the opposition of symbolic notions of *civilization-barbarity* (barbarity taken as *naturalness, primitiveness*, nearness to the *origin*) is clearly seen. Echoes of this implication are heard in the reasoning of R. Kipling, Gr. Robakidze, D. Merezhkovsky and many others. They emphasize the differences in the *attitude to the world* of the carriers of "western" and "eastern" cultures.[2] In this period the increasing interest in the heritage of ancient civilizations and Greco-Roman mythology and literature, the characters of which

---

1 "The East and the West are two different worlds not only in the geographic respect but, using the apt expression of the Russian thinker Chaadaev, – in the very way things are [...] it should be mentioned that in the being of the East the accent is made on the sprout, whereas in the being of the West the plant itself goes to the forefront. The East dissolves its essence, its "ego" in the origin: for it any beginning is the origin. And the West develops into the personal monade and for it the beginning almost always means the only possible new origin [...]. The East is fragrant with the origin. All objects in the origin are a single whole (Robakidze 2001:61). "The soul of the Russian people remains an eternal enigma for Europe. We resemble you as the left hand resembles the right hand: the right hand does not coincide with the left one in one and the same plane ... According to Kant, your area is phenomenal, ours is transcendental; according to Nietzsche – you have Apollo in you, we have Dionysis ... Not in the mind and feeling [...] but in our innermost will we are mystics" (Merezhkovsky 1999: 57-58), etc.

2 "Medea" by S.Shanshiashvili is included in the cycle of poems ("Demetica", "Jason and Reno" "Golden Fleece", "Medea" and "Beautiful Helen") written by him in 1911-1912 (in so-called Swiss period of his work) and devoted to antiquity.

often represent specific human qualities, also attracts attention. In this atmosphere the myth about Medea emerges. It is a poem based on the Greek tragedy of the same name, written by the Georgian poet and playwright S.Shanshiashvili (1888-1979). The poem reflects the significance of Medea's character from the standpoint of Georgian cultural mentality in the beginning of the 20th century.[3]

The character of Medea in ancient mythology and literature is complex and by no means unambiguous: she is the granddaughter of Helios, minister of the godess Gecata, and a powerful enchantress. Contrary to her father's wishes, using her magic, Medea helps Jason steal the Golden Fleece and take it away from her motherland of Colchis. She marries Jason., and leaves her paternal house for the sake of love. She is a wife devoted to her husband's interests. She does not stop at murder (Glauce and Creon). Abandoned by Jason, she kills her own children in terrible revenge.

This character has exerted a magical attraction on poets, writers, playwrights, painters, and composers since the time of Ancient Greece to the present day. Medea is a character in the works by Pindar, Euripides, Apollodorus, Seneca, P. Veroneze, E. Delakrua, P. Cornel, F. V. Gotter, F. M. Klinger, Z. Anua, J.B. Niccolini, F. Choker and many others. For centuries, the image of a princess from Colchis preserved by ancient mythology has also been exciting for Georgian writers and poets, for whom it had a special attraction. First and foremost, they regard her as a native of Colchis.[4]

The unification of the old Kartveli (old Georgian) tribes, first known as Eya (Αια) or Colchis (Κολχίς) and later Lazika (Λαζική) played a part in Greek mythology in antiquity, and was the scene of action of many legendary events. Colchis was of considerable importance in the history of the Greeks and later for the Romans. In the dialogue "Phedon" it is said: "The earth is very big and we inhabit only a minor part of it, from Phasis to the Pillars of Hercules" (μέγρι Ἡρακλείων στηλων άπό Φάσιδος), (Platonis 1931:LV1I1) i.e. from the banks of Rioni to the Strait of Gibraltar. The recognition of Phasis (present river Rioni) as one of the borders of the ancient cultural world known to Plato, the author of the dialogue, was not purely coincidental. For Greek and Roman authors Colchis and its tribes were part of their history (Urushadze 1980:21-28). However, it should be mentioned,

3 Without going into details, it can be stated that in Georgian literature the character and the name of Medea has been repeatedly used both in poetry and in prose during its centuries-old history to the present day. In particular, such famous writers and poets as Ak.Tsereteli, K.Kapaneli, G.Tabidze, O Chiladze, L.Sanikidze and many, many others also did not deprive Medea of their attention. In 2008.

4 Comparison of various translations makes it possible to suppose that working on the poem S. Shanshiashvili used the text of tragedy of Euripides "Medea" in Innokenti Annensky's translation (1856-1909) into Russian, issued in 1909.

in their opinion Colchis was the "outskirts" – the most distant borderland of ancient civilization, a world inhabited by "barbarians"...

In ancient mythology Colchis/Eya appears as a legendary country, the home of the Golden Fleece, ruled by the formidable king of Eetes/Aeetes, the son of the God Helios, and his daughter, the enchantress Medea. It was to this place, the kingdom of Aeetes, that Phrixus (son of king Athanas) had been brought by the Ram with a Golden Fleece, the gift of the God Hermes. The ram was sacrificed to Zeus, and the Golden Fleece was hung by Aeetes on the tree in the sacred grove of Ares. We know the story of Jason and Medea from the myths about the expedition of Agronauts for the Golden Fleece to the banks of Phasis (river Rioni). Here, in ancient Colchis, by the will of Gods, Aeete's daughter Medea became enamoured of Jason (according to some versions of the myth, the passion for Jason was inspired by Aphrodite by order of Hera) and from this fatal moment began the most tragic period in her life.

Of all the aspects of the myth about Medea the greatest attention in Georgian literature has traditionally given precisely to the Corinthian period, in particular, to the story of the child murder. Such a murder committed by a mother is unacceptable in most cultures, including the Orthodox Christianity of the Georgia. In this context the poem by S. Shanshiashvili is not an exception, a fact which is unequivocally shown by its subtitle "Medea in Corinth, Marriage of Jason to Creuza, Medea's vengeance."

Such abilities of Medea's as her power to raise the dead and to fly suggest that initially Medea was respected as a goddess. Probably the image of Medea combined the features of the sun goddess, the powerful witch of Thessalian fairy-tales respected in Colchis, and one of the characters of the Corinthian epic, where Medea and her father were regarded as natives of Corinth. In Greece Medea became a symbol of a cruel and treacherous foreigner with a magical gift, and therefore a dangerous figure. The fabulous abilities of Medea underwent substantial changes in the creative work of Greek and Roman writers. The theme of the unrequited love of Medea for Jason, outlined already by Pindar, was developed in the tragedy of the same name by Euripides where Medea became a killer of her children. Seneca (tragedy "Medea") describes her as a harsh avenger, acting with cruel consistency (Mythological Dictionary 1990: online). Thus, as far back as ancient times a fixed tradition to interpret the tragic triangle Medea ↔ Jason ↔ Creuza from the standpoint of foreignness, the other-ness of the "dangerous" foreigner to Greek culture was created. It is exactly this point that becomes especially significant in the poem by S. Shanshiashvili.

As is known, there are several versions of the Corinthian period of Medea's life. S. Shanshiashvili, generally following the plotline of the Euripidean tragedy, gives his own interpretation of the tragic events. Emphasizing the opposition

Civilization (Jason) – Barbarity (Medea), the poet develops and emphasizes the theme of Medea's foreignness in the Hellenic society outlined by Euripides:

A good Greek land hath been Thy lasting home, not barbary. Thou hast seen Our ordered life, and justice, and the long Still grasp of law not changing with the strong Man's pleasure.	ველურ ქვეყნით მოგიყვანე ბარბაროსი და ურჩხული, და უწვრთნელმა ელლინთ მხარეს გაიცანი სწორე სჯული	(I've) brought from the wild country (world) a barbarian and monster and (you) untrained, in the country of ancient Greeks got familiar with the just rule.
(Euripides1912:30) (4)		(Shanshiashvili 1964:191)

In the previous poems of the cycle Jason's lack of sincere feelings is emphasized (in Colchis he is driven only by profit and does not conceal this from the Colchis princess). Therefore, in the poem by S. Shanshiashvili Jason's intention to marry Creuza receives a clear motivation: Jason abandons Medea not because of love for Creuza, not for fear of her magic abilities and the cruelty of her "barbarian" nature (as is interpreted in some monuments) and even not because of her "barbarian" origin (which is repeatedly emphasized by S.Shanshiashvili), but again for profit: a marriage to the heiress of Corinth opens for Jason a road to power and wealth, to the desired throne. In this connection, of interest is the interpretation of Euripides' dialogue between Medea and Jason when the woman in despair makes the last attempt to call her husband back. Jason tries to explain to Medea that she should be glad of his new prospect since the accession of Jason to the throne in Corinth will strengthen the position of her own sons:

I sought to rear Our sons in nurture worthy of my race, And, raising brethren to them, in one place Join both my houses, and be all from now Prince-like and happy.	და თუ ეხლა ცოლად ვირთავ მე კორინთის მეფის ქალსა, – ეს შენც უნდა გახარებდეს<...> რადგან შენ შვილთ სამკვიდრებელს მივცემ დიდსა და მაღალსა	And if I am marrying a daughter of a Corinthian king, – It should make happy you too […] For I will give to your children the hereditary domain great and lofty
(Euripides 1912:31)		(Shanshiashvili 1964:191)

So, the prudence and egoism of Jason are transformed into *reason* as opposed to *emotion*. However, this is not an argument for Medea's being carried away by love. On the whole, S. Shanshiashvili's Medea repeats the same reproaches as the Medea of Euripides, but blaming Jason with insincerity, she generalizes this feature, and spreads it to all carriers of the western culture:

To me it seemeth, when
A crafty tongue is given to evil men
(Euripides 1912:32)

'Tis like to wreck, not help
them. Their own brain

დასავლეთში ხართ ვერაგნი
და ნიღაბში ავაზაკნი,
თეთრი კბილით იღიმებით,
და შავს გულში გიძევთ მანკი!

Tempts them with lies to dare
and dare again,
Till ...

In the west you are treacherous
and masked brigands (robbers)
(You) show white teeth when you smile,
but your black heart is full of vice!
(Shanshiashvili 1964:192)

The matrimonial conflict develops into the collision of different behavioral models (emotionality – restraint/*mask*). Here, the echo of reasoning about the East-West, typical for the European cultural context at the turn of the 19th-20th centuries, is clearly heard: the opposition of two types of attitudes toward the world (sensitive and rational), and the problem of the possibilities-impossibilities of an interpenetration of two types of cultures also comes out. Besides, from the standpoint of a modern reader, the opposition *white-toothed smile – black hearts* in Medea's remark attracts attention. On the one hand, breaking the fixed stereotype *white-toothed smile, black-skinned face* not only imparts to the picturesque colors the traditional symbolic filling – moral categories (white/black – Good/Evil), but also closely associats them with no the less stable stereotype *white-toothed smile → American smile*, i.e. a kind of a symbol-marker of the behavioral model determined by western civilization.[5]

S. Shanshiashvili intentionally varies the development of the main plotline: while in Euripides' work Jason, who decided to marry again, "forgets" his former family ("Old love burneth low / When new love wakes, men say. He is not now / Husband nor father here, nor any kin" – Euripides 1912:7) and makes up his mind to banish Medea with the children from Corinth, in the poem by S. Shanshiashvili, both Jason and Creuza show love and concern for Medea's children. Creuza with kindness, fruit and sweets, tries in every way to gain their love and she succeeds. Jason does not want to part with the children at all. Medea alone must leave Corinth. The culmination takes place when on hearing the

5 "In the western world in general and in the English-speaking world in particular, a smile is a symbol of culture (naturally, culture in ethnographic terms), this is a tradition, a custom: to stretch one's lips in the proper position to show that you have no aggressive intentions, you are not going either to rob or to kill. This is a formal demonstration to the other people that you belong to the given culture, to the given society" (Ter-Minasova: online). Of course, both in the West and in the East the smile is first of all a demonstration of politeness (see Sternin: online). Eventually, this is the same mask used to hide the difficulties or negative feelings of an individual behind the outward restraint, demonstrating buoyancy and optimism, or affability, sociability and friendliness. However, so-called official smile of an American or a European is associated, as a rule, precisely with the expression a "white-toothed smile".

order to leave the country Medea asks the permission to take at least one son with her – the son who wants to stay with his mother. However, the sons (young Hellenes) reject their "low-born" mother. For them the origin of Medea – the princess from distant Colchis (a barbarian from the outskirts of civilized Oikumena), even though she is the granddaughter of Helios, is much lower than that of Creuza – the princess of Corinth:

მსწრაფლ შვილებსა დაუძახეს
დედა თქვენსკენ მოგიხმობდათ.
მაგრამ ზურგი შეაქციეს,
გლახ ნაშობი მშობელს გმობდა...

Children were called swiftly
mother was calling them to her.
But they turned their backs,
badly born (ones) denounced their parent.

(Shanshiashvili 1964:197)

Unlike Euripides, S.Shanshiashvili creates vivid characters of the children: he gives their names (Akimel and Tesal), describes their children's games, etc. All this allows him to enhance the psychological motivation of the Medea's act – the despair of a mother who has been rejected by her own children is increased by the realization of the deception and treachery of her unfaithful husband to the point of rage. Precisely in this moment Medea makes up her mind to kill Creuza by presenting her with poisoned jewelry.

რადგან შენის ქალიშვილის
ეგრე მდიდრობს სიყვარული,
რომ შვილები მას ეტრფიან,
დედა ვიქმენ დაგმობილი, –
მსურს სახსოვრად მას
გარდავსცე
ძვირფასი რამ სამკაული

Since your daughter's
love is so rich (ample)
that her children adore (worship) her.
I, the mother, was rejected, –
I would like to present
a precious adornment to her

(Shanshiashvili 1964:198)

In addition to Jason's insults, Medea blames him for "kidnapping" her children. On the other hand, her attitude to her sons also changes. She regards them as a continuation of their father – Jason and projects to their future a behavioral model that brings only grief to other people. So, in the bitter insanity there takes place a complete estrangement of mother from her own children which emphasizes the motivation of their murder as "Jason's sons". If in the Euripides' tragedy we read: "Unfathered children, God hate you / As I am hated, and him, too, / That gat you, and this house and all!" (Euripides 1912: 8),[6] S.Shanshiashvili's Medea comes to the conclusion that:

6 Compare with translation into Russian of Innokenti Annenski: Вы, дети... / О, будьте ж вы прокляты вместе / С отцом, который родил вас! / Весь **дом наш** погибни! (Еврипид

მებაღემა რაც ხე დარგო, ისეთს ნაყოფს ჩაიბარებს; მისთა შვილთა ყოფა–ქცევა სხვას სიცოცხლეს გაუმწარებს!..	A gardener will get the kind of fruit similar to a tree he planted; Behavior of his children will embitter the life of others!…

(Shanshiashvili 1964:199)

Thus, the murder of the children by their own mother takes on the significance of a final estrangement from the society of the Hellenic civilization as personified by Jason. "Not to be quite shut out from home … alas, / She knoweth now how rare a thing that was!" (Euripides 1912:4).[7] S.Shanshiashvili also adds a feeling of guilt towards her native people, on whom descended a lot of troubles after the Golden Fleece was stolen (this is told by a new character – a pilgrim, a stranger from Colchis). When she sees that her love and hope for happy life with Jason were a complete failure, Medea recalls her happy youth and her native country. She begins to recover from the power of delusion and deeply repents of her misdeeds. The poet also introduces a completely new episode into the plotline – heaving learnt about the disasters that descended upon her native people after the loss of the Golden Fleece, Medea realizes all the consequences of her misdeed. She comes to the conclusion that stealing the Fleece it still has not brought any good to anyone. Wishing to return the stolen Fleece and thereby to correct, at least partially, the harm done to her own people, Medea scatters the golden wool in the air: "*Let every country has it // will revive and flourish//through wisdom, delight, art / let the good find its way to them*!" (Shanshiashvili 1964:193). The poet gives a new interpretation of the mystic function of the Golden Fleece – the divine gift bringing welfare to the people who possess it. The story as interpreted by S.Shanshiashvili is opposed symbolically to the Centrist idea: at the end of the poem Medea, scattering the Fleece in the air, declares that it should belong to all mankind, to all peoples with equal right to prosperity whether they belong to the world of the Hellenic "civilization" or to the world of "barbarians". So, in the poem a new motif appears: the feeling of guilt toward the motherland awakens a sense of responsibility in the woman infatuated with love. It should be mentioned that patriotism is one of the characteristic features of Georgian literature during the whole history of its development. Therefore, we consider the manifestation of this implication a straight projection of the fact that for S.Shanshiashvili Medea is first of all a Colchis princess with a "Georgian appearance" (Euripides) whose behavior he tries to motivate with allowance for this position.

1999: 114-117) – "You, children…/Oh, damn you together/with your father who gave birth to you! / **Let our house be lost**! (Euripides 1999: 114-117).

7 Compare with translation into Russian of Innokenti Annenski: «Несчастие открыло цену ей/ Утраченной отчизны" (Еврипид 1999: 35) – "The misfortune showed her value/of the lost motherland" (Euripides 1999: 35).

Since in the poem there is no episode of meeting of Medea with Enei, Medea, in the gust of revenge, having killed the children of Jason, who has broken his conjugal oaths and all his promises, finds herself in complete solitude, in a strange land, faced with the fact that her life is destroyed. She is a victim of Fate, which makes her image even more tragic. It is significant that precisely in this way the version of the baby-killing suggested by the poet was assessed by a contemporary of S.Shanshiashvili, the famous Georgian critic, Kita Abashidze (1879-1917)[8] who considered the interpretation of the well-known plot given by the poet from the standpoint of a "fatal passion" and vengeance on the unfaithful husband who "[…] loves the children more than his fiancée, more than himself; therefore, according to the critic – precisely here the source of this terrible revenge should be sought" (Abashidze 1971:462). In particular, K.Abashidze says that it is a "fatal feeling" which, making a man lose his mind, prudence, turning him into a slave of only one passion, makes him pay for it" (Abashidze 1971:451). The critic calls this "fatal passion" "mijnuroba", the notion used in eastern and medieval Georgian literature to denote "reckless, frantic love/passion": "A man infatuated with this passion becomes a somnambulist. He does not belong to himself and completely submits to an uncertain magic power" (Abashidze 1971:45). According to him, "the feeling powerful as death, "hot as the hell" is an unambiguous attribute" of Medea who is "so dizzy with her feeling, bewitched so much, that she loses her mind and thus forgets everything" (Abashidze 1971:457). In his opinion, the Medea of S.Shanshiashvili, unlike the "treacherous and vindictive" Medea of Euripides and the "sentimental" Medea of Apollo of Rhodes, is nearer to human psychology (Abashidze 1971:462). However, noting that the ancient tradition regarded Medea as a "barbarian", the critic assessed this factonly from the moral point of view, i.e. from the standpoint of the awful crime – the baby-killing committed by her: "according to the legend, Medea, seized with vengeance lust, kills her children, this episode is described in gloomy shades, to put it mildly, by the great Greek tragedian Euripides in his "Medea", "because of this awful crime Greek legends regard Medea as a foreigner, a barbarian, therefore any crime could be easily ascribed to her" (our italics – I.M.) (Abashidze 1971: 461). At the same time, Colchis, from the standpoint of the notions of antiquity, was the extreme borderland of the Hellenic civilization, the boundary region between the Hellenic and other world – the "world of Barbarians," as the Greeks would say. We think that our comparative textual analysis not only reveals common features and differences in motivation and behavioural models in the tragedy by Euripides and in the poem by

---

8 The article "Our young writers" was first published in the newspaper "Sakhalkho Gazeti" ("Peoples' Newspaper" in 1913, №888-905 – in Georgian).

S.Shanshiashvili, but also to interpret the conflict between the characters of the poem of the Georgian author of the beginning of the 20th century as a development of the theme of the collision of two different mentalities, already outlined by Euripides – i.e. between the Hellenic civilization fixed by “law” and the “barbarian”, “uncivilized”, world of uncontrolled passions…

Thus, the character of Medea created by S.Shanshiashvili not only differs significantly from the mythological archetype, but also from of the character of Euripides’ tragedy. The Georgian author focuses on the difference of psychological motivation and behavioural models that led to the tragedy and baby-killing. Interpreting the ancient drama from the standpoint of the conflict of different cultural worlds, the poet imparts to it the significance of a collision of mentalities and defends the right of any people to whom “the good will find its way” to welfare.

References

Abashidze კიტა აბაშიძე /Abashidze Kita/. ჩვენი ახალგაზრდა მწერლები // კიტა აბაშიძე. *ცხოვრება და ხელოვნება /Our young writers* // Kita Abashidze. *Life and Work*/- თბილისი: თსუ /Tbilisi: TSU/, 1971 (in Georgian).

Еврипид/ *Медея* /Evripid. *Medea* // Еврипид. Трагедии в 2-х тт., т I, «Литературные памятники” /Evripid. Tragedy in two volumes, v. I, ” Literary monuments”/ – Москва: Наука /Moscow: Nauka/, 1999, (in Russian).

The Medea of Evripides – Oxford University Press, New York, 1912.

Мережковский Д. /Merezhkovsky D./. Предисловие// Д.Мережковский. З. Гиппиус. Д. Философов. *Царь и Революция*. /Foreword// D. Merezhkovsky, Z.Gippius, D.Filosofov. *King and Revolution*/ – Paris,1907; Москва /Moscow/, 1999 (in Russian).

Мифологический словарь/Гл.ред. Е.М. Мелетинский /*Mythological Dictionary* /Editor-in-Chief E.M.Meletinski/ – Москва: Советская энциклопедия /Moscow: Soviet Encyclopaedia/, 1990, (in Russian): http://myths.kulichki.ru/enc/item/f00/s22/a002209.shtml.

Platonis dialogi ed. Hermann. I. Lipsiae, 1931. Phaedo, LV1I1.

Робакидзе Гр. /Robakidze Gr./. Чувство жизни на Востоке и Западе // Григол Робакидзе. *Демон и миф. Магический калейдоскоп.* /Sense of life in the East and West // Grigol Robakidze. *Demon and myth.. Magic kaleidoscope*/ – Тбилиси /Tbilisi/, 2001 (in Russian).

ლევან სანიკიძე /Sanikidze Levan/. *ამბავი კოლხი ასულისა /Story of a Colchis girl/.* – თბილისი:თსუ /Tbilisi: TSU /, 1963 (in Georgian).

Стернин И.А. /Sternin I.A./. *Улыбка в русском коммуникативном поведении /A smile in the Russian communicative behavior/*, (in Russian): http://comm behavior.narod.ru/RusFin/RusFin 2000/Sternin4.htm.

Тер-Минасова С. /Ter-Minasova S./. *Язык и межкультурная коммуникация /Language and interculture communication/*, (in Russian): http://www.gumer. info/bibliotek_Buks/Linguist/Ter/_22. php.

Урушадзе Л. В. /Urushadze L.V./. Страна волшебницы Медеи // *Кавказ и Средиземноморье.* /The Country of the entantress Medea // *The Caucasus and the Mediterranean/* – Тбилиси: ТГУ /Tbilisi: TSU/, 1980, (in Russian): http://liberea.gerodot. ru/a_quest/medea.htm#1.

სანდრო შანშიაშვილი / Shanshiashvili Sandro/. *რჩეული*, 4 ტომად, ტ.4 (*Selected works in 4 volumes*, v. 4) – თბილისი: საბჭოთა საქართველო / Tbilisi: Sabchota Sakartvelo/, 1964 (in Georgian).

The Holy Grail, Whore of Babylon (or Rome), Mother Earth, and the Purifying World Conflagration in the Works of Nikolay and Lev Gumilyov[1]

Yordan Lyutskanov
(Bulgaria)

Ethnoses are not like snakes:
they shed not skins, but their souls

I. I will start with three statements which I consider commonplaces. First, apocalyptics and sophiology, on the one hand, and ecology, on the other, share certain common characteristics.[2] Similarly, certain points in common can be found between the movement of counter-Eurocentrism and in the 'conditional mood' of history.[3] Finally, between a father and a son one should expect not only genetic, but intellectual ties.[4]

Now I will proceed to a proposition that I consider to be less trivial. All three possibilities already mentioned may be taken separately, one by one. But they could also coincide within one single case, one pair of human fates. And this is just what happened with the Gumilyovs, father and son, Nikolay Gumilyov, an outstanding modernist poet, and Lev Gumilyov, an outstanding historian of the Soviet time.

This paper proposes one more point of inquiry. It hypothesizes that Lev Gumilyov, adopting and developing an Eurasianist vision of history, stumbled upon or arrived at his father's "talents", which he "multiplies" (I mean to suggest the Parable of the "talents," Matthew 25: 14-30). The logic of such an inquiry requires that revealing evidence be produced pointing to L. Gumilyov's intellectual connecti-

---

1 I express my gratitude to Tatyana Megrelishvili and to Zaal Andronikashvili, whose conversation(in December 2008, and in April 2010) served as the moral impetus for writing this work.

2 Gumilyov: Ethnogenesis. (First published 1979) – Or: Лев Гумилев, Этногенез и биосфера Земли [Ethnogenesis and the Biosphere of the Earth]. [Chapt.] XIX. Филогенез или онтогенез? [Philogenesis or Ontogenesis?] [§] Антропосукцессии [Anthroposuccessions] (para. 3 of 3).

3 Ecology evokes responsibility towards all living beings, approachable as *real*, as Creation permeated by the presence of the Creator (cf. Sophiology: Sophia – it is the Creation in the face of the Creator, and in the state of being permeable to Him); the inevitable – bearing in mind human free will and moral feebleness – *ir*responsibility results in a just retribution, known as Apocalypse.

4 The common denominator is the refusal to identify the due with the disposable.

on to Eurasianism. Second, it must compare that evidence with what Lev intellectually shared with his father. I am ommitting the first step in the hope that the similarities (and differences) between Lev and the 'classics' of Eurasianism (mainly P. Savitsky, N. Trubetskoy) are well known. I will focus on the similarities and differences between father and son. Within this paper I will restrict myself to comparing the manifestations of four archetypal symbols in Lev's and Nikolay's works.

II. 1. The archetypal symbol of the Holy Grail is the earliest and the most clearly visible feature in N. Gumilyov's lyrics. In the widely known first poem of his first book, the sonnet "I am a conquistador in an iron helmet ...", ("Я конквистадор в панцире железном ...", 1905),[5] the Grail takes the appearance of a "star of the valley, the blue lily." I must say, I employ an extremely wide notion of the "Grail." Following Ernst Robert Curtius, I identify it with the mystical aim of long-distance travel. Adhering to this wide notion of the Grail, I consider the whole early lyric of Gumilyov as a variation on the theme of looking for the Grail. Ernst Robert Curtius, a historian of European literature, cautions against a groundless widening of the Grail's symbolical meaning, At the same time he indirectly sanctions by it pointing out that medieval writers already had a vague idea of its primary meaning (Curtius 1953: 112). The kernel of the Grail legend is the following: a young protagonist arrives at a wasteland ruled by an old and sick priesly king. The king's illness and the land's devastation seem to be a euphemism for impotency, and an elixir from a vessel named Grail can cure the illness.[6] As far as I can ascertain, this original layer of the Grail legend is noticeable in a few verses in N. Gumilyev's work: "The Sun Virgin" ("Дева солнца", 1903-1905), and "Tale About the Kings" ("Сказка о королях", 1903-1905).[7]

Regarding L. Gumilyev's commitment to the legend, I may summarize: his book *on Prester John*,[8] entitled "Поиски вымышленного царства" ("Searching for an Imaginary Kingdom", 1970), is in fact a demystification of the Holy Grail legend in several respects.

First, the legend of Prester John might be regarded as a historical projection of the Grail legend, and Lev Gumilyev demonstrates the incoherence between

5 A (re)consideration within the theory of autotextuality is possible; see below.
6 English-Russian translation, if not specified, mine (Y.L.); works are dated after the e-collection.
7 Ibid. And further on: "Ancient vegetation cults seem to have coalesced with the symbolism of the Eucharist in late Antiquity and to have survived esoterically into the Middle Ages".
8 The work narrates allegorically the failures of the old king and the young protagonists to get the Grail.

the legend and the factual situation in Inner Asia of the 12-13th centuries (a situation recognisable through historical reconstruction).

Second, I may functionally identify the Europeans who credited the Prester John legend and expected the aid of his troops with the young protagonist of the Holy Grail legend; it occurs, however, that within this historical fulfilment of the legend, it is not the old king-priest but the young protagonist who is impotent – insofar as the latter, instead of hastening to lend a hand, waits for the help of the former. The legend entered history, but the agents who embody its protagonists proved incompetent. Thus Lev performs a dramatic turn in the interpretation of the Grail legend. Needless to say that I have no reason to expect him to have pointed out the similarity between the two legends, the dependence of Prester John on the Grail – he might have not even noticed it. It is enough that his subconscience noticed and dictated him the idea of that book, “Поиски”.

To resume, Western Christians credited the fable of Prester John’s kingdom because they didn’t want – or, rather, lacked the moral strength – to cope with their own problems on their own. This is the moral of L. Gumilyev’s book. It seems as if Nikolay Gumilyev taught that lesson when he abandoned the image of the knight as a lyrical protagonist’s self-identification (cf. his “Я и вы”, “Me and you”, 1917) Third, Lev succeeded in overcoming the worldview immanent to both legends, overcoming the view that sees the ‘Path’ as the constituting “archetype” of personal existence. The archetype of the world in his works is identifiable not with a ‘Path’, but with a ‘Home,’ with a ‘Home’ which has been stretched out upon the whole of Eurasia as if it were a tent embracing the Earth and the top of its dome pierced the stratosphere. The drift from ‘Path’ to ‘Home’ happened already in his father’s works, being concisely represented in the poem “Пятистопные ямбы” (“Five-foot Jambs”, 1915; publ. in “Колчан” (“Quiver”, 1916)): “Лишь изредка надменно и упрямо / Во мне кричит ветшающий Адам, / Но тот, кто видел лилию Хирама, / Тот не грустит по сказочным садам, / А набожно возводит стены храма, / Угодного земле и небесам”.[9] Lev Gumilyev’s Eurasia has been prefigured in Nikolay’s collection “Шатер” (“Tent”, 1921).

2. The whore of Babylon (or Rome).[10] Some contemporary researchers consider the Whore of Babylon to be the arch-symbol of what they call the “occidentalist”

9 Informally, that was the title given to the book by the author – “Priest John” (“Поп Иван”). See: Трилистник письменного стола [Trifolium of the writing desk]. 1. Преодоление филологии. Комментарий [издателя] [Transcending philology. A commentary [of the publisher]]. <http://gumilevica.kulichki.net/SIK/sik01.htm>).

10 “Just rarely – haughty and stubborn – / The declining Adam cries in me – / But he, who has seen Hiram’s lily / Is not grievous for legendary gardens, / And piously erects the walls of temple / Pleasing to both earth and heaven”.

perception of civilisation. I consider "Occidentalism"[11] to be a concept polemically promoted to counterbalance the effect of Edward Said's "Orientalism". Not without simplification, I understand Occidentalism here as a complex of animosity against urban culture, the latter being conceived as a source of evil, and, particularly, of vice. The Old Testament embodies the most powerful of its ancient manifestations: the images of Sodom and Gomorra, of Babylon, and, to some extent, of Egypt, are fine examples.[12] If we revisit the symbol from the viewpoint of E. R. Curtius's history of literary topoi, we could associate it with the Young Girl/Old Woman topos. The corresponding symbol has been used in late antiquity to designate the Great Mother Goddess (and her hypostases), the goddess of Rome (Roma), and the Church as well.[13] Literary studies, analytical psychology, and culturology, each in its own way, arrive at one and the same phenomenon.

In Nikolay Gumilyev's early lyric, the Whore of Babylon comes into being gradually. In a number of poems within his first collection, "Путь конквистадоров" ("The Path of Conquistadors", 1905), the image is of a world in which architectural forms are limited to castles and to temples, without settlements. Parallel to this, the feminine personages also lack signs of any fault ("С тобой я буду до зари ...", "Песня о певце и короле": "With you I'll be till dawn …", "Song about the Poet and the King", both written 1903-1905). Nevertheless this world is not necessarily a/the world preceding Original sin. It is rather a state, or a stage, characteristic of the prenatal condition of the male protagonist. He has not left a/the womb (probably the Mother Goddess's) yet, and has not recognized the womb in her as a hypostasis of the Whore of Babylon. He is just imaginarily leaving it for short periods and then retreating. But as early as in the last stanza of "Греза ночная и дневная" ("A Dream of Day and of Night", 1903-1905) one may notice the shadow of civilization. The text hints at the proposition that enjoying the comfort of woman's embrace/ basking in a woman's embrace impedes the protagonist from being involved with and acting in the world. He undergoes a gradual emancipation from the feminine womb, and the feminine presence splits into several personages. They are identifiable with an intimate friend, a mysterious Maiden who lives far away, Mother Earth, and others. Mother Earth is

11 In Russian – plainly Город-блудница, that is, without specifying a city's name.

12 See the book, or the culturological pamphlet (as we understand it), of Ian Buruma and Avishay Margalit (I. Buruma, A. Margalit. Occidentalism: the West in the eyes of its enemies (2004); translated into Bulgarian in 2006).

13 Later manifestations of the worldview pamphletised there are Russian Slavophilism and in general all ideologies which confront Westernisation, that is, the import of the combination between a parliamental democracy, a (rhetoric of) free trade, and sets of beliefs and arguments claiming universal validity for Western culture.

almost unnoticeable in “Рассказ девушки” (“Maiden’s Story”, 1905) – yet it preserves the maiden’s innocence here. In “Осенняя песня” (“Autumn Song”, 1903-1905) an image of Mother Earth in a sacred marriage with the sun (Sun) emerges, and the text immediately hints at her potential career as a whore (through likening her to Eve).

Further on in this work the virginity of the world is spoiled in a somewhat different and more profound sense: a wood nymph, having dbeen seduced, betrays her friend (also a wood nymph) in the name of love. It is not the contamination of original sin in the Christian sense, nor the sin of fratricide that interests us here, but rather the result: the poem’s message is that friendship is “higher” than love, from the viewpoint of the implicitly promoted ethical judgment.[14] I have paid particular attention to these early works of N. Gumilyov in order to revisit the common origin of such symbols as the Whore of Babylon and Mother Earth. They come into existence with the separation of the male self from the womb, who until then was an individual and ambivalent (or pre-ambivalent) female being. Concurrently, a new attitude to the hypostases of the female being appears – we may call it ethical. To simplify, the Whore of Babylon is associated with Evil, while Mother Earth comes to represent Good. The first is conceivable as a hypostasis of the Jungian archetype of the “Shadow”, and the second – as a hypostasis of the “Anima.” Simultaneously, the female being is divided gnosiologically: a part of her rests in the image of a known, near-living, and fundamentally uninteresting (insofar as inaccessible) woman, and a part is projected into a far and mysterious Virgin of the earth, Virgin of the sun, Virgin of the Rainbow gates (Дева Радужных ворот), who is, of course, notoriously desirable and unintelligible.

Now I am turning from the issue of the psychology of the subconscious to the filogenesis of culture. The second hypostasis, retaining its gnosiological profile, settled in the idea of the Anima mundi, incorporates in a sublimated way the first hypostasis (an example from Christianity: Virgin Mary, or Mother of God, has ‘adopted’ Mary, the mother of Jesus, Joseph’s wife). In the wasteland of bourgeois protestant civilisation (I am recalling Jung’s critique of the symbolic pauperisation of the protestant West) the hypertrophy of the far, mysterious hypostasis of the female being might acquire the form – and the formula – of “love to the [depersonalised] distant”. The vital feat in such a situation appears to be not the repersonalisation of the far Virgin (by the way, an enamoured imagination would not have left her to manifest herself), but rather in recognizing her in the uninteresting girl who lives next door, *one’s neighbour*. The correlation Shadow–Anima still

14 Curtius: 101-105. – The scholar approaches the phenomenon aware of depth psychology and of its roots in archaic psychology (105), and recognises the Jungian archetype of Anima in the image of Goddess-Natura (122-123).

possesses its actuality here… Recurring to our main discourse, I will summarise our topic-relevant observations on Nikolay Gumilyov's lyric (simplifying so as to catch the mainstream). Beginning probably with the "Alien Sky" ("Чужое небо", 1912) collection, one may distinguish a drift from love of the distant towards love of the close of one's neighbour (an abrupt shift being visible in the "Quiver"'s "Five-feet Yambs", 1915). An ethical ambivalence of the female persists, but another shift occurs. The protagonist's soul-mate, "Друг" (she or he, who is addressed via "Thee" – but it might not be God), tends to lose the characteristics of 'femaleness' (feminine gender).[15] The relationship with the Anima is more and more rarely expressed via the symbol of love towards a woman, and more and more frequently – via the symbol of friendship. An analogical shift – but regarding the images representing the archetype of the Shadow – is discernible in Lev's works: the image of the voluptuous and treacherous woman does not occur there, even when the historiography material allows for such a choice.[16] It is a symptomatic shift, from the viewpoint of C.G. Jung's analytical psychology...

The Whore's symbolic extension, the City-Whore (the Whore of Babylon, Rome, etc.), appears in Nikolay's works as early as the poem "Masquerade" ("Маскарад", 1907), within his *second* collection, "Romantic Flowers" ("Романтические цветы", 1908). The image still lacks magnificence, it is given in the semi-profile of a synecdoche: "Мазурки стремительный зов раздавался, / И я танцевал с куртизанкой Содома" ("[…]/ And I danced with a courtesan of Sodom"). ...In "Terror" ("Ужас") instead of a town or a city the image of a building is displayed, and the Whore is symbolically identified with Death. ... In "Contagion" ("Зараза") contagion means death, and (insofar) as death (Death) and whore (Whore) are identical, we may assume that the whore (Whore) enters the city (the city of Cairo, the City) to reign.[17] The theme meets a trans-temporal

15 "В ее душе зажглись слова / И манят огненные строки. / (...) «Но если ты желаешь Дня / И любишь лучшую отраду, / Отдай объятиям огня / Твою сестру, твою дриаду." / (...) Теперь открылися миры / Жене божественно-надменной, / Взамен угаснувшей сестры / Она узнала сон вселенной" ("In her soul the words ignited / And the flaming lines draw [her]. / (…) «But if you want the Day / And if you like finer a delight, / Give up to fire's embrace / Your sister, your dryad.» / (…) Now worlds have been revealed / To woman godly haughty, / Instead of her sister who faded away / She faced the dream [or sleep] of universe").

16 .In this respect the poems of the last one third (I mean the linear sequence) of the "Quiver" collection (1916) deserve particular attention.

17 See the indulgent characterisation of the Mameluk sultan's wife, that "poor foolish woman" ("бедной глупой женщины"), who ordered the murder of her husband, and then killed herself in a most cruel way, in the "Black Legend" ("Черная легенда", publ. 1989). <http://gumilevica. kulichki.net/articles/bl04.htm#para70>. Cf. the role of women in the Genghisids' court (as characterised by Lev); an instance of woman reigning over the Kara-Khitan Khanate (as depicted by him)… A symbolical equation of lie and snake in Lev's works is possible, but one of woman and snake (in general rather frequent) is highly improbable. One of the symbolic valences of the

axis, being reiterated in a number of global horizons: within the horizon of Hellenism (in "Incantation", "Заклинание"), and of the Caliphate (in "Contagion") ... Insofar we speak of this collection, the theme of the City-Whore bursts out after stumbling upon Roman material – it permeates the so called Roman cycle of poems: "The Founders", "Manlius", "Games", "To the Emperor", "Caracalla", "The navigator Pausanius" ("Основатели", "Манлий", "Игры", "Императору", "Каракалла", "Мореплаватель Павсаний..."). (In fact the archetypal symbol of the Whore of Babylon, reconsidered as the Whore of Rome, is one of the collection's leitmotivs. A sequential reading of the collection, letting the meanings of the manifestations produce their cumulative effect, sustains the conclusion. Here I have been able to afford myself only a syncopic series of references, instead of a consequential analysis.)

A bundle of metonymies in "The Fouders" make the reader ready to face the Whore of Rome, imbued with death (Death). The elements of this symbol (and not allegory) being the following: Rome; the couple Romulus–Remus (cf. with earlier poems: friend betrayal as an opportunity for love; that is, fratricide originates from seduction); circus (the loci of circus and masquerade have enough in common to be semantic 'rhymes'; cf. "Masquerade" – where the image of the City-Whore appeared for first time); a house open to everyone (an ambivalence); tombs (associable with cave and with death, cf. "Beyond the Grave", "За гробом"). For some reason in "The Founders" Roma has nothing in common with a female wolf. Instead the dispersed presence of a bitch is felt (but just to mark that in Russian the association is more subtle, 'a she-wolf' and 'a whore' do not share room within one and the same word). Rome turns out to be a Whore-City by constitution. And this is not an old man – or an old woman's – fate, nor the fate of old age, of 'civilisation', in the sense of decadence. "Manlius" comes as an explanation. In the City-Whore the murder of the saviour (of the city), under the acclamation of the people is a norm. And so is blood. If we go back to the poems from the "Path of Conquistadors", to "The Virgin of sun" for example, we will understand: blood in Rome results from the **un**successful attempt to conquer the Virgin… Rome is a historical illustration of the *trans*-historical, archetypal *Failure* of the king, who has conquered the whole world through bloodshed. The 'king' turns out to be a captive of the Whore, the Whore of Rome – is it worth getting the Grail for the Roman "king"?

Biblical archetype has been de-activated, but another (or the other) has come to the fore (it looks like a compensatory stress): Satan in Lev's works is not only a fallen angel, but the Father of lies (see Lev Gumilyov: Ethnogenesis, XXI. Сумма противоречий, [§] Клио против Сатурна, para. 9 of 16. [Summa oppositorum. Clio against Saturn] <http://gumilevica.kulichki.net/EBE/ebe 05.htm#ebe05chapter21>), and, of course, he is not the figure to deserve sympathy.

The future fate of the Whore of Rome in the world of Gumilyov is displayed in the "A Baby Elephant" ("Слоненок", 1920; "Огненный столп" ("Pillar of Fire", 1921) coll.), and its disposition has been prefigured in the "Games." Let us focus for a while on the latter. The games last for three days. The crowd anticipates with pleasure the next murder.[18] But the Alamannic chieftan (who is the next to fall), calms the hungry beasts down. The public hasn't had such an experience before. This is the "Game's" plot (sujet). Because of a similitude in fabulae the "Games" could be included in a certain series of texts: "Games", "Barbarians", "A Baby Elephant". The Alamannic chieftan is a captive, but he does what is unheard of. The role of the whore is being performed by the crowd, and the consul is the souteneur. The contagion has permeated the whole of Rome's social body. In the "Barbarians" the chieftan of the victorious barbarians, who despised the volupuous act of the queen or empress (царица), has no name, and they are anonymous too. In the "Baby-elephant" one hears the name of Hannibal, and sees him on his elephant approaching the trembling Rome. Gumilyov drifts away from actual history (the Germanic forces that destroy Rome) into a history which is hypothetical. He sways into another, into an alternative stream of history. In Nikolay's version of history it is not the Germanic king who avenges Carthage (in 455 the vandal Genseric entered Rome and, as the tradition says, sacked it, declaring himself an avenger of Carthage – Lev Gumilyov writes about this),[19] but Hannibal for the Alamann. The alternative history involves cooperation the offended and the defeated. The interest in the "conditional mood" of history, hardly distinguishable in some works of Nikolay, bursts out in Lev's, on the material concerning Rome (the same associative chain: Hannibal – Genseric) and Eastern Christianity. But it might be an object of a separate scholarly concern ....

In Nikolay Gumilyev s third collection, "Pearls" ("Жемчуги", 1910) the imagery of the City-Whore intersects with the theme of global holocaust. The "Queen", or the "Empress", or why not the "Shahbanu" ("Царица")[20] is woven of semantic

18 Almost immediately afterwards (in the linear sequence of poems within the collection), in "Lake Chad" ("Озеро Чад"), the theme is treated inversely. Woman (with a capital letter) becomes plainly a woman, to end her descent (kenosis) to the verge of slavery and prostitution...: as a "boring and unwanted mistress […] in Marseille". The symbol of City-Whore has hardly attained the size of an archetypal menace, Shadow, cast upon the whole world, when it (or she) shrinks to cause pity, to regain moral ambivalence, to match the image of the New Testament whore and, at the same time, the archetype of Anima ....

19 An English translation from Carl Proffer exists.

20 See "Ethnogenesis", [Chapt.] XXV. Субпассионарии, [§] "Вырожденцы", "Бродяги", "Бродяги-солдаты", para. 3 of 6. [Sub-passionaries. "Renegades", "Vagabonds", "Vagabonds-Soldiers"]. <http://gumilevica.kulichki.net/EBE/ebe06.htm#ebe06chapter25>. – In the works of Gumilyovs the theme of barbarians invading the city-*orbs* appears not to display the cruelty of barbarians, but to supplement the theme of the decomposition of civilization, or, to say it in

and visual threads, tying together the early "Incantation" (1907), the late "Sahara" ("Сахара", 1918), and the chronotope of most of Lev' Gumilyev's works: Inner Asia, in the glow of fires and in the yellow mist of Buddhist propagation, the one that crushed both Nestorianism and Eastern Mithraism (the Tibetan religion Bon).

The poem immediately following the "Queen" – "A Friend" (or a "Comrade"?) – is an attempt at writing on the topic of fraternal love. The montage sequence accumulates an extra meaning: the implicit author goes away from the "Self" captured by the female beauty and therefore prone to deserting his duty (or, by metonymy, his friend)...

The theme of the City-Whore is revived and revitalised in the late works of Nikolay Gumilye's in his tragedy "The Poisoned Tunic" ("Отравленная туника", 1917-1918). Though the issue deserves special attention, here I will confine myself to the note that the work represents itself an interpretation of Vladimir-Solovyov's idea of Byzantium.[21] Half a century later the 'epilogue' of this tragedy of Byzantine self-identification was examined by Lev Gumilyov in his "Black Legend" ("Черная легенда", 1989), and it is an examination evidently evoking the predecessors' attempts. (In fact it is an epilogue conceivable as a next tragedy, as a next historical collision.)

One should not and, probably, could not fail to notice that Lev pushes forward the possibility of dramatising the historical material. Neither would he fail to notice the joky gallantness of intonation, characteristic of several Nikolay's, and Solovyov's, works having a historiosophical (or sophiological) subtext. In an earlier book, "Searching for an Imaginary Kingdom" (the book on Prester John) Lev Gumilyev's has worked out, on separate historical material, another aspect of the tragedy displayed by Nikolay in the "Poisoned Tunic"; the aspect, or the common denominator, being a/the *failed marriage*. In addition, Lev deepens the ethical quest of the situation: he examines the failed marriage between an unjustly *forgotten* (Nestorian church) and a *calumniated* people (the Mongols).

In Lev Gumilyev's works only a distant echo of the City-Whore theme is detectable. It is thus probably because Lev has freed himself from the female image in recalling the archetype of Shadow (Shadow has not the guise of a woman here). The Whore of Babylon (or rather of Rome) has been echoed in two themes in his work. It is, first, the theme of the civilised – or not so civilized – lie: it is exemplified (or personified) by historical sources (in "Ethnogenesis and the

---

Lev's terms, the theme of the triumphant "subpassionaries" within a given ethnos (in the phase of "obscuration").

21 "Царица" extends the group of Nikolay's poems about distant Maidens, incorporating a non-semantic accent and one more intertextual presence: of Vl. Solovyov's poem "Газели пустынь ты стройнее и краше..." ("You are more graceful and lovelier than a gazelle from the deserts ...").

Biosphere of Earth", in "Priest John", in "Black Legend"), the Templiers (in "Black Legend"), the Holy (Papal) seat (in the same book). And it is, second, the theme of the aggressiveness of civilisation, of the Chinese in particular; an adequate figurative representation of the latter theme would be the following: the Dragon menaces Mother-The Great Steppe.[22] Within the second theme I recognise an urge for "rehabilitation" of the so called steppe barbarism and barbarians. Within the first one I notice an impulse for demystifying secret societies throughout human history. There is such a judgement in the "Black Legend", after we have read several lines narrating about knightly orders, on the assassins: where and when secret societies reside and act, the lie has the real opportunity to rule over people, and, moreover – the conscious lie. At this point Lev transcends his father, who has demonstrated an ambivalent attitude toward orders ....

Lev Gumilyev's concern with the power of hearsay (that is, the material consequences of the power of imagination), being the hidden engine of two of his works, "In Search of the Imagined Kingdom" and "Black Legend", might originate from his father's: Nikolay's unfinished story (повесть) "The Merry Brothers" ("Веселые братья"), which tells about a secret society that fabricates falsified historical (primary) sources and scientific discoveries in order to slip them whenever needed.

Expressing his creed as a historian, Lev Gumilyov does mention the mendacity of sources, the unreliability of the methods employed by some historians. Listing what the "Father of Lies" whispers into the "credulous ignorant man's" ear, Lev Gumilyev, of course, differentiates his position from his fellows' historians. But, more importantly, he draws the silhouette of an enemy worldview or, rather, of his religious antagonist. It is not an accident that he chooses to exemplify his argument with a case from the history of religious propaganda: Buddhism tries to penetrate Tibet, and it is prevented from doing so by Bon, that is, Mithraism.[23] Lev takes over the opposition against "Buddhist non-resistance to evil",[24] but retains affinity or indifference to other religions of the East, thus

22 See Lev Gumilev, "Searching for an Imaginary Kingdom", [Part IV.] Трилистник мышино норы, [Chapt.] 12. Двуединный (Окончание). [§] Поиск источника веры. [Trifolium of mouse hole. The Dual (The End). Searching the source of faith] <http://gumilevica.kulichki.net/SIK/sik04e.htm#sik04chapter12-6>. Cf. the short article "Страна Шамбала в легенде и в истории" ("Country of Shambala in Legend and in History"; 1968) <http://gumilevica.kulichki.net/articles/tibet12.htm>.

23 It was made explicit in "On the Reasons of Decline of Medieval Worldview" ("О причинах упадка средневекового миросозерцания", 1891), "Byzantism and Russia" ("Византизм и Россия", 1896). It is not uncharacteristic of Dmitry Merezhkovsky as well, see his 1900s essay (or piece of travel writing) "Hagia Sophia" ("Св. София").

24 In Nikolay's poem "Dragon" ("Змей", 1915-1916; "Bonfire" coll., 1918) the Dragon still pertains to the Steppe, one that still has feud with Rus'... Lev, departing, as it seems, from Solo-

following his father. (Fatalism, just like determinism, is a deadly enemy of the idea of alternative history and the multiplicity of worlds.)

The Whore of Rome has transformed into the Father of Lies.

3. Mother-Earth. As far as Nikolay's works are concerned, the most characteristic and symbolically profuse manifestations of Mother-Earth are to be found in "Andrey Rublyov" ("Андрей Рублев"), "Nature" ("Природа") ("Bonfire", or "Костер" coll., 1918), "Sahara", and the "Introduction"[25] of the "Tent" collection. Mother-earth comprises the whole of Creation, permeated and inspired by divine energies. It is this Mother-Earth, a personification of femininity in which the unity of Mother and Virgin (image of Sophia and the wisdom of God) is restored, which prefigures the Earth of Lev Gumilyov, the globe breathing with its biosphere and anthroposphere, the globe excited with a burst of passionarity: "As if someone lashes the globe, and blood rushes to the scar and it becomes inflamed" (<http://gumilevica.kulichki.net/EBE/ebe04.htm#ebe04chapter17>).

4. The Purifying Global Holocaust. In the early lyrics of Nikolay Gumilyov, flame (or the burning, 'flamability') is the inner characteristic of the protagonist. Sometimes flame becomes the constituant or the distinctive feature of the female being, and also the symbol of love. Later on, in "Костер", fire symbolises the Creation, permeated by energy, and also the energies penetrating the Creation. And alongside all the lyric collections of N. Gumilyov, fragmentary views on Zoroastrian cosmology or the cult are clear evidence of this (Люцканов 2007.). In the "Pillar of Fire" (1921) fire refers to the Apocalypse. In the "Tent" (1921) it remodels the Apocalypse as an event recurring in the history of Earth ("Sahara"). "Sahara" has been prefigured by an early poem – "A Forest Fire" ("Pearls", "Жемчуга" coll.): "Ветер гонит тучу дыма, / Словно грузного коня / [...]" ("The wind hounds a cloud of smoke, / As if [hounds] a heavy horse").

Now I will cite a definition of passionarity to help us see the commonality between those images of Nikolay and Lev Gumilyov work: "The starting moment of ethnogenesis, as well as the reaching of its highest phase and the phase of regeneration requires from the population to extra-efforts [...] This is the "X-

---

vyov's works ("Panmongolism", "Three Conversations" – see the Politician's rejoinders, – and other), steadily distinguishes between the Steppe and China. It is thereby noteworthy that the aggressor, threatening the existence of other historical actants of Eurasia, turns out to be China. Furthermore, it occurs that in the epoch of Romans and Parthians it was up the Steppe to save the West from a Chinese intervention. The "Yellow menace" attained a concrete identification. The theme is easy to trace in the book on "priest John".

25 Этногенез и биосфера Земли. [Chapt.] XXI. Сумма противоречий. [§] Клио против Сатурна, para. 10 of 16. <http://gumilevica.kulichki.net/EBE/ebe05.htm#ebe05chapter21>. – On Bon and Mithraism see above, n. 23.

factor" which we have searched for!" (http://gumilevica.kulichki.net/EBE/ebe05.htm#ebe05chapter21>). The ""X-factor" that has interested us projects itself into the realm of human psychology" (Ibid.); and the generator of passionarity as an "important hereditary characteristic" has to be looked for in the "vast realm of the subconscious–not the individual, but the collective" (http://gumilevica. kulichki.net/EBE/ebe06.htm#ebe 06chapter24). Insofar as fire is identifiable with the energy of the Creation, and insofar the Apocalypse is a fatally destructive, but also a purifying release of that energy, fire appears to be conceivable as a potential for extra-exertion, and an Apocalypse – as a burst of extra-effort.

III. It is time to elucidate what the archetypal symbols I have examined so far and the archetypes in the sense of C.G. Jung have in common. The Whore of Babylon (or Rome) and Mother-Earth are relatable to the Jungian archetypes of Shadow and Anima, Conflagration – with the archetype of the Wiseman, and of transfiguration (transformation).[26] The Holy Grail, as well as the *potential* archetypes of Path and Home (commanding the experience of space which Nikolay Gumilyov's works generate) could be referred at as symbols of transformation too.

I consider an interpretation of Nikolay and Lev Gumilyov's works in the light of Jung's analytical psychology highly heuristic, but it has to be postponed for another occasion.

The reader will probably ask the question what my reasons were for choosing these four archetypal symbols (the Grail, the Whore, Mother-Earth, and the Conflagration) to represent the Gumilyovs' works in terms of the collective subconscious[27] I am not going to give my answer a scholarly guise. I have juxtaposed two series of items (probable symbolical representations of archetypes, to be found in

26 The adhering of the early "Eurasianists" to this tradition is best witnessed in Nikolay Trubetskoy's article "The Religions of India and Christianity" ("Религии Индии и христианство", 1922).

27 The following fragments are noteworthy: "[л]ик жены подобен раю" ("[w]oman's face is like heaven"). – "Земля, к чему шутить со мною: / Одежды нищенские сбрось / И стань, как ты и есть, звездою, / Огнем пронизанной насквозь!" ("Oh, Earth, why are you joking with me: / Cast off your beggarly clothes / And be, as you are, a star, / Permeated by fire"). – "Ты, на дереве древнем Евразии / Исполинской висящая грушей." ("You, on the ancient tree of Eurasia, / Hanging (as if an) immense pear"). – "Аравия, Сирия, Гоби, – / Это лишь затихание сахарской волны, / В сатанинской воспрянувшей злобе / [...] И когда, наконец, корабли марсиан / У земного окажутся шара, / То увидят сплошной золотой океан / И дадут ему имя: Сахара." ("Arabia, Syria, Gobi, – / They are merely a calming down of Saharan wave, / Arisen in a Satanic fury / […] And when, at last, the ships of Marsians / Approach the globe, / They will see a limitless ocean of gold / And will name it: Sahara"). – In her Saharan representation, Mother-Earth is similar to Yahweh and to the angry and threatening God of the Apocalypse. – A group of relevant V. Solovyov poems deserving a parallel Solovyov–Gumilyov, investigation contains, among others, the famous "Милый друг, иль ты не видишь …" ("Dear friend, or you don't see …").

Gumilyovs' works, and *the main* archetypes of the collective subconscious manifest in the experience of a male, to be found in Jung's) relying on my *personal* and cumulative experience as a reader of the Gumilyovs' works. Yet in some other respects my discourse has tried to be disciplined, even rigorist: I have tried to follow Jung's distinction between "archetype" and "archetypal symbol (motive, etc.)".

IV. The observations made and the generalisations drawn in this paper suggest that between Nikolay and Lev Gumilyov (and probably Vladimir Solovyov) there exists an intellectual continuity. This conclusion could be developed. It could be sustained by a more or less convincing argument, and it could be denied; but anyway, the observations that unite them would remain raw material. They have to be rethought from the viewpoint of a relevant theory of their explanatory force. Now I am able to point out three such theories. It is, first, the theory of the collective subconscious of C.G. Jung. It is conceivable that the case of father and of son could represent a specific curve of a burst of the collective subconscious, and a specific rhythm of efforts aimed at self-analysis. It is probable that between father and son, even if they live apart, there exists a psychic connection which makes it possible to examine them as a relatively autonomous group of personalities (or as a kind of multiple personality). This is reminiscent of Jung's assertion of the fragmentariness of the individual conscience, of the multiplicity (multipersonality) of the individual self. This makes possible to examine the two as such a group that has its peculiar regime of "inheriting" neuroses and its peculiar regime of healing them.[28] I have cut off the things before attempting such an approach here, for in fact I have dealt with the archetypes in the works of Gumilyovs, and not in their lives. It is Lev Gumilyov's theory of ethnogenesis – it is its episteme (or perspective) of the "mouse hole" which is employable here above all. An inspection of texts, deeds, and the subconscious impulses of a father and his son would be, probably, somehow symptomatic for an inquiry on the Russian ethnos in the phase of, may be, its climax. Correspondingly, attention would be focused on the selection and on the rhythm of such manifestations of the subconscious which could be regarded as referring to the functioning and evolution of a given ethnic stereotype. A symbiosis of Jung's and of Gumilyov's theory would meet such an agenda. It is, third, remaining in the field of literary criticism, the autotextual theory, the theory of dialogical relations between the works of a single author (Коларов 2009: 7) that is of assistance. Autotextuality has been defined, in a broader sense, as a self-charging, "autarkic"

28 Cf. Юнг 1991: para. 358-440. – Об архетипах коллективного бессознательного. (Transl. from German by A. Rutkevich, from: C.G. Jung, **Bewusstes und Unbewusstes**. Fischer. Frankfurt am Main, 1971, p. 11-53).

*inter*textuality (Ibid. Lucien Dällenbach, "intertextualité autarcique").[29] We may assume that each group of texts has a certain potential for auto-interpretation, but usually this potential is neutralized by opposite forces. The notion of autotextuality seems to be applicable to those infrequent cases when in a group of texts the centripetal forces prevail over the centrifugal. From the viewpoint of biology and of the (post)renaissance philological tradition one would expect such a group to coincide with the mass of texts belonging to a single author. Nevertheless, texts pertaining to some particular groups of authors – master and disciple, father and son – may be added.[30] What is the intellectual concern of autotextuality in a narrower sense of the word? It is to examine "the auto-reminiscences, the principles and mechanisms, through which new texts are generated – in the traces of texts already created, via transformation, via performing their creative potential: meanings left underexposed, alternative variants left encoded in memory, principles of construction resting underrun. Texts are considered productive nuclei emitting creative energy in the realm of author's works, a block conceived as a complexly organized, balanced and, at the same time, auto-disputing work" (Коларов 2009: 9). It is a programme worth employing for a study of Gumilyovs' works.

References

Гумилев, Л.Н. *Труды Льва Гумилева.* <http://gumilevica. kulichki.net/>.

Gumilev, L.N. *Trudy L'va Gumileva.* <http://gumilevica. kulichki.net/>.

Гумилев, Н.С. *Электронное собрание сочинений.* <http:// gumilev.ru/>.

Gumilev, N.S. *Jelektronnoe sobranie sochinenij.* <http://gumilev.ru/>.

Коларов, Р. Повторение и сътворение: Поетика на автотекстуалността. София: Просвета, 2009.

Kolarov, R. Povtorenie i s#tvorenie: Poetika na avtotekstualnostta. Sofija: Prosveta, 2009.

Люцканов, Й. *Огненият стълп преди "Огнен стълп" (Лириката на Николай Гумильов и огнепоклонничеството).* Реката на времето: Сборник статии

29 I was asked such a question when presenting a version of this paper orally.

30 Our considerations here are, inevitably, preliminary. We are not acquainted with the corpus of Jung's works (with the exception of the small selection already referred to, note 2), nor do we know the works of his followers. Therefore we cannot point out investigations which probably already exist and would have confirmed or modified our supposition.

31 A contemporary Bulgarian scholar employs a relevant approach to such a cluster of texts, as "Russian classical literature" (Нейчев 2009). He examines it within a framework of self-charging intertextuality, of self-interpreting group of texts, without referring to that term (and concept), "autotextuality."

в памет на проф. Людмила Боева (1934-2001). Съст. А. Вачева, И. Чекова. София, УИ "Св. Климент Охридски", 2007, 338-344.

Ljuckanov, J. *Ognenijat st#lp predi "Ognen st#lp" (Lirikata na Nikolaj Gumil'ov i ognepoklonnichestvoto).* Rekata na vremeto: Sbornik statii v pamet na prof. Ljudmila Boeva (1934-2001). S#st. A. Vacheva, I. Chekova. Sofija, UI "Sv. Kliment Ohridski", 2007, 338-344.

Нейчев, Н. Литература и месианизъм: Руското литературно месианство през XIX век. Пловдив: УИ "Паисий Хилендарски", 2009.

Nejchev, N. Literatura i mesianiz#m: Ruskoto literaturno mesianstvo prez XIX vek. Plovdiv: UI "Paisij Hilendarski", 2009.

Соловьев, В.С. *"Враг с Востока".* Сочинения в 2-х томах. Т. 2 (Чтения о богочеловечестве; Философская публицистика). Москва: Правда, 1989. 432-444.

Solov'ev, V.S. *"Vrag s Vostoka".* Sochinenija v 2-h tomah. T. 2 (Chtenija o bogochelovechestve; Filosofskaja publicistika). Moskva: Pravda, 1989. 432-444.
Юнг, К.Г. *Архетип и символ.* Москва: Ренессанс, 1991. <http://www. psyinst. ru/library.php? part=article&id=34>.

Jung, K.G. *Arhetip i simvol.* Moskva: Renessans, 1991. <http://www.psyinst. ru/library.php?part=article&id=34>.

Curtuis, E.R. *European literature and the Latin Middle Ages.* New York: Pantheon books, 1953.

Part 7
Archetypical images as a way of constructing identity

The Archetype of Construction Sacrifice in the Formation of a City's Identity: from a "City-Factory" towards a "City of Consumer Goods Exhibition"

Igor Yankov, Larisa Piskunova (Russia)

The paper investigates the mechanism of transition from the soviet to the post-soviet life experience through visual images of a city's space. We find it interesting to observe this problem via a prism of anthropological approach by using the mythologem of a "construction" sacrifice.

Social reality is revealed both on the verbal and visual levels. The specificity of a visual representation is based on its ability to show society from a more objectivised view, more observant and uninterested imagination. City streets, movements, posters, buildings and show programs can inform us more about unspoken social relations. In other contexts visual images can be used as a proof or negation of theoretical generalizations. Certainly, the objectivity of visual evidence can be recognized only in the frame of methodologically correct constructions.

From an anthropological point of view, sacrifice is the central element of mytho-ritual methods of world structure. Scrifice plays a constitutive role in the process of cosmogenesis. The body of a primary sacrifice is a building material for the creation of the Cosmos. Sacrifice is a special "way" of relation with a mystery, a manner of structuring social relations and as it was shown by R. Girard (Girard 2000), a method of channelling violence. Sacrifice incorporates into itself violence and provides for its overcoming in an emotionally represented ritual.

The mechanism of creating the world through sacrifice is not limited by traditionally sacrificing a human or an animal to God. There is also a mechanism of ritual exchange with gifts (symbolic exchange) within the frame of this sacrificial matrix, which acts as a basis pf archaic economy and a method of building social order. Sacrifice is a mechanism for renewing life and death, a method providing for the circulation of symbols. (Baudrillard J. 2000)

One type of sacrifice is a "construction" sacrifice, which plays a central role in the process of the building a house, a temple or a city. In ancient times a construction sacrifice ensured the safety of buildings, forts, cities at the expense of children, young virgins, or the casual passersby. It provided for the relations of a city or a house, and in archaic times it provided tribes with a spirit of place or ancestral totemic figures. (Zelenin D. 2004:15-175)

For the following discussion, it is significant to notice that the image of sacrifice constructs mythological designs through interaction with which the form of symbolic exchange with life and death, the identity of a society (ethnic, national and urban) and its subsequent existence is built. This interaction takes the form of a historical narrative – a story or description about the foundation of a society and its existence in time. The dominant narrative extracts from a variety of historical incidents only those that fit into the corresponding matrix. Extracted incidents are interpreted according to a given semantic field. If an archaic myth and ritual define a primary semantic matrix, in the following stages of social development, many different texts not necessarily connected with the archaic pretext appear. But they often retain a semantic core that organises the text, not in direct, but in a hidden, reduced form. Therefore, any historical myth, a story about the founding of a society and its essential features, is mythological by definition and based on the idea of sacrificial events.

In historical dynamics, sacrificial mythological events that set out the examples, the benchmarks, do not always work by linear logic of mere imitation. Since a historical existence is a problematic existence, and in the process of renewing itself a society must always build a new type of relationship with the mythological basis, based on the principle of a coexistence of "a multiplicity of local narratives". In psychological discourse such new readings are a way of "acting out" the problem and options for transforming the dominant narrative, opening new perspectives, creating new contexts and new spaces for the nascent, renewed action or sense. However, if the problem is not "acted out" (resolved), it is pushed into the unconscious and only is seemingly overcome. That leads to the possibility of a social explosion in the future.

The city as a concrete social body finds its identity in relation to the basic archetypical images embodied in the text of the mythological city, which is formed like a plot by its architectural style, the citizens' behavior, as well as its literature, legends, rumors and the media.

The specificity of a city is expressed in the principal variations of behavior and the interpretations of their meanings. However, in cities of the modern industrial era, this variation is shaped and generalized by a unified ideology. For example, the concept of a socialist city is quite intelligible to contemporaries: utopian, but meaningful.

Obviously, under modern conditions of the post-Soviet era, post-modern Russian cities recreated their mythology. They cannot be reduced to a single basis (ideological, cultural, religious). According to the experience of western urbanism, the main principle behind the functioning of urban mythology is based on a non-generalized variety. Thus, the specificity of the cultural space of the modern city generates a coexistence of different narrative strategies and discourses which are not combined into a single linear sequence. As a result the formation of several local intertextual narratives defining urban space takes place. *Mythological characters and plots become the connecting elements* of this diverse and multi-directional unity.

The formation of the post-Soviet, post-socialist identity of modern cities passes through different strategies: the rejection of the Soviet past, opposition, and repression and neglect; or its adaptation or rejection with qualitative changes.

A good example of the coexistence of different strategies towards the Soviet past is the space of Yekaterinburg. The most visible embodiment of the idea of construction sacrifice laid at the foundation of a new world, the "new city", is the Temple-on-the-Blood, built on the place of the execution of the royal family. The fact of the death of the Emperor, Empress and their children in Yekaterinburg, (July 1918) is one of the fundamental meaningful contemporary events for the modern positioning of the city. It is a specific foundation for constructing the urban mythology, the formation of a local identity (the city where the King was killed.)

There are several overlapping options for the usage of this mythologem. For the Soviet period killing the king and the subsequent destruction of the exploiting classes, as well as the victims of the purges, repressions and various difficult tortures are constitutive elements of the existence and prosperity of Soviet society. Therefore, Sverdlovsk (Yekaterinburg) was a special Soviet city and had a special status at the center of the Ural region. A semantic inversion and the transformation of the myth of the murder of the Tsar and his family, which found its visual expression in the Temple-on-the-Blood, happened in the post-Soviet period. One of the narrative options works within church and religious discourse, the second in official-public discourse and "national consciousness," and the third as a touristic landmark. The appearance of a massive church built in Byzantine style captures the formal significance of the event and states the "presence" of official authority. The governor E. Rossel actively contributed to the creation of such a pompous, expensive building and has long fought for the preservation of the king's remains in the Sverdlovsk region. The temple emphasizes the political, federal importance of Sverdlovsk region, as one of the centers of revived post-bolshevist Russia, and visually represents the claim of Yekaterinburg to the role of a third capital. The temple became the center of mass, religious activities and cultural events, and one of the "obligatory" local tourist attractions. The temple is a typical replica, all its furniture, its location, as well as its ways of positioning as a center of "revived" spirituality, speaks about its instrumental focus. The main purpose of its construction is to connect the existing socio-political structure with a mythological spiritual past and adopt them as a permanent feature. This approach forces the Soviet period out of historical line, making it spoiled godless, etc.

However, it is impossible to completely overthrow the Soviet mythology. It is too strong. It left many imprints, and is still too fresh in the memory of most of population. The signs of the Soviet period constitute the most important and inescapable element of the modern urban body. One option towards the Soviet past can be an interpretation of the entire Soviet period as a **sacrificial period**.

A variant of the interpretation of the Soviet period as sacrificial is the existence of a metonymic relation with those of its aspects that can be the subject of "pride" in the present. The characterists of this sacrificial mythology can be found in the following statement:

"Yes, we tolerated and suffered hardships, but we build the cities and factories, and won the war ...." The "real", "material", "living" figure which embodies this strategy is Marshall Zhukov. Monuments to Zhukov have quickly begun to fill the urban space of Russian cities. There is a memorial to the famous marshall, who after the war was commander of the Urals Military District in Yekaterinburg as well.

Increased attention to Zhukov in the post-Soviet period is an indicator of the growing influence of this second strategy (where the Soviet period is conceived as a heroic sacrifice). Zhukov is the hero of the victorious World War II. In the minds of Russians, the joy of victory and the victory itself merged with the figure of Zhukov. Identification with him helps to overcome the complex of state and national inferiority. And if we remember the Marshall's character, to succeed despite loss, then one can see the attempt to adopt in the public consciousness the typical motif of victory through sacrifice. In the mythology of war, Zhukov emerges as a double in relation to Stalin. On the one hand, he is Stalin's comrade and stands next to him, and he also connects the figure of Stalin with modernity. On the other hand he is the antithesis of Stalin. As he was the one who warned Stalin about the Nazi threat before the war. He argues with Stalin in the critical moments of war, and in fact he was also exiled by Stalin after the victory.

As a mythological character, G.K.Zhukov is an actualized hero, connecting the heroic past and the legitimized present. He is a figure reconciling us to the Soviet era. This reinterpretation of history is defined within a narrative removed from the immediate Soviet ideology, focusing on productive heroic sacrifice. Because of its duality, the character becomes of a common strand with the Soviet Stalinist myth, and also a way to "digest" it in new conditions. According to this interpretive doctrine, Zhukov's further glorification can be assumed to continue in the nearest future. For the urban mythology of Yekaterinburg Zhukov becomes an iconic character, also, because he commanded the Ural Military District at the time of his disgrace. Therefore referring to Zhukov as "our own" is typical for discursive and visual strategies of the urban and regional authorities.

Another option towards building relationship with the Soviet experience is neglect, the submersion of the Soviet history into the background, deleting it from history. Expanding this doctrine is also possible at several levels: you can declare the Soviet past to be illegitimate like the Baltic countries try to do. But there is another more convenient option. The main idea of it is simply to ignore history. Plunging into the post-historical state it is possible to dismiss history as a series of **significant** events and the images associated with them. Historical events of the past have been sacrificed for the sake of unproblematic present.

The most vivid example of this strategy is removing the old town. By destroying the old town and its personal history one erases the city's stylistic originality as well. A living form of attitude towards the past is the "playful" interpretation of mytho-ritual schemes. One of the options for implementing this strategy was celebrating the birthday of the Rosa Luxemburg's tree, conducted by a Ekaterinburg theater formerly located on the street named after this well-known activist of the communist movement. Ironically the "playful" "game" mythology, created by the theatre about the tree, which some media naively accepted as real, argues that in the beginning of the century, Rosa Luxemburg had secretly visited Yekaterinburg and had planted a tree in the courtyard of the future theatre. The tree served as symbolic, sacrificial totem.

Post-Soviet glossy history appears as if from out of nowhere. However, it had a real basis due to the redistribution of property, and a bloody struggle with the victims of this conversion. The components of the story are also involved in the construction of the modern world. The most spectacular traces of the era of the nineties are burial complexes left from the gang fights and wars of the period of the primary accumulation of capital. Tombstones are large-scale presentations of wealth and are built according to the specific cultural taste of their "owners." They have become the subject of special analysis (O. Matic). Shirokorechenskoe cemetery in Yekaterinburg is now a tourist attraction place, which is included in all the online guides for foreign tourists. The monuments symbolize the victory of life over death, however not an eternal victory, but a profane one. In this case, they symbolize a heaven on this side of the world. Also, bandit memorials are a form of direct approval of the violence in this world, wich was reflected in the dominant trends of public life in the early nineties in Russia. The attitude of the city authorities is that the bandit monuments discredit the city. They ruin the city's reputation. However, it should be noted that the perception of the sites as aesthetic objects, objects for observation, transforms them from actual experiences of the past into ta past already overcome, "experienced." Their perception as cultural objects promotes the overcoming and acting out of the problematic situation. Thus, the bandits are becoming a construction sacrifice of a new city, new order, new world.

Creating the identity of the new city passes through the embodiment of the iconic figures of the "game" world. In modern Russian cities particular importance is given to pedestrian streets, local versions of the Arbat in Moscow, as a means of visual organization, the structure and content of cultural space. Weiner Street plays this role for Yekaterinburg. A series of sculptures was built along this street, which immediately became the centre of attraction for residents and tourists, creating meeting and sightseeing places. This was followed by immediate creation of a modern mythology and a general tradition to leave the coins for figures. Coins and small bills are a "devalued" legacy of a profaned sacrificial ritual. The rapid revival of the old and the emergence of new ritual forms speaks about the necessity for sacrificial space among modern city dwellers, for whom idolatry in a soft "semi-game" form is "natural." As a result a specific phenomenon appears. On the one hand such pleasurable and "sacrificial" places embody the "soul" of the city, "enliven" the urban space, and give it its individuality. On the other hand, the typical, standard, uniform figures transform the modern city into one part of the "glossy" culture, reprinted in the vast territory of Russia.

The city can also be interpreted and perceived through such images as a showcase and exhibition. A man lives either in the factory, in the Soviet city, or at an exhibition of consumption.

Thus, the modern city is the intersection of different texts in different directions. Modern urban identity is built through a comparison of the different variants of the interpretation of Soviet past mythologies. The problem is that the dominant ways of working with the mythological basis tend to push aside the sacrifice from the actual historical experience and move it into a prehistoric, pre-actual time. As a result, the modern festive, but pseudo-sacrificial city, pushes the themes of violence and other social problems into the "unconscious" of the urban narrative. The lack of self-sacrifice or pseudo-sacrifice leads to the fact that the problems are avoided, become potent and irrational.

The prospects for constructing the city's identity are seen in the search for the mechanisms for "acting out" the past problems. This can be the adoption or "game" re-formation of sacrificial practices, but the phenomenon of sacrifice cannot be eliminated from actual experience.

References

Baudrillard J., *Symbolic exchange and death.* M.: Dobrosvet. 2000.

Girard R., *The Violence and Sacred* M.: New literatural outlook. 2000.

Zelenin D. Construction Sacrifice, Selected works. The articles on spiritual culture. 1934-1954. M.: "Indrik", 2004.

Matich O. Successful mafiosi – death mafiozi: the culture of культура funeral rituals. New literary outlook. № 33.

Riker P. *The time and the story.* M., СПб.: University book, 1998, p. 1.

The Archetype of the Four in the Architecture of the Four-*īwān* Building Tradition

Elena Paskaleva
(The Netherlands)

The four-*īwān* scheme, marking the four cardinal points with majestic porches surrounding a courtyard, has been traced down to the Parthian palaces of Hatra and Assūr, 2nd c. AD (Figure 1) and is associated with the Sasanian period (224-637 AD). Originally, the scheme was used as a palace plan representing royal and divine power. Later on, with the advent of Islam and after the 10th c. AD, the four-*īwān* plan was widely adopted for religious compounds such as open-courtyard mosques (Figure 2) and madrasas, and centrally-domed mausoleums, tombs and Sufi *khānaqāhs*.

Fig. 1: Assūr, first known four-*īwān* usage, Parthian palace 2nd c. AD, plan after Kleiss

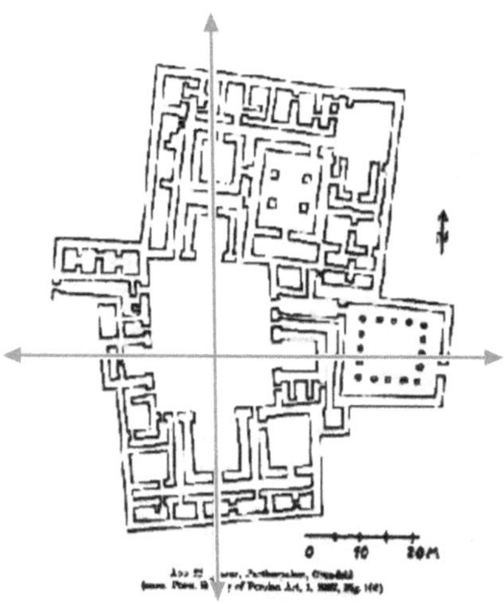

Source: Kleiss: Palästen und palastartigen Wohnbauten In Iran, 1989, Fig. 22

Fig. 2: Samarqand, Bībī Khānum Mosque, plan after Ratiia

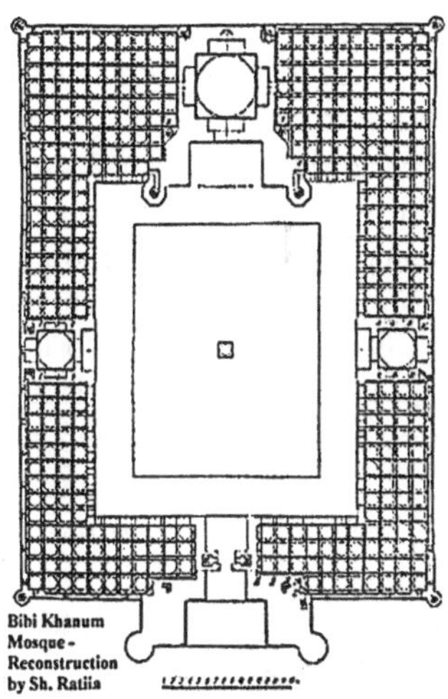

Source: http://depts.washington.edu/silkroad/cities/uz/Samarqand/bibi.html [Accessed on 1 April 2010]

Initially, the *īwān* was associated with a gate or an arch to a sanctuary, going back to the first fire temples from the 5th c. BC. It developed in later times as a sacred passage to a holy site: a passage, related to crossing the border between the profane (the urban fabric) and the sacred (the holy building). Although the religious reality of the *īwān* in the four-*īwān* mosque is very different from the Zoroastrian fire temples, the archetype of a holy gate, transpositioning the human being from its temporal realm into the divine realm, has remained intact. Similar to other religions, the religious essence of Islam can be found exactly in the intersection of those two worlds: the divine and the temporal. This makes the *īwān* the most appropriate choice of an architectural feature to mark the sacred space of the mosque and to define it strictly from the profane surroundings of the hectic outside world.

The building tradition of the four *īwāns* remained virtually unchanged after the 2nd c. AD. The structure has been widely used for palaces, open courtyard mosques, madrasas and caravansarays and for centrally domed tombs and *khānaqāhs*. Furthermore, the four-*īwān* plan was the main architectural choice of the ruling dynasties in Central Asia as late as the 19th c. AD.

In my work, I analyse the four-*īwān* plan as a dynastic architectural tool marking the centre of the world, from which power spreads along the cardinal points to all corners of the macrosomos. The concept of recreating Paradise on earth is further developed in line with dynastic supremacy and the role of the ruler as cosmocrator. Examples of this concept can be found in the architectural heritage of two imperial triads: the Tīmūrids, represented by Tīmūr (1336-1405), Shah Rukh (1377-1447) and Ulugh Beg (1393-1449) and the Mughals, in turn represented by Akbar (1542-1605), Jahangir (1569-1627) and Shah Jahan (1592-1666). These triads are formed by the grandfather – the great emperor, "King of the World" (Tīmūr, Akbar), the pious and modest son (Shah Rukh, Jahangir) and the ingenious grandson, who tries to surpass his grandfather by reviving the dynastic iconography and the megalomaniac aspirations of the grandfather, acting as "the supreme King of the World" (Ulugh Beg, Shah Jahan). The architectural activities of these two royal triads can be analysed as a representation of their power aspirations, whereby each ruler is recreated as a representative of God on earth, an *Axis Mundi* in himself, mediating between the divine and the mortal realities. The emperor as a cosmocrator can be compared to God and his ultimate creation: Paradise. All Tīmūrid and Mughal quadripartite architectural and landscape paradisiacal settings adopted the geography, the geometry and the stylistic features of Paradise based on the archetype of the four.

A plausible explanation shedding more light on the lack of evolution in the four-*īwān* building tradition is the fact that the four-*īwān* plan was used only for representational buildings, commissioned by the supreme imperial and local rulers. The four-*īwān* plan was a power statement, rediscovered by the subsequent ruler trying to relate his power to a previous undisputed chief patron. Since the Tīmūrids fostered good relations with the Sufi community, the four-*īwān* compounds were a symbolically acceptable setting both for the Sufi orders and for the *ʿulamāʾ*. For the four-*īwān* plan is an architectural representation both of the cosmologies of Sufism and of orthodox Islam.

For the first time, I discuss the four-*īwān* plan in terms of the archetype of the four. This approach offers comparative analysis with Buddhist and Hindu cross-axial monuments, encompassing the current descriptive research (Golombek and Wilber 1988; O'Kane 1987; Koch 2002 and Koch 2006) that regards the four-*īwān* plan only as a strictly Islamic phenomena. If we assume that the archetype of the four defines the core of the four-*īwān* plan, the most obvious conclusion will be that its origin and essence are not Islamic.

The archetype of the four has emerged as a visual image from the hieropahny of the four, the latter being the primary one in my view. The two terms "hierophany" and "archetype" should be shortly explained here. The concept of the hierophany is used to differentiate between the elements of sacred order (the ideal world believed to be created by the primordial God) and the items of profane experience (the perception of the real world as seen by man). Further, the hierophanies are the means of man to construct a "sense of cosmic harmony" as put by Coupe (Coupe 1997: 62.). This cosmic harmony is opposed to the experience of profane time according to Eliade (Eliade 1971), whereby the sacred and the profane are dichotomously interrelated.[1] So, the hierophany is a tool to experience sacred order in a profane reality. Via the hierophany, the human transcends time and space and is transpositioned into the *illo tempore*,[2] the mythical time when the world was created. In a way, the hierophany in itself is a microcosmic Axis Mundi, a sacred channel that assures man's access to the realm of divine creation. The visual representation of the hierophany is a mimetic process that denotes either a certain aspect of God (manifestation of the sacred) or an element of God's creation (sacred rivers and mountains, the cosmic ocean, etc.). In the course of time, the hierophanies overlap and are being rediscovered in a process of hierophanic palimpsest. The hierophanic palimpsest in turn establishes the hierophany as a stable image throughout time. The archetype emerges when the visualised hierophany is recurrently reused and perceived by man. Thus the process of hierophanic visualisation in the case of the four evolved in the archetype[3] of the four. This archetype denotes an attempt to reproduce God's creation on earth by profane means and in a profane environment. The image represented by the

1 However, Islam does not differentiate between the concepts of sacred and profane.

2 Term coined by Eliade.

3 According to Coupe: literally, an original image, or founding figure, Coupe: *Myth*, p. 4.

archetype acquires the status of a sacred entity and the previously profane environment described by the archetype is attributed qualities of the sacred.

The basic archetype of the four elements combined with a central element can be found in all mythologies and religions of the world. The most prominent representations are related to the four cardinal points: the cosmic cross (horizontal dimension) and the cosmic centre: the *Axis Mundi* (vertical dimension) (Figure 3). The archetype of the four has anthropomorphic origin that can be explained with the symmetry of the human body and its position and orientation in the horizon. Furthermore, the number four derives from the symmetry of the human body, which suggests a quadripartite division of the horizon: a front and a back, left and right side. It might have been an attempt to describe the "unknown" world in a manner closer to man in order to understand the primordial world and to come to terms with the fears and the calamities related to the powers of nature.

Fig. 3: Spatial orientation of the archetype of the four (horizontal dimension) and the *Axis Mundi* (vertical dimension)

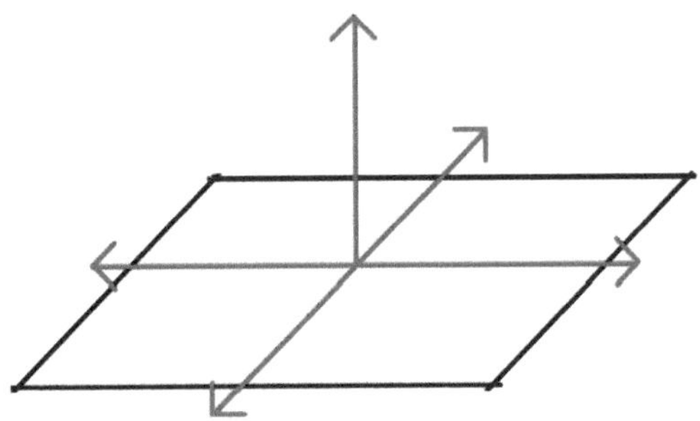

In the mythological thought, the archetype of the four can be found in the representations of the four winds, the four seasons, the four elements, the four humours of the human body, the four regents of the world, the four giants holding the world, etc.

In the polytheistic thought, the archetype of the four evolved in the representation of the four major deities plus one omnipotent central deity (Figure 4), the four castes, the four Vedas, the Vāstu Shastra Mandala (Figure 5), etc.

Fig. 4: Osiris within a temple scriptorium. Papyrus Salt 825. Ptolemaic Period (305-30 BC), British Museum

Fig. 5: 9x9 Vāstu Shastra Mandala and the Vāstu-Purusha Mandala

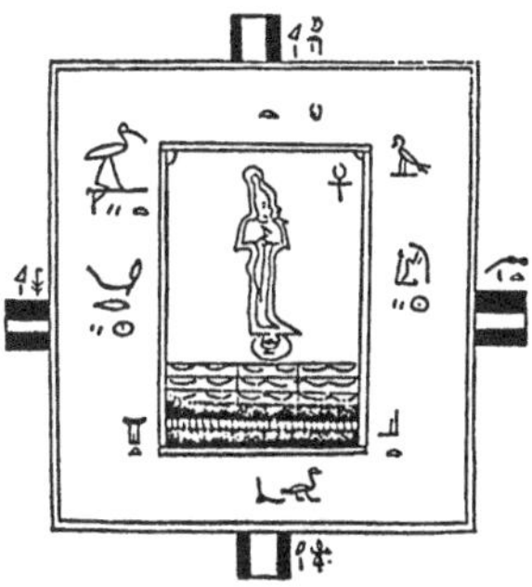

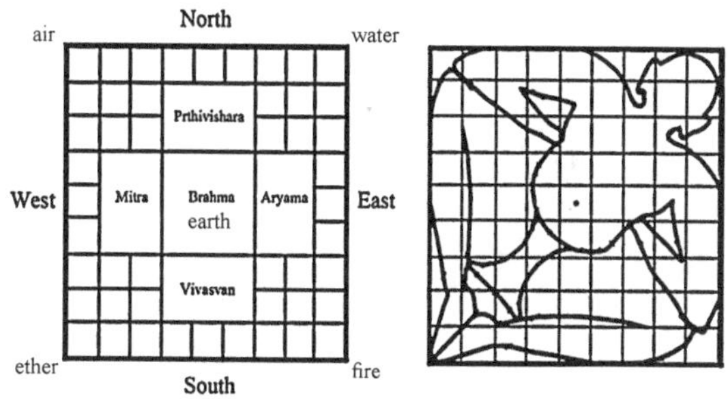

9x9 Vaastu Shastra Mandala

Vaastu Purusha Mandala

Source: Wilkinson: Symbol and Magic in Egyptian Art, 1994, p.144

Source: Drawing by En-Yu Huang

Upon the ascension of monotheistic beliefs, the archetype of the four developed further as a representation of the four evangelists (Christianity) (Figure 6), the four pillars (angels) holding the Throne of God (Islam) (Figure 7), Muḥammad and the first four Caliphs, etc. In the Old Testament and in the Quran, there are the four rivers of Paradise, emanating from one source (Genesis 2:10 and Sūra 47:15), the four "animalia" and the four major prophets. In the New Testament, there are the four evangelists and the four Gospels that spread across the world, the four *mysteria Christi*, the four cardinal virtues and the vision of the Throned Being amid the four living creatures (Revelation 4).

Fig. 6: Four evangelists after the Book of Kells, 800 AD

Source: http://www.uni-due.de/DI/Manu scripts.htm [Accessed on 1 April 2010]

Fig. 7: Four angels surround the Throne of God. Al-Qazwini, 1475 AD, British library, Persian 178, fol. 57A.

The angels are in the form of a man, a bull, an eagle and a lion.

Source: Rustomji: The Garden, 2009, p.137, Fig. 7.4

In the mystical beliefs that accompanied monotheistic thought such as Manichaeism and Sufism, the archetype of the four remained constant and acquired extra imagery such as for example *The Universal Tree and the Four Birds* discussed in a treatise by Ibn ʻArabī (Ibn ʻArabī 2006.). In Sufi cosmology, the fortification of the four world directions has cosmic dimensions, whereby the four spiritual masters (*awtād*, "pegs" or "pillars") are related to the east, west, north and south (Akkach 2005: 95.). Ibn `Arabī postulates that God preserves one pillar for every direction and one central "pole", *al-qutb*, which can be interpreted as the cosmic axis (the equivalent of the *Axis Mundi* in the archetype of the four).

Along this central axis, humans can transcend through the three cosmic zones: 1) starting from the underworld, the unholy zone (as in the case of tombs, in which the sarcophagus is placed underground, as for example in the Ishrat Khaneh and Gur-i Amir in Samarkand); 2) experiencing the horizontality of the earthly world, the first holy zone, where the earth meets the Heavens (i.e. the building itself, the intersecting axes of the four *īwāns* marking its centre), and 3) proceeding to the verticality of the Heavens, the second or heavenly holy zone (which can be associated with the dome, rising above the point of the intersecting axes as in the *khānaqāhs*). Akkach (Ibid., p. 95.) argues that the verticality in Sufi teachings (the representation of the archetype of the *Axis Mundi*) is an expression of human uniqueness, while the stressing of the geographical directions (i.e. the archetype of the four, i.e. the cosmic cross) stands for the comprehensiveness of human reality.

In this article I argue that the four-*īwān* plan with the four gates (*īwān*s), ideally denoting the four cardinal points, is a visual representation of the archetype of the four: the cosmic cross and the archetype of the *Axis Mundi* – the cosmic centre. As I have shown above, the archetype of the four is very complex and includes many different visual representations, which have evolved in a hierophanic palimpsest throughout time and beyond mythological and religious thought. In their sacred essence, the four *īwān*s are no different from, for example, the four pillars supporting the Throne of God in Islam. That is why, to analyse the existence and the quintessence of the four-*īwān* plan in terms of exclusively Islamic iconography and architectural morphology would be a limitation, depriving the archetype of the four of its broader and extremely complex meaning.

Since the origin of the archetype of the four is related to the spatial orientation of man in the world, it acquired spatial, strictly geometrical, representations that were adopted in the construction of quadripartite cities (e.g. *urbs dei*), palaces, temples (e.g. Buddhist stupas, Hindu temples, Christian cruciform churches and martyria, Islamic four-*īwān* mosques and madrasas, and Sufi domed four-*īwān* *khānaqāhs*, etc.), tombs and gardens (e.g. *čahār bahr*s). All these architectural and landscape sites had clear rectangular boundaries, defined by two intersecting orthogonal axes marking the four corners of the world. The geometrical principles of symmetry were applied everywhere to create a representation of the built environment as similar as possible to the creation of the world by God. The geometrical organisation of space (as attributed to God) is opposed to the chaos of the profane, unorganised space (in opposition to God's perfection). Creating order in the chaos by means of symmetry is regarded as an ideal topography, the only one that fully represents order and is subject only to God's rules of perfection.

The architecture of the four-*īwān* compounds can be also analysed as a representation of the hierophany of Paradise, which is derived from the archetype of the four (i.e. the four rivers of Paradise springing from a central source). Paradise is directly associated with Islamic prayer and it is in Paradise, where the human Muhammad reaches Allāh. In a similar way, the human worshipper, who will never visit the real Paradise in his/her lifetime, can reach Allāh only in prayer, in a setting, similar to the domain of Allāh, e.g. Paradise. So, the four-*īwān* plan, based on the archetype of the four – the four rivers of Paradise, symbolically marked by the intersecting orthogonal axes along the four *īwāns* – seems to be the most suitable setting for prayer that presupposes and allows for direct contact with Allāh.

The construction of the four-*īwān* compound can be regarded as a sacred act, repeating the creation of the world by God. The vertical aspect of the archetype of the *Axis Mundi* coincides with the geometrical centre of the compound and creates a representation of cosmogenesis: the single point of all creation.[4] The orthogonal axes, radiating from the centre as a cosmic cross, mark the created world in its totality. The archetype of the *Axis Mundi* can thus be interpreted as a clear spatio-temporal representation of the built environment as it defines space, vertically emanating from the centre and spreading along the horizontal axes of the cosmic cross (Figure 3).

The geometric centre, defined by the intersecting axes, is ubiquitous, without any direct reference to a certain point in time or space. As such, the centre, i.e. the *Axis Mundi* is identified with the primordial unity of the creation. On the other hand, the radiating axes from the centre represent the diversity and multitude of the world as a divine, time-governed manifestation by using the human coordinates as an architectural tool.

Another aspect related to the symmetry is that God's perfection, evoked and represented by perfectly organised building and landscape schemes, is in contrast with humanity's imperfections. The human being is seen as subordinated to the divine organisational principles. The four-*īwān* plan, as opposed to the sporadically evolved urban fabric, can be regarded as a perfectly organised system based on geometrical symmetry. In this way, we have two juxtapositions: on the one hand, human imperfection in contrast to divine symmetry; and on the other hand, the urban, quasi-unstructured frames in contrast to the place of divine presence and worship i.e. the mosque or the madrasa. Further, the asymmetrical "chaos" of the urban fabric versus the symmetrical "cosmos" defined by the four-*īwāns*. The cosmos (from the Greek κόσμος, meaning "ordered world") being created by God to generate order is recreated on earth by the commissioner of a four-*īwān* compound, who in turn assumes the role of God on earth in a sort of hierophanic mimesis and utilises the archetype of the four as an architectural concept to recreate God's realm on earth.

The four-*īwān* plan is based on a geometrical grid, very similar to the grid of the mandala. This relates automatically the four-*īwān* plan to Buddhist, Hindu

4 This term is used by Snodgrass with regard to the Buddhist stupa.

and Jain sacred monuments also based on the mandala. All these settings have cross axial design based on the archetype of the four: the cosmic cross and the *Axis Mundi*.

The geometrical similarities between the mandala and the four-*īwān* plan, both of them based on the archetype of the four, are:

- the orthogonal symmetrical outline,
- the grid, based on which the compound is organised,
- the central organisation and cross-axial design (stressing the four cardinal directions, be it with deities, staircases or colours in the buildings based on the mandala in stupas, Hindu and Buddhist temples; or with *pishtaqs* in the case of the *īwāns*),
- the anthropomorphic organic unity and four directions of the world.

The closed rectangular ensemble, both in the Buddhist stupa and in the four-*īwān* compound is based on orthogonal symmetry. The spatial controlling factor of hierophanic geometric patterns is symmetry. The metaphorical interpretation of architecture has generated orthogonal symmetry to God's perfection and transcendent purity.

The straight lines in Islam have been considered to represent *tawhid* – the divine unity and sacred order between man and nature. This order, created by the divine geometrical patterns was expressed in mathematical regularity. Another aspect related to orthogonal symmetry is that God's perfection, evoked and represented by perfectly organised building and landscape schemes, is in contrast with human's imperfections. The human being is seen as subordinated to the divine organisational principles. The four-*īwān* plan within the urban fabric can be regarded as a perfectly organised system based on orthogonal symmetry.

While in the Hindu temple the *Axis Mundi* is clearly represented by the horizontal centre of the mandala and by the verticality of the mountain-like tower, the four-*īwān* plan reveals two potential *loci* for the *Axis Mundi*. The one is of course in the centre of the courtyard, which is the geometrical centre of the compound and the intersecting point of the two orthogonal axes, the second one is the *mihrāb*, situated in the sanctuary. On the one hand, the imam or the shaykh carrying out the service assumes the function of the cosmic man in the *mihrāb* and connects metaphorically with the Heavens. On the other hand, the congregation in the courtyard as a whole acts as an *Axis Mundi* and unobstructed by any architectural settings (lack of a cupola) directly connects with the divine reality. These two architectural centres: the centre of the courtyard and the *mihrāb* can be explained with the hierophanic palimpsest. Primarily, the orthogonal centre of the courtyard was also the locus of the *Axis Mundi* and the most sacred place. However, with the advent of monotheistic thought and with the Islamic necessity to incorporate the *mihrāb* in the *qibla* as the most sacred locus in the compound, the four-*īwān* plan acquired two hierophanic centres: 1) the centre of the courtyard, marked by the water basin, related to the archetype of the four in terms of representations of Paradise and the *al-kawthar*, and 2) the *mihrāb* niche as the most sacred part of the *qibla.*

This schematic comparison between the Jain temple and the Buddhist stupa with the four-*īwān* plan (Figures 8-10) shows that the basic compositional features such as the orientation along two orthogonal axes, situation of the sanctuary in their crossing point, four massive gates, etc., with all of them based on the archetype of the four, are similar. Although there is not a direct historical link between the two architectural settings, the archetypes of the *Axis Mundi* and the cosmic cross, of the navel of the world, of the holy mountain, etc. are basically the same. They represent different architectural traditions based on the same anthropomorphic and physiomorphic beliefs and cosmological schemes evolved throughout the process of hierophanic palimpsest.

Fig. 8: Plans of stupas with four stairways or four Buddha images in the cardinal points after Snodgrass

Source: Snodgrass: The Stupa, 1985, p. 132, Fig. 75.

Fig. 9: Plan of the Jain Chaumukh Temple of Ranakpur, 1439 AD after Peter

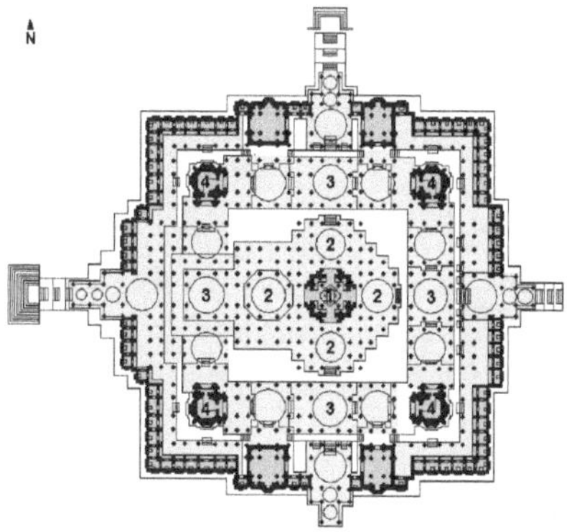

Source: http://de.wikipedia.org/w/index.php?title=Datei:Grundriss_Adinatha-Tempel_Ranakpur.gif&filetimestamp=20070814132327 [Accessed on 1 October 2009].

Fig. 10: Bukhārā, the covered market Taqi Zargaron, 16th c. AD after Borodina

Source: Borodina: Central Asia, 1985, p. 122.

The main aim of this article is to show that the four-*īwān* plan can be analysed as an architectural representation of the archetype of the four. It was used to represent political agendas and imperial ambitions. The ruler professes his omnipotent divine power as a commissioner of a pious building based on a paradisiacal plan. The four-*īwān* plan, based on the archetype of the four, has been used prior to the advent of Islam and its essence is not Islamic but hierophanic.

References

Akkach, S.: *Cosmology and Architecture in Premodern Islam*. New York: State University of New York Press, 2005.

Architecture of Manasara. Translated from original Sanskrit. Manasara Series: Volume IV. Prasanna Kumar Acharya. New Delhi: Munshiram Manoharlal Publishers Pvt. Ltd., 1934.

Ardalan, N. and Bakhtiar, L.: *The Sense of Unity. The Sufi Tradition in Persian Architecture*. Chicago: Chicago University Press, 1973.

Borodina, I.: *Central Asia. Architectural Monuments from the 9th -19th c.* Photo album. Moscow: Science Publishing House, 1985. (Russian edition)

Coupe, L.: *Myth*. London: Routledge, 1997.

Esmeijer, A.C.: Divina Quaternitas. A preliminary study in the method and application of visual exegesis. Assen: Van Gorcum, 1978.

Ibn ʻArabī: *The Universal Tree and the Four Birds*. Translated by A. Jaffray. Oxford: Anqa Publishing, 2006.

Kleiss, W.: *Die Entwicklung von Palästen und palastartigen Wohnbauten in Iran*. Wien: Verlag der Österreichischen Akademie der Wissenschaften, 1989.

Mekking, A.J.J.: "The Architectural Representation of Reality. The Built Environment as the Materialization of a Mental Construct". In The Global Built Environment as a Representation of Realities, ed. A.J.J. Mekking and E. Roose. Pallas Publications, 2009.

Snodgrass, A.: *The Symbolism of the Stupa*. New York: Cornell Southeast Asia Program, 1985.

Rustomji, N.: The Garden and the fire. Heaven and Hell in Islamic Culture. New York: Columbia University Press, 2009.

Volwahsen, A.: *Islamisches Indien. Weltkulturen und Baukunst*. München: Hirmer Verlag, 1969.

List of the Authors

Kamal Abdullayev (Azerbaijan)
Professor, writer. Rector of Baku Slavic University, Correspondent Member and Academic-Secretary for Humanities and Social Sciences branch of Azerbaijan National Academy of Sciences. PhD from Linguistics Institute, Academy of Sciences of Soviet Union, Moscow. Research interests: archetype plots in Turkic and Greek epics, epics *Kitabi Dede Gorgoud* and *Nibelungenlied,* theoretical syntax in Azerbaijani language, syntax parallels in Turkic languages

E-mail: bakslavuniver@hotmail.com

Rahilya Geybullayeva (Azerbaijan)
Professor, head of the Department of Azerbaijani Literature at Baku Slavic University. Founding Head of Azerbaijan Comparative Literature Association. PhD from Lomonosov Moscow State University. Research interests: literature in crossroads of history, religion, culture, society; concept of national culture and national identity; pagan elements in monotheistic religions; between religious book-epic-chronicle, myth and history. Served as Visiting Professor as Fulbright Scholar at the University of Wisconsin-Madison (USA), UNESCO scholar at SOAS, London, and Carnegie scholar at the University of California-Berkeley.

E-mail: rahilya_g@hotmail.com

Izabella Horvath (China-USA)
Visiting scholar, Art Education Research Institute, *Hangzhou Normal University, China*

ESL Faculty at DePaul University, USA, free lance writer. MA from University of Illinois, Chicago.

Research interests: Hungarian and Turkish folktales, cultural anthropology, comparative ethnography.

E-mail: ihorvath3@gmail.com

Aslan Mamedly (Azerbaijan)
Professor, Department of General Lingustics, Baku Slavic University
PhD from Linguistics Institute, Azerbaijan National Academy of Sciences
Research interests: lexicology and phraseology, cognitive lingusitics, language and natioinal worldview relations, translation and misinterpreation of sacred books (mainly Bible)
E-mail: mamedli_aslan@yahoo.com

Simon Sorgenfrei (Sweden)
PhD Student, Department of Literature, History of Ideas and Religion, University of Gothenburg,Sweden. Research interests: Islam, Sufism
Email: simon.sorgenfrei@lir.gu.se

Tatiana Megrelishvili (Georgia)
Professor, Department of Litearture, Georgian Technical University
E-mail: tatamegre@mail.ru

Angelina Saule (Australia)
MA Slavic Studies student at Monash University, English Instructor
E-mail: angelina_orit@hotmail.com

Gorkhmaz Guliyev (Azerbaijan)
Professor of Foreign Literature of Azerbaijan University of Languages.
PhD from Azerbaijan National Academy of Sciences.
Research interests: postmodernity, French literature, Jalil Mamed-kuluzadeh, myths in contemporary literary works

Gonul Bakay (Turkey)
Associate Professor, American Language and Literature department of Bahçeşehir University- Istanbul. B.A.from London University, PhD from İstanbul University. Research interests: 18th century English literature, Gothic novel, Black studies and Feminist studies. Published five books in Turkish.
E-mail: gonulbakay@gmail.com

Mamed Godjaev (Azerbaijan)
Professor, Head of Classic Russian Literature Department, Baku Slavic University
Research interests: F. Dostoyevsky, L. Tolstoy, Nizami, concept of human in literature, ideal of beauty in XIX Russian literature

Khuraman Mursalieva (Azerbaijan)
PhD, Assistant Professor of the Modern Russian Literature Department, Baku Slavic University.
Research interests: Anna Akhmatova, Mariya Tsvetayeva, srebryaniy vek (silver century) of Russsian literature.

Sevinj Bakysh (United Kingdom)
Independent researcher, academic translator PhD from Literary Institute, Azerbaijan National Academy of Sciences MA in European Thought, University College of London, United Kingdom Head of Literature Department at Azerbaijan University of Languages (2001-2002)
E-mail: sevincb@rambler.ru

Saddik Gohar (UAE)
Professor at the UAE University. PhD/MA in English Literature and Critical Theory from Indiana University (USA), undergraduate degrees in English language and literature from Egyptian University. Published eleven books , six of them in Europe and translated fifteen books into Arabic/English in the areas of comparative literature , Middle Eastern studies, American literature, translation studies , Arabic/Islamic literature and critical theory journals in North America, Europe, Australia, New Zealand, India and South Africa.
E-mail: s.gohor@uaeu.ac.ae

Khalida Isa-zada (Azerbaijan)
PhD from Baku Slavic University, Head of the History and Grammar of English Department, Baku Slavic University
E-mail: khalida_is@yahoo.com

Hatice Övgü Tüzün (Turkey)
Assistant Professor
Department of American Culture and Literature, Bahçeşehir University, Turkey
PhD from University of Kent, UK
MA in Modern Literature and Culture, University of Kent, UK
E-mail: otuzun@hotmail.com

Elnare Garagyezova (Azerbaijan)
PhD student, Literary Institute, Azerbaijan National Academy of Sciences
Teaching assistant at the Azerbaijani Literature Department, Baku Slavic University
Research interests: mythology in modern literature and culture, literature and history
E-mail: e.garagozova.bsu@gmail.com

Gunay Garayeva (Azerbaijan)
Associate Professor, Azerbaijani Literature Department, Baku Slavic University
PhD from Literary Institute, Azerbaijan National Academy of Sciences
E-mail: g.garayeva@yahoo.com

Anuar Galiev (Kazakhstan)
Professor, Kazakh National University named Al-Farabi
Research Interests: etnosemiotics of Central Asia and Caucases; history in myths of Turkic people
E-mail:agaliev@hotmail.com

Irina Modebadze (Georgia)
Dr., Theory of Literature and Comparativistic Department, Institute of Georgian Literature named after Shota Rustaveli
E-mail: irinamodeb@gmail.com

Tamar Tsitsishvili (Georgia)
Dr., History of Georgian Literature Department, Institute of Georgian Literature named after Shota Rustaveli
E-mail: t.tsitsishvili@yahoo.com

Yordan Lyutskanov (Bulgaria)
Researcher, Institute for Literature, Bulgarian Academy of Sciences (Section of Russian Literature, 2006-2010, Section of Comparative Literature, since 2010)
PhD in Russian Literature from the Higher Attestation Commission of Bulgaria (2006)
MA in Russian Philology, Sofia University "St. Kliment Ohridski" (2000)
E-mail: yljuckanov@gmail.com

Igor Yankov (Russia)
PhD, Onthology Department, Ural State University
E-mail: iyankov@yandex.ru

Larisa Piskunova (Russia)
PhD., Assoc. Prof. of Aesthetic, History and Theory of Culture Department, Ural State University

E-mail: reklama-urgu@yandex.ru

Elena Paskaleva (The Netherlands)
Dr. Elena Paskaleva, the research profile Asian Modernities and Traditions at Leiden University, The Netherlands. She studied Architecture at the University for Architecture and Civil Engineering (Sofia, Bulgaria), Bauhaus University Weimar (Weimar, Germany) and Art History at the Friedrich-Schiller University (Jena, Germany). In 2001-2002 she attended the Manchester School of Architecture (United Kingdom) on a Socrates Scholarship by DAAD (German Academic Exchange Service). She obtained her MA degree (*cum laude*) in Comparative World Architecture from Leiden University, The Netherlands (2004), and PhD from the same university (2010. Her research interests are Tīmūrid architecture, as a dynastic architectural tool to legitimize extreme and universal power.

E-mail: elpask@gmail.com

Index

FSC
www.fsc.org
MIX
Papier | Fördert
gute Waldnutzung
FSC® C083411

Kolibri 360 GmbH
Ferdinand-Jühlke-Straße 7
99095 Erfurt, Deutschland
produktsicherheit@kolibri360.de